Emotional Dimensions of Educational Administration and Leadership

Emotional Dimensions of Educational Administration and Leadership explores foundational theories for emotional dimensions of educational administration and leadership as they influence our understanding, analysis, and practice in the field. It covers a broad range of topics, such as ethics, authority, personality, social justice, gender discrimination, organisational culture, decision-making, accountability, and marketisation.

The first section, 'Theoretical foundations', includes discussion of the early modern romantic philosophy that produced the heroic notion of leadership, the idealist philosophy of Hegel, existential concerns through Kierkegaard, the contributions of psychoanalysis, and Habermasian critical theory. The second section, 'Types of emotional analysis', includes examinations of the material culture, emotional economies, the politics of emotion, and the relationship between emotion and rationality. The last section, 'Critical and contemporary issues', includes critiques of the fear arising from accountability regimes, the political economy of the market model, a feminist critique of ideologies reflecting emotional investments, narrative expressions for the emotional context of teamwork, the problem of narcissism, and the emotional dimensions of role engagement.

This volume explores an area that is only just re-emergent in the last few years. The collection demonstrates the relevance to practical issues and problems internationally, both within the organisational context and extra-organisationally with a focus on the application of emotional factors as they affect our understanding of, and practice in, educational organisations. The emotions of education affect the implementation of political values and culture within organisations.

Eugenie A. Samier, formerly Associate Professor in Leadership and Administration Studies at the Faculty of Education, Simon Fraser University, Canada, is Guest Researcher at Humboldt University of Berlin. **Michèle Schmidt** is Assistant Professor and Associate Director of Graduate Programs at the Faculty of Education, Simon Fraser University, Canada.

Emotional Dimensions of Educational Administration and Leadership

Edited by Eugenie A. Samier and Michèle Schmidt

LONDON AND NEW YORK

First published 2009
by Routledge
2 Park Square, Milton Park, Abingdon, Oxon OX14 4RN

Simultaneously published in the USA and Canada
by Routledge
270 Madison Ave, New York, NY 10016

Routledge is an imprint of the Taylor & Francis Group, an informa business

Typeset in Garamond by Wearset Ltd, Boldon, Tyne and Wear
Printed and bound in Great Britain by TJI Digital, Padstow, Cornwall

British Library Cataloguing in Publication Data
A catalogue record for this book is available from the British Library

Library of Congress Cataloging in Publication Data
A catalog record for this book has been requested

ISBN10: 0-415-47697-6 (hbk)

ISBN13: 978-0-415-47697-3 (hbk)

Contents

Illustrations

Figures

Tables

Contributors

Terryl Atkins is a Lecturer in the Visual and Performing Arts Department at Thompson Rivers University, Canada, where she teaches Photography, Visual Culture, Gallery Studies, and Art Theory. She is near finishing an interdisciplinary PhD on imagination and embodied perception in relation to the creation of two-dimensional works of art focusing on the evolution of pictorial space and imaging processes of schizophrenics and autistics, as well as a critical evaluation of the process of art in therapy.

Richard Bates is Professor of Social and Administrative Studies in the Faculty of Education, Deakin University, Australia. His international reputation rests primarily on his contributions to the debate over the New Sociology of Education, on his work in developing an alternative 'cultural' tradition in Educational Administration and on his contributions to Teacher Education. He has published some 70 papers and books as well as being on the editorial boards of numerous journals.

Jill Blackmore is a Professor of Education (Personal Chair) in the Faculty of Education, Deakin University. Her research interests include feminist approaches to globalisation, education policy and governance, educational leadership and reform, organisational change and innovation, teachers' and academics' work, and the changing relations between the individual, community, family and the state.

Cheryl L. Bolton held various management positions in the private sector in the UK before leaving it to pursue a career in post compulsory education where she developed courses and curricula across a wide range of business and management programmes. Later she transferred to Teacher Education. Currently she is a Senior Lecturer in Post Compulsory Education in the Institute for Education Policy Research at Staffordshire University, UK.

Megan Crawford is a Senior Lecturer in the London Centre for Leadership and Learning, Institute of Education. Before moving into Higher Education, she worked as a primary school teacher in a variety of schools in southern England, and was a deputy headteacher for the latter part of her career in schools. She is also an experienced school governor, having been chair of governors of a small church primary, and a large primary in special measures, as well as helping to set up two new primary schools. Currently, she is Chair of Governors of a new secondary school, where she has been involved since the beginning of her career. She also has extensive experience of looked after children, through Local Authority voluntary work. Her research interests include all aspects of working with people, including emotions and leadership, governing bodies, Continuing Professional Development (CPD), and headship preparation, practice and sustainability.

Fenwick W. English is the R. Wendell Eaves Senior Distinguished Professor of Educational Leadership in the School of Education at the University of North Carolina at Chapel Hill. He has been both a practitioner in K-12 education (principal and superintendent) since 1961 and a professor, department chair, dean and vice-chancellor of academic affairs in higher education since 1984. He has served as the General Editor of the *Handbook of Educational Leadership* (2005) and the *Encyclopedia of Educational Leadership and Administration* (2006).

Peter Gronn is Professor of Education, Faculty of Education, University of Cambridge. Previously (2007–8), he was chair in Public Service, Educational Leadership and Management at the University of Glasgow, prior to which (2003–7) he was Professor of Education (personal chair) in the Faculty of Education, Monash University. His research interests cover all aspects of leadership, including policy, distributed leadership, leadership formation and the development of leaders, leadership models and types, and the connection between organisational culture, and leadership and organisational learning.

Sheri Klein is a Professor of Art Education at the University of Wisconsin–Stout, Menomonnie WI where she teaches undergraduate art education and master's level education courses. She earned a BFA and MFA in Painting from the School of the Art Insitute of Chicago and a PhD in Curriculum and Instruction from Indiana University, Bloomington. She has published numerous articles in national and international education, curriculum, art education, and leadership journals (*Art Education*, *International Journal of Leadership in Education*, *Reflective Practice*, *Studies in Art Education*), and serves on the editorial boards for several journals. Her areas of scholarship cover aspects of art and teacher education and higher education issues that include leadership.

Peter Milley holds a PhD in Leadership Studies from the University of Victoria, BC. He is a Senior Advisor in Curriculum and Leadership at the Canada School of Public Service in Ottawa where he conducts research on public administration, leadership and management, and provides advice nationally and internationally to senior public officials on how to encourage leadership and learning in their organisations.

Eugenie A. Samier concentrates her research and writing in administrative philosophy and theory, Weberian foundations of administration, theories and models of educational leadership, and comparative educational administration. She currently holds a Guest Researcher position at the Humboldt University of Berlin, was Visiting Professor in the Department of Administrative Studies at the University of Tartu, Estonia (2003) and has been a guest lecturer at universities and institutes in Germany, Estonia, Russia, Norway, and Finland.

Michèle Schmidt is Assistant Professor and Associate Director of Graduate Programs in the Faculty of Education at Simon Fraser University. Her research interests and publications are in the areas of the emotions of teaching and leading, leadership within a context of educational change and accountability, and socio–cultural perspectives of education that focus on the implications of capital on children's school experiences in small schools.

Yaroslav Senyshyn is Professor in the Faculty of Education at Simon Fraser University, Past-President of its Faculty Association and Member-at-Large of the Canadian Association of University Teachers (CAUT) Executive Committee. He teaches philosophy of music, aesthetics, curriculum theory and moral education.

Nigel Tubbs is Professor of Philosophical and Educational Thought at the University of Winchester in England. His most recent publications are *Philosophy's Higher Education* and *Philosophy of the Teacher*. He has published philosophical work on the teacher in the *Journal of Philosophy of Education*, *Educational Studies*, and *Educational Theory and Practice*.

Janice Wallace is Associate Dean, Undergraduate Teacher Education and an Associate Professor in the Department of Educational Policy Studies, the University of Alberta, Edmonton, Alberta. She received her PhD at OISE/University of Toronto in 2000 and was awarded the Thomas B. Greenfield Award by the Canadian Association for the Study of Educational Administration. Her scholarship focuses on equity issues in educational organisations and the particular effects of globalisation on the work of administrators. She was a faculty member at the University of Western Ontario, has been a visiting lecturer at the University of Victoria, and an invited Visiting Scholar at the University of British Columbia.

Michalinos Zembylas is Assistant Professor of Education at the Open University of Cyprus and Director of Curriculum Development at CARDET, Cyprus. He earned his BS in Elementary Education and MEd in science education from the University of Texas at Austin and his PhD in Curriculum and Instruction from the University of Illinois at Urbana-Champaign. His research interests lie in the area of exploring how discursive, political, and cultural aspects define the experience of emotion and affect in curriculum and pedagogy. He is particularly interested in how affective politics intersect with issues of social justice pedagogies, intercultural and peace education, and citizenship education.

Editors' introduction

Eugenie A. Samier and Michèle Schmidt

> Emotions shape the landscape of our mental and social lives. Like the 'geological upheavals' a traveller might discover in a landscape where recently only a flat plane could be seen, they mark our lives as uneven, uncertain, and prone to reversal.
>
> Nussbaum 2001: 1

Martha Nussbaum set herself a monumental task recently when she wrote *Upheavals of Thought: The Intelligence of Emotions*. Her 700-plus page opus adopts the possibility of emotions serving as an intelligent response to value posed by Proust, a view that regards emotions as part of ethical reasoning rather than the tendency in Western philosophy to regard them as either 'support[ing] or subvert[ing] our choice to act according to principle' (2001: 1) (not to be confused with Gardner's comparatively simplistic and narrower Emotional Intelligence theory), particularly according to moral values. Her exploration takes her through a revisiting of philosophical, literary, and social thought, an intellectual voyage, from the Greek Stoics to the most recent economic and political theories grounded in compassion. Her criticism extends into two areas of current educational critique: first, the harnessing of emotion by a market-place imperative to which educational organisations are 'relatively vulnerable'; and a mass media 'held hostage to market standards' thereby diminishing the potential they have to serve the public good (see 2001: 433–5). What is also apparent from her comprehensive survey is that the study of emotion has an ancient and relatively continuous history, carried up through intellectual traditions that include political and other social institutional considerations. A consideration of emotions is central to influential texts on the state and its agencies, notably in Plato's *Republic*, Aristotle's *Politics*, Locke's *Two Treatises of Government*, Hobbes' *Leviathan*, Rousseau's *Discourses*, Kant's political writings, Hegel's political writings, and Mill's writings on liberty and government, all of which shaped Western notions of the state and its administration, that is, the public sphere in which most of education is located or regulated.

The purpose of this volume is to explore foundational theory for the emotional dimensions of educational administration and leadership, an area that is only just re-emergent in the last few years. The collection is also intended to demonstrate the relevance of this foundation to practical issues and problems internationally, both within the organisational context and extra-organisationally. As such, the focus is on the application of emotional factors as they affect our understanding of, and practice in, educational organisations. Emotions are fundamental to ethics, governance, policy, management and power issues, gender, ethnic and race relations, affecting organisational climate and culture, and the quality of interpersonal relations that form micropolitics.

The emotions of education affect the inculcation and implementation of basic political values and rights as they pertain to organisations, as well as the deep visceral character that organisational politics and culture can take. For example, what are the emotional explanations for those who fear and avoid authority positions and those who lust after the status and privilege of leadership positions (here Plato's dictum that power positions should only go to those who do not desire them is relevant). And what are the distinguishing emotions associated with formal administrative positions and informal leadership roles? Are the emotions activated by charisma (as with any authoritative role), dangerous, unstable, and immoral, while at the same time engendering enthusiasm, engagement, and commitment? Is it possible to develop a rigorous theoretical foundation for emotions that complements other explanatory and hermeneutic dimensions and structures of experience without succumbing to emotional reductionism? Is emotion something that can be shaped towards organisational purpose without being manipulative? There are many questions involving the recognition and use of emotions at all administrative and organisational levels that cannot be adequately answered by uni-dimensional or simplistic explanations.

The study of emotions in organisations, administration, and leadership

One of the first tasks in considering theories (and value and uses) of emotions is definitional. This in itself is not straightforward; it is highly complex and contentious, involving many disciplines and traditions within them, problems that are well beyond the scope of this collection to address in a comprehensive manner. But each author must explicitly or implicitly choose to follow some definitional construct. Are emotions the same as feelings (from perspectives adopting an unconscious activity, emotions is the broader term)? How are emotions related to values, including moral and political values that are at the heart of educational administration? How are emotions and their causes distinguishable (involving emotions that are without external cause, and those that arise inherent to the human condition, as well as cognitive and non-cognitive theories)? How are emotions related to behaviour and expression (in other words, is the behaviour necessary to experiencing the emotion)? How does one account for conflicting emotions, if, in fact, it is possible to even experience only one emotion at a time? How do culture and gender affect emotion? How do emotions affect the fundamental functions of administration and leadership: awareness of others, self-awareness, decision-making, learning, consciousness, interpersonal relations, character development, personality, concept formation (e.g. social justice, ethics, organisation design)? What is there in administration and leadership that is not affected by, or rooted in, emotion?

Even identifying and classifying emotions is not simple. Are there primary emotions from which others are derived (see Ekman 1999) or do some basic emotions blend into others (see Plutchik 2001)? Are emotions discrete or variable across bi-polar dimensions? Which are emotional episodes and emotional dispositions? Among the many approaches are somatic theories, cognitive theories, perceptual (a hybrid of somatic and cognitive), sociological, psychotherapeutic, anthropological, and the list goes on. From an organisational functional perspective, there are emotions that serve to advance humane administration, such as love, joy, hope, and courage that on the surface would appear to promote a sense of community, sympathy and empathy, and serve individuals' political rights to fairness and equality, as well as the general growth and development of staff. There are other emotions that would appear to be harmful, such as anger, dejection, fear, disgust, and distress. However, these are also circumstantial in terms of their value to organisational experience. Aren't anger and disgust important in opposing injustice or an abuse of authority? Meta-emotion, our feelings and thoughts about emotion, are critically central to administrative authority: how a senior administrator reacts to the emotions of others is part and parcel of the power wielded in legitimation and response. From Weber's point of view, one of the most important critiques of bureaucratised organisations is that they bleed out of bureaucrats the capacity for emotional response (largely through suppression and repression) rendering them virtually sociopathic in their organisational role:

> No one knows who will live in this cage of the future ... mechanized petrification, embellished with a sort of convulsive self-importance. For of the last stage of this cultural development, it might well be truly said: 'Specialists without spirit, sensualists without heart; this nullity imagines that it has attained a level of civilization never before achieved'.
>
> (1930: 182)

Approaches to emotion vary considerably across psychological theories. At the physiological end, primary emotions such as happiness, sadness, fear, anger, surprise, and disgust are seen to be produced in the brain and manifested by distinctive facial expressions (Ekman and Friesen 1971). This definition of emotion lends itself to interpretation best when studying patterns of emotional experience, expression, and emotionally-influenced behaviour (Kidd

2004). The functionalist interpretation has recently made inroads in organisational literature where the focus is on the individual's relationship to the environment involving emotions that influence their cognitive processing, social interaction, and physical experience leading to either maintenance or change in their actions when aspiring to particular goals. Other psychologies have also played a strong role in organisation, administration, and leadership studies, from the depth psychologies of psychoanalysis and analytic psychology, through to the humanistic psychologies influenced by existentialism and phenomenology. These have emphasised to a much higher degree in meaning, identity, the personal and subjective, and self-actualisation. The humanistic psychologies and depth psychologies, in particular, derive also from the broad range of influences found in societal context, culture, politics, and other conditions that shape the worlds in which personality and character are formed.

Commentary on the nature of emotion and its effect on organisational performance is as old as studies on rulership and military strategy. Sun Tzu, in *The Art of War*, regards emotions as strategic and tactical means; Machiavelli, in *The Prince*, intended as a guide during extreme conditions of siege and warfare, also evaluates emotions in terms of their role in maintaining order and dominance. Plato takes quite a different approach. While concerned primarily with social order and rulership in *The Republic*, he counsels against the rampant exercise of emotions that distort rational thought, yet is dependent upon courage in the protective class of society.

In the early modern disciplinary period, from the early to mid-twentieth century, leadership studies were influenced mostly by experimental and behavioural psychologies. One of Terman's earliest articles, 'A Preliminary Study of the Psychology and Pedagogy of Leadership' (1904), draws on animal studies and anthropology to determine if leadership attributes are selectively recognisable. By the 1940s and 1950s, the psychological investigation of leadership was well established. In the 1940s, most leadership studies were dominated by trait theory (Cowley 1931; Stogdill 1948) and situational leadership styles, for example, Knickerbocker (1948) who viewed emotions as functional, dependent upon the character and circumstances of the followership. During the same period Gibb (1947) and Hollander (1964) viewed the role of emotions as socially constructed through interaction. In the 1950s and 1960s considerations broadened to encompass many perspectives on leadership: as an aspect of organisation (Stogdill 1950; Bavelas 1960); as a function of group decision-making (Bales and Slater 1955); as a function of follower perception of personality attributes (Clifford and Cohn 1964); as having an effect on the organisational hierarchy of leadership (Pelz 1951); as containing personality variables (Mann 1959); as having an influence on leadership work style and group performance (Fiedler 1965); and as revealing the dual leadership of formal and informal in complex organisations (Etzioni 1965); and the democratic ethics of leadership (Brameld 1955).

In the 1960s and 1970s, much of the emotional dimension of administration studies was included in organisational behaviour, mostly using psychoanalytic approaches (e.g. Karen Horney), industrial psychology of Herzberg, behaviourism, and trait theory that informed the human relations school. The major focus for the latter three was on motivation – how to motivate workers to be more productive. A significant impact was made at this time by Simon's *Administrative Behavior* (1947), imposing the notion of 'bounded rationality' that relegated emotions to the 'irrational', ushering in the dominance of cognitive studies and reinforcing scientific and mechanistic management.

A lesser used tradition is that of psychoanalysis, empirically a more qualitative and interpretive approach, in the work of Bettelheim, Horney, and Adorno (on the authoritarian personality), more recently receiving significant attention in organisation studies through Hirschhorn's *The Workplace Within* (1988), Diamond's *The Unconscious Life of Organizations* (1993), Obholzer and Roberts' *The Unconscious at Work* (1994), and Gabriel's *Organizations in Depth* (1999). However, for the last 20 years, it is Manfred Kets de Vries who has dominated the management field treatment of emotions in the workplace, beginning with *The Neurotic Organization* in 1984 (co-authored with Danny Miller). A representative article of his psychoanalytic approach is 'Beyond the Quick Fix' (1998, co-author K. Balazs), which examines the personal changes on a conscious and unconscious level required for organisational change to take place. The main focus is a critique of those writers who assume a superficial, 'quick fix' approach, ignoring underlying psychodynamics such as resistance, the importance of 'focal events' and public commitment, as well as the complexity of inner journeys that individuals undergo in organisational transformation.

Currently organisation studies has seen a resurgence of this topic, however, in radically altered form. In psychology, Salovey and Mayer have argued for two issues that underlie the emotional turn in administrative studies: that not all emotions are 'chaotic, haphazard, and something to outgrow', and that emotional intelligence may have as important a role to play as social and cognitive intelligence (1990: 186). They explore the value of development and harnessing emotions for physiological, cognitive, motivational, and experiential reasons, in both understanding and monitoring one's own emotions (1990: 189), and, through empathy, and understanding others' in creating more constructive interpersonal relations (1990: 193). Vince and Saleem (2004) examine how the dynamics of caution and blame create micropolitics that inhibit organisational learning.

One of the first to address this 'muted' area in organisational and management studies was Stephen Fineman in *Emotion in Organizations* (1993), followed shortly thereafter by a series of three collections: Ashkanasy *et al.*'s *Emotions in the Workplace: Research, Theory, and Practice* (2000), Ashkanasy *et al.*'s (2002) *Managing Emotions in the Workplace* (2002), and Härtel *et al.*'s *Emotions in Organizational Behavior* (2005). Their first collection introduced a number of aspects that were further explored in the subsequent collections: the nature of emotion and its place in organisation studies, the ways that emotions structure organisational life, how a study of emotions can help in the interpretation of organisational dynamics, the effects of emotions, and emerging research approaches. Lord *et al.*'s *Emotions in the Workplace* (2002) complements these volumes with additional exploration of conceptual foundations, emotional regulation, and various problems in the workplace.

By 2000, emotions had become a sub-division of organisation theory, producing regular papers and symposia at major organisation and management conferences, with articles appearing regularly in major journals, and, as just reviewed, collections. Fineman provides a thorough overview of topics in his introductory essay: the relationship between aesthetics and emotion (e.g. Gagliardi 1999; Strati 1999), a range of approaches from psychoanalysis to social constructivism, emotional labour (e.g. Hochschild 1983) and emotional intelligence (Goleman 1995). Although Fineman claims a decline in psychoanalytic approaches, this can be challenged by the popularity of Kets de Vries' and other psychoanalytically oriented work, and the current importance of narcissism as a destructive element in management, most of which have a psychoanalytical orientation.

A related field particularly important for educational leadership, political studies, has also recently seen a number of new books on the emotions of political behaviour. George Marcus' *The Sentimental Citizen* (2002) was one of the first to open the recent discussion, in a period that seems, at least in the US, to be dominated by sensationalism, hyperbole, scare tactics, and scandals (2002: 2–3). Neuman *et al.*'s *The Affect Effect* (2007) examines a number of important aspects of political activity that overlap into educational administration concerns: cognition, judgement, evaluation, voting, identity construction, surveillance, and cultural symbols. The collection also covers emotions that can have a damaging effect such as fear, anger, and anxiety. Another major source for leadership, although usually found outside the educational field, is the political biography.

There are many other traditions in psychology (and related fields) that have yet to be used for our understanding of emotion in administrative and leadership practice, even though their nature speak centrally and clearly to human interaction. Analytic psychology is one that has received some attention. Mark Chater has contributed a recent article to the field, 'Archetypes of Destruction: Notes on the Impact of Distorted Management Theory on Education Communities' (2005), that employs the Jungian theory of archetypes through the 'gods of mismanagement' type to effectively critique aspects of education management. Existential, Gestalt, and phenomenological psychologies also promise great potential in illuminating the role of emotions in the pursuit of higher order values, humane social interaction, and the complexity of the leadership experience.

The study of emotions in educational administration and leadership

The study of emotions in educational administration and leadership covers a range of approaches. The sociological is one that has been commonly used to view emotions as a social construct (Hochschild 1979; Kemper 1978; Turner 1962), embedded in social interactions (see Averill 1980; Parkinson 1995) and shaped by context (White 1993), enabling researchers to explore the role of emotion in interpersonal communication (Kidd 2004; Hargreaves 1998). This perspective distinguishes emotions 'from their essential interiority' (White 1993: 31) by considering the contingent effect of social influences, acknowledging individuals 'as actors whose subjectivity is continually formed in, and through, interactions with others' (1993: 29). Emotions, in other words, are contextual, political, and relational phenomena as well as psychological properties of unique individuals (Hargreaves 1998). They exist as inter- and intra-personal constructs (Denzin 1984), deeply embedded in, and configured by, people's ability to define and achieve their purposes, by their experiences of power and powerlessness, and in their relationships with others (Hargreaves 1998; Schmidt 2000). Within this more constructivist paradigm, we find appraisal theories of emotion, where events are either related to an individual's well-being or examined for their emotional meaning in any random context (Lazarus 1999). Adopting a sociological perspective, Hartley (2004) draws primarily from the Durkheimian and Weberian traditions (although overlooks the psychological dimension that Weber attributed to his multi-disciplinary notion of understanding) to examine the 'emotional revival' taking place in management studies. Based on a concern for the emotional effects on a group level in sociology, that is, 'collective emotions', and on organisational conditions like bureaucratisation in suppressing the emotional, part of Weber's definition of 'disenchantment', Hartley explores the moral implications of the relationship between emotions and a culture of consumption.

On a social psychology level, the theory of emotional contagion offers an important insight for leadership. Those who are able to visibly express emotions have the potential to achieve much more influence over others in their emotional states – for good or for evil – effective in creating a more humane and conducive environment or in establishing power (Domagalski 1999: 842–3). The theory of emotional labour, first appearing in the field in Hochschild's seminal 'Emotion Work, Feeling Rules, and Social Structure' (1979), also contributes to an understanding of the dynamics surrounding administrative and leadership roles, shaping the emotional climate, including emotional commodification in market-oriented organisations (Domalgalski 1999: 844–5). Some (e.g. Lee *et al.* 1999) see the need to view emotions from a multi-paradigm perspective drawing on psychological and social constructivist perspectives. In this way, it is possible to identify emotions that are influenced by organisational settings and conditions that lead to anger, anxiety, fear, guilt-shame, envy-jealousy, hope, happiness, joy, pride, love, and compassion (Lazarus and Cohen-Charash 2001). Kidd (2004) explains, for example, that anger may be a common response to a demeaning offence or misuse of managerial power leading to decreased organisational commitment and eventual resignation. Martin *et al.* (1998) found in their research of individuals' experiences that often emotional expression was constrained by what was deemed acceptable or unacceptable responses. On a more positive note, studies have also shown evidence of 'bounded emotionality' where members of an organisation develop feelings of community (Kidd 2004).

Day and Leitch (2001) have explored the role of emotions in teacher professional practice, examining its relationship to good practice, rational decision-making, effective careers, cognitive health and various contextual factors, and the passion of vocation, drawing on a number of authors, but most prominently Goleman's (1995) theory of emotional intelligence. They include an examination of powerful emotions like 'hurt, guilt, resentment, fear, injustice, and shame' (2001: 403) that affect professional identity and its world, as well as some of the most appropriate interpretive research approaches for emotions, such as narrative, critical incident, and biographical methods and the relationship between emotions and organisational culture. Blackmore (2004) has also explored the emotions associated with performativity in educational leadership, and Zembylas (2003; 2005) the emotional dimensions of identity-building.

Kovan and Dirkx (2003) have examined how emotions, among other factors, affect commitment and a sense of personal development necessary for vocation in a transformative learning environment for adults. Ashkanasy and Dasborough (2003) have begun empirical studies on the value of emotions in teaching leadership undergraduate courses, demonstrating a strong relationship between emotional awareness and development and performance, including team activities. One source of negative emotions in the university setting is bullying (or mobbing), a phenomenon that has received more recent attention, including its impact on the workplace. Ferris argues that mandatory training for organisational representatives (that is, anyone whose responsibility is to respond to employee problems) is necessary in reducing the harmful effects of bullying, due in part to the 'escalating number of cases' (2004: 390), and the usual reluctance of employees to seek help due to the risks they incur as a consequence. Lewis has examined bullying in the university and college environment where market-oriented management has taken hold, redefining inappropriate treatment of employees as 'tough managerial styles' or 'macho management' (2004: 281–2).

Emotions as a theoretical construct in education are often overlooked when examining the impact of educational reform and leadership (Spillane *et al.* 2002). In particular, what seems to be missing is an examination of how emotions shape and are shaped by the work of educators. Some are engaged in researching the topic of educators' emotional lives and the impact of high-stakes accountability (Jeffrey and Woods 1996), as well as stress-inducing reform strategies (Dinham and Scott 1996). Yet little has been done to illuminate how emotions are embedded in, and shaped by, reforms, and how these emotions manifest themselves in, and affect, educators' work (Schmidt and Datnow 2005). Campos *et al.* (1994) regard as relevant to education those ranging from physiological and psychological to more sociological and anthropological perspectives that examine constructivist notions of how culture relates to emotions. Geijsel and Meijers (2005) have contributed to these issues by demonstrating that a major responsibility of administrators and leaders in organisational change is to create the conditions and provide emotional support for a more creative and meaningful identity construction, requiring a commitment strategy, conducive culture, and the establishment of a learning community. Parkin (1993) has explored problems associated with emotion, organisational change and reform for gender equity: in the public realm of organisation where rationality dominates, emotional expressiveness, associated more with women, disadvantages them to the pathologisation, marginalisation, and trivialisation of emotions.

Chapter overviews

The first section, 'Theoretical Foundations', includes discussion of early modern romantic philosophy tradition that later influenced a number of scholarly traditions, the idealist philosophy of Hegel, Freudian theory, and the existentialism of Søren Kierkegaard, and Habermas' Critical Theory. Eugenie Samier's 'The Romantic Philosophy of Mind: The Elevation of Emotion to the (Anti-)Heroic Ideal' focuses on one of the historical predecessors to psychological and socio-cultural approaches to emotion, the philosophical movement of Romanticism that emphasised individual uniqueness, intuition, and the unconscious, elevating emotional experience to an importance as great as that of reason. It united imagination, reason, connecting the individual's inner world with the socio-historical context, including that of educational organisations, introducing the modern heroic ideal as the highest expression of individual authenticity and the source of socio-political change, as well as the dangers of the 'dark' heroicism.

Nigel Tubbs explores how Hegel's master and servant relationship, found in his *Phenomenology of Spirit*, can be brought to bear on issues of authority in 'Philosophy and Authority: Passion in Ambivalence'. This involves looking at the philosophical and spiritual significance of fear and anxiety and how this is played out in issues and dilemmas relating to the educational professional who is prepared to reflect upon the nature of professional freedom and autonomy, and ways in which authority and freedom have been related to the soul. The kinds of emotions that can be located within such a treatment of the Western philosophical canon are those concerned with anxiety, courage, despair, curiosity, and vulnerability.

In 'Kierkegaard, Emotion, and the Individual: Passion of the Infinite as the Truth for Educational Leadership', Yaroslav Senyshyn examines Kierkegaard's use of the term 'individual', as a leader who must struggle to resist the levelling of the masses. The profound significance of the levelling process lies in the predominance of the category 'generation' over the category 'individuality'. He felt that people in his time lacked the emotional moral stamina to act on decisions – even trivial ones – individually and thus sought the framework of the committee to dare themselves into acting collectively.

Eugenie Samier, in 'Unconscious Dynamics in the Educational Organisation: Psychoanalytic Contributions to Administration and Leadership Studies', reviews the contributions of Freudian theory to uncovering unconscious processes that affect personality and interpersonal behaviour in educational administration and leadership. Important aspects include: ego and superego development informing morality, just action and self-respect; defence mechanisms, particularly projection, denial, resistance, and sublimation in both positive and negative forms; and neurotic dispositions that produce problematic organisational cultures and destructive micro-politics. These can be used to explain a number of problems such as abuse of power and authority, excessive management control, groupthink, and the transference reactions of emotions onto colleagues and superordinates leading to demonisation or idealisation.

Peter Milley's 'Towards a Critical Theory of Emotions in Educational Leadership and Administration: Building on Concepts from Jürgen Habermas' explores the contribution Habermas' work can make in analysing and interpreting the emotional dimension of education and its administration. Critical Theory provides a useful lens for investigating the emotional dimensions of freedom, equality, and social justice that are at the heart of this school of thought. Habermas' typology of human interests and corresponding forms of rationality, his concepts of communicative and strategic action, and his model of lifeworld and system all provide a role for emotion as it relates to happiness and well-being, from a critical view of negative and destructive emotions through to positive and constructive emotions in human interaction.

The second section of this book, 'Types of Emotional Analysis', includes examinations of artefactual expressions, emotional economies, the politics of emotion, and the relationship between emotion and rationality. Sheri Klein's 'Desks and Office Spaces: Personal, Emotional, and Organisational Sites for Leading', examines the desk as a site for the development and refinement of humanistic leadership practices that can result in a union of heart and head, the emotion and the intellect, thinking, feeling, and senses. It is also a site where the aesthetic merges with the emotional, the sensory, and the imaginative dimensions of leaders. How desks are designed, organised, and placed, in addition to the artefacts and images displayed on and around desks, communicate leaders' visions, their professional identity, and the emotional connections to or in their work.

Michalinos Zembylas, in 'The Politics of Emotions: Affective Economies, Ambivalence, and Transformation', analyses the politics of emotions through the lens of emotional economies, and how they serve as places of ambivalence and transformation. Emotional economies refer to relations, practices, and discourses about emotions, how they are constructed and how they constantly change. The aim is to sketch a theory that has a place for *ambivalence* and *transformation*, that shows the relations between emotions on the one hand and personal and institutional enactments of power on the other, thereby extending beyond the 'emotional rules' that individuals accommodate or resist in expressing, suppressing, or neutralising emotions. Emotional economies may establish, assert, subvert, or reinforce power differentials, playing an important political role in enabling resistance, something that is currently missing from many accounts of emotions.

In 'Measures of Hope and Despair: Emotionality, Politics, and Education', Jill Blackmore focuses on how emotions are often a surface manifestation of contestation over politics and power as well as relations of subordination and domination. This chapter argues that cultural and value shifts of educational reforms have led to significant transformations in students as well as professional identity among teachers, academics, and trainers that have challenged their individual and collective emotional investments in education as a field. These transformations are examined in the context of wider social changes that have produced new anxieties in high-risk globalised societies in which overt and covert mechanisms of blame and shame are routinely used by governments and institutions to manage institutions, staff and students, through audits, ranking and individualisation of risk and responsibility to individuals, both students and teachers. Drawing on a range of social theorists and empirical case studies, Blackmore explores how emotions are inseparable from issues of what we value, how we value ourselves and others, and of social justice.

Cheryl Bolton and Fenwick English's 'My Head and My Heart: Deconstructing the Historical/Hysterical Binary that Conceals and Reveals Emotion in Educational Leadership' challenges current leadership preparation that places premium emphasis on rational thinking, decision-making models, organisational structures, and technology, with leadership encounters in which very logical and rational thinkers suddenly encounter a different part of themselves when they have unexpected personal experiences, oftentimes taking the form of the 'wounded leader'. The discussion is illustrated through the experiences of Thomas Jefferson, empirical studies, and the authors' own empirical research. They argue that understanding the role of emotion and culture becomes more significant as we respond to the influences of the global market. This means becoming increasingly productive and competitive, requiring that leaders act in ways that are contrary to their rational training as they increasingly work outside their experience or understanding. The implications for gender stereotyping that has shaped our understanding of what makes an effective leader are also examined in order to pose alternative perspectives in preparing educational leaders not only in strategic and tactical terms, but in approaches that draw upon the full range of the arts and humanities in coming to terms with leadership challenges.

The last section of this collection, 'Critical and Contemporary Issues', includes critiques of the fear arising from accountability regimes, the political economy of the market model, a feminist critique of ideologies reflecting emotional investments, emotional contexts for teamwork, the problem of narcissism, and the emotional dimensions of role engagement. Michèle Schmidt's 'Accountability and the Educational Leader: Where Does Fear Fit in?' explores the emotions fuelled by fear in an accountability era that seems to be defined primarily by test scores, raising student achievement, and school rankings that lead to either rewards or sanctions. This includes the fear of being publicly identified as a 'poor performing' or a 'high performing' school as the media, parents, and the community increasingly reify the power of test data, leaving school leaders the unexpected victims or heroes of an accountability system within which emotional involvement is often one of the most difficult aspects to deal with. Schmidt reviews a number of theories that illuminate this problem of fear in school leadership that explain the sociological, political, and institutional factors that mitigate or militate educational leaders' feelings of fear within a context of accountability.

In 'The Political Economy of the Emotions: Individualism, Culture and Markets, and the Administration of the Self in Education', Richard Bates examines the emotional dimension of the search for authenticity in contemporary life, bedevilled by the doctrine of individualism on the one hand and collectivism or managerialism on the other. Setting aside the psychologistic search for the true emotions of the inner self that characterised much popular commentary during the mid-twentieth century, he explores two contemporary sources that dominate the search for emotional security and provide for sources for the self. On the one hand, modern markets seem to allow for an unfettered individualism which itself has emotional consequences of a profound and perhaps disorienting kind. On the other hand cultures would seem to offer ready-made solutions to emotional dilemmas. Each requires of education a differing conception of curriculum, pedagogy, and evaluation, each requires a different approach to the management of the self, and each has a different trajectory for the emotional management of both managers and managed. This chapter explores the role of education in such emotional management and the consequences for educational administration.

Janice Wallace uses a feminist post-structural policy analysis framework informed by Foucault's theories of governmentality to examine the emotional experiences of three gender equity employment officers in '"Let's Get Personal": Disrupting Gender Norms in Educational Organisations'. The ideological and structural resistance to their organisational position as agents of policy change represents the resistance to a discursive interruption in gendered norms, especially by those in power, mostly men, who enjoy the material benefits of dominant ideologies and, therefore, have little motivation to give up the privilege they enjoy. The author argues that personal resistance is a phenomenon enabled by the ways in which gender equity work is constructed in opposition to the dominant understandings of organisations in which the personal is shunned by masculinist meta-narratives. The 'places of emotion' that are revealed in the tensions and resistances experienced by gender equity officers is the focus of this chapter.

Megan Crawford's 'The Leader and the Team: Emotional Context in Educational Leadership' examines the personal and emotional sides of leadership in schools arguing that leadership is reliant on both the personal emotional quality of those in leadership roles, and is a necessary quality of social work relationships in schools. Drawing on a social constructionist approach that presents the stories that people tell gives substance to the feelings held by the participants, and at the same time actively constitutes the emotional form of work life. How educational leaders experience, and talk about, emotion and meaning in their daily interactions is discussed, and the impact it has on the emotional context of work. This leads to a discussion of narratives and emotion, and how the leader forms an emotional context within which the narrative of education is carried out. Leaders' knowledge of their own emotional selves enables them to visualise how they want others to relate to each other within the school – an emotional coherent context.

In 'Emotional Engagement with Leadership' Peter Gronn looks at the emotional engagement with, and disengagement from, the work of leaders as role performance. Central to potential leadership engagement is a series of challenges concerned with identity, aspirations for self, career development and mobility, and what it means to exercise the responsibilities entailed in leading others. Negotiating each of these demands may entail serious psychological and emotional working through for prospective leaders, during which time individuals confront a calculus of risk. This is a broad configuration or mix of anticipated rewards, incentives, possibilities, costs, and consequences that have to be identified, weighed up and mulled over in both internal and public forms of conversational reasoning. This chapter considers some of the key features of leadership engagement, including the positioning of oneself in relation to anticipated challenges; identification of one's personal resources, strengths, and weaknesses; reliance on peers, mentors, and coaches; testing of self in light of experience; and coping with vulnerability and the potential for failure. Like disengagement, leadership engagement is influenced by various cultures and contexts producing expectations of leadership performance and accomplishment that have broad significance for systemic policies and organisational processes of leader formation, succession, and recruitment.

In the final chapter, the problem of narcissism in educational administration and leadership is examined in Eugenie Samier and Terryl Atkins' 'The Problem of Narcissists in Positions of Power: The Grandiose, the Callous, and the Irresponsible in Educational Administration and Leadership'. Positions of power and influence provide motive and opportunity for the damaging character of this personality disorder to negatively affect the work life of colleagues and sabotage organisational effectiveness. The chapter reviews the theoretical foundation for narcissism in organisational settings, identifying its typical traits and behaviours. These include an illegitimate sense of entitlement, inappropriate need for admiration and attention, a lack of empathy, the projection of negative traits onto others, and an objectified use of people. This is followed by a discussion of the recommended strategies on the part of individual organisational actors in protecting themselves from the harmful effects of those in authority positions who bear responsibility for the behaviour of their subordinates.

References

Ashkanasy, N. and Dasborough, M. (2003) 'Emotional awareness and emotional intelligence in leadership teaching', *Journal of Education for Business*, 79, 1: 18–22.

Ashkanasy, N., Härtel, C., and Zerbe, W. (eds) (2000) *Emotions in the Workplace: Research, Theory, and Practice*, Westport: Quorum Books.

Ashkanasy, N., Zerbe, W., and Härtel, C. (2002) *Managing Emotions in the Workplace*, Armonk: M.E. Sharpe.

Averill, J.R. (1980) 'A constructivist view of emotion', in R. Plutchik and H. Kellerman (eds) *Theories of Emotion*, New York: Academic Press.

Bales, R. and Slater, P. (1955) 'Role differentiation in small decision-making groups', in T. Parsons and R. Bales (eds) *Family, Socialization and Interaction Processes*, Glencoe: Free Press.

Bavelas, A. (1960) 'Leadership: Man and function', *Administrative Science Quarterly*, 5: 491–8.

Blackmore, J. (2004) 'Leading as emotional management work in high risk times: The counterintuitive impulses of performativity and passion', *School Leadership & Management*, 24, 4: 439–59.

Brameld, T. (1955) 'Ethics of leadership', *Adult Leadership*, 4: 5–8.

Campos, J.J., Mumme, D.L., Kermoian, R., and Campos, R.G. (1994) 'A functionalist perspective on the nature of emotion', in N.A. Fox (ed.) *The Development of Emotion Regulations: Biological and Behavioural Considerations*, Monographs of the Society for Research in Child Development, 59 (2–3 Serial No. 240).

Chater, M. (2005) 'Archetypes of destruction: Notes on the impact of distorted management theory on education communities', *International Journal of Leadership in Education*, 8, 1: 3–19.

Clifford, C. and Cohn, T. (1964) 'The relationship between leadership and personality attributes perceived by followers', *Journal of Social Psychology*, 64: 57–64.

Cowley, W. (1931) 'The traits of face-to-face leaders', *Journal of Abnormal and Social Psychology*, 46: 589–95.

Day, C. and Leitch, R. (2001) 'Teachers' and teacher educators' lives: The role of emotion', *Teaching and Teacher Education*, 17: 403–15.

Denzin, N.K. (1984) *On Understanding Emotion*, San Francisco: Jossey-Bass.

Diamond, M. (1993) *The Unconscious Life of Organizations: Interpreting Organizational Reality*, Westport: Quorum.

Dinham, S. and Scott, C. (1996) *The Teacher 2000 Project: A Study of Teacher Motivation and Health*, Pinrith: University of Western Sydney Press.

Domagalski, T.A. (1999) 'Managing stress: Emotion and power at work', *Human Relations*, 52, 6: 833–52.

Ekman, P. (1999) 'Basic emotions', in T. Dalgleish and M. Power (eds) *Handbook of Cognition and Emotion*, Sussex: John Wiley & Sons.

Ekman, P. and Friesen, W.V. (1971) 'Constants across cultures in the face and emotion', *Journal of Personality and Social Psychology*, 17: 124–9.

Etzioni, A. (1965) 'Dual leadership in complex organizations', *American Sociological Review*, 30: 688–98.

Ferris, P. (2004) 'A preliminary typology of organisational response to allegations of workplace bullying: See no evil, hear no evil, speak no evil', *British Journal of Guidance and Counselling*, 32, 3: 389–95.

Fiedler, F. (1965) 'Leadership – a new model', *Discovery*, 12–17.

Fineman, S. (ed.) (1993) *Emotion in Organizations*, London: Sage.

Gabriel, Y. (1999) *Organizations in Depth*, London: Sage.

Gagliardi, P. (1999) 'Exploring the aesthetic side of organizational life', in S. Clegg, C. Hardy, and W. Nord (eds) *Studying Organizations*, London: Sage.

Geijsel, F. and Meijers, F. (2005) 'Identity learning: The core process of educational change', *Educational Studies*, 31, 4: 419–30.

Gibb, C. (1947) 'The principles and traits of leadership', *Journal of Abnormal and Social Psychology*, 42: 267–84.

Goleman, D. (1995) *Emotional Intelligence*, New York: Bantam Books.

Hargreaves, A. (1998) 'The emotional politics of teaching and teacher development: With implications for educational leadership', *International Journal of Leadership in Education*, 1, 4: 315–36.

Härtel, C., Zerbe, W., and Ashkanasy, N. (eds) (2005) *Emotions in Organizational Behavior*, Mahwah: Lawrence Erlbaum Associates.

Hartley, D. (2004) 'Management, leadership and the emotional order of the school', *Journal of Education Policy*, 19, 5: 583–94.

Hirschhorn, L. (1988) *The Workplace Within: Psychodynamics of Organisational Life*, Cambridge: MIT Press.

Hochschild, A. (1979) 'Emotion work, feeling rules, and social structure', *American Journal of Sociology*, 39: 551–75.

—— (1983) *The Managed Heart: The Commercialization of Human Feeling*, Berkeley: University of California Press.

Hollander, E. (1964) 'Emergent leadership and social influence', *Leadership Groups and Influence*, Oxford: Oxford University Press.

Jeffrey, B. and Woods, P. (1996) 'Feeling deprofessionalised: The social construction of emotions during an OFSTED inspection', *Cambridge Journal of Education*, 26, 3: 325–43.

Kemper, T.D. (1978) *A Social Interactional Theory of Emotions*, New York: Wiley.

Kets de Vries, M. and Balazs, K. (1998) 'Beyond the quick fix: The psychodynamics of organizational transformation and change', *European Management Journal*, 16, 5: 611–22.

Kets de Vries, M. and Miller, D. (1984) *The Neurotic Organization: Diagnosing and Changing Counterproductive Styles of Management*, San Francisco: Jossey-Bass.

Kidd, J.M. (2004) 'Emotion in career contexts: Challenges for theory and research', *Journal of Vocational Behavior*, 64: 441–54.

Knickerbocker, I. (1948) 'Leadership: A conception and some implications', *Journal of Social Issues*, 4: 23–40.

Kovan, J. and Dirkx, J. (2003) '"Being called awake": The role of transformative learning in the lives of environmental activists', *Adult Education Quarterly*, 53, 2: 99–118.

Lazarus, R.S. (1999) *Stress and Emotion, a New Synthesis*, London: Free Association Books.

Lazarus, R.S. and Cohen-Charash, Y. (2001) 'Discrete emotions in organizational life', in R.L. Payne and C.L. Cooper (eds) *Emotions at Work: Theory, Research and Applications in Management*, Chichester: Wiley.

Lee, T.W., Mitchell, T.R., and Sablynski, C.J. (1999) 'Qualitative research in organizational and vocational psychology, 1979–1999', *Journal of Vocational Behavior*, 55: 161–87.

Lewis, D. (2004) 'Bullying at work: The impact of shame among university and college lecturers', *British Journal of Guidance and Counselling*, 32, 3: 281–99.

Lord, R., Klimoski, J., and Kanfer, R. (2002) *Emotions in the Workplace: Understanding the Structure and Role of Emotions in Organizational Behavior*, San Francisco: Jossey-Bass.

Mann, R. (1959) 'A review of the relationships between personality and performance in small groups', *Psychological Bulletin*, 56: 241–70.

Marcus, G. (2002) *The Sentimental Citizen: Emotion in Democratic Politics*, University Park: Pennsylvania State University Press.

Martin, J., Knopoff, K., and Beckman, C. (1998) 'An alternative to bureaucratic impersonality and emotional labor: Bounded emotionality at The Body Shop', *Administrative Science Quarterly*, 43: 429–69.

Neuman, W.R., Marcus, G.E., MacKuen, M., and Crigler, A.N. (ed.) (2007) *The Affect Effect: Dynamics of Emotion in Political Thinking and Behavior*, Chicago: University of Chicago Press.

Nussbaum, M. (2001) *Upheavals of Thought: The Intelligence of Emotions*, Cambridge: Cambridge University Press.

Obholzer, A. and Roberts, V. (1994) *The Unconscious at Work*, London: Routledge.

Parkin, W. (1993) 'The public and the private: Gender, sexuality and emotion', in S. Fineman (ed.) *Emotion in Organizations*, London: Sage.

Parkinson, B. (1995) *Ideas and Realities of Emotion*, London: Routledge.

Pelz, D. (1951) 'Leadership within a hierarchical organization', *Journal of Social Issues*, 7: 49–55.

Plutchik, R. (2001) 'The nature of emotions', *American Scientist*, 89, 4: 344–50.

Salovey, P. and Mayer, J. (1990) 'Emotional intelligence', *Imagination, Cognition, and Personality*, 9: 185–211.

Schmidt, M. (2000) 'Role theory, emotions and identity in the department headship of secondary schooling', *Teaching and Teacher Education*, 16, 8: 827–42.

Schmidt, M. and Datnow, A. (2005) 'Teachers' sense-making about comprehensive school reform: The influence of emotions', *Teaching and Teacher Education*, 21: 949–65.

Simon, H. (1947) *Administrative Behavior: A Study of Decision-Making Processes in Administrative Organizations*, New York: Macmillan.

Spillane, J.P., Reiser, B.J., and Reimer, T. (2002) 'Policy implementation and cognition: Reframing and refocusing implementation research', *Review of Educational Research*, 72, 3: 387–431.

Stogdill, R. (1948) 'Personal factors associated with leadership: A survey of the literature', *Journal of Psychology*, 25: 35–71.

—— (1950) 'Leadership, membership and organization', *Psychological Bulletin*, 47: 1–14.

Strati, A. (1999) *Organization and Aesthetics*, London: Sage.

Terman, L. (1904) 'A preliminary study of the psychology and pedagogy of leadership', *Journal of Genetic Psychology*, 11: 413–51.

Turner, R.H. (1962) 'Role-taking: Process versus conformity', in A.M. Rose (ed.) *Human Behaviour and Social Processes: An Interactionist Approach*, London: Routledge & Kegan Paul.

Vince, R. and Saleem, T. (2004) 'The impact of caution and blame on organizational learning', *Management Learning*, 35, 2: 133–54.

Weber, M. (1930) *The Protestant Ethic and the Spirit of Capitalism*, London: Unwin Hyman.

White, G. (1993) 'Emotions inside out: The anthropology of affect', in M. Lewis and J.M. Haviland (eds) *Handbook of Emotions*, New York: Guilford Press.

Zembylas, M. (2003) 'Interrogating "teacher identity": Emotion, resistance, and self-formation', *Educational Theory*, 53, 1: 107–27.

—— (2005) 'Discursive practices, genealogies, and emotional rules: A poststructuralist view on emotion and identity in teaching', *Teaching and Teacher Education*, 21, 8: 935–48.

Part I

Theoretical foundations

1 The romantic philosophy of mind

The elevation of emotion to the (anti-)heroic ideal

Eugenie A. Samier

One of the predecessors to psychological and socio-cultural approaches to emotion is the late-eighteenth and early-nineteenth-century philosophical movement of Romanticism that emphasised individual uniqueness and intuition, elevating emotional experience to an importance as great as that of reason. It is a philosophy of being predicated upon a pursuit of freedom and equality achieved through self-realisation and a transcendent process uniting imagination, reason, and conscious and unconscious emotion. It laid a foundation for many later intellectual movements of social and political critique, particularly those connecting individuals' inner worlds and the socio-historical context, including that of educational experience: the dialectic idealism of Hegel, historicism, existentialism, phenomenology, hermeneutics, psychoanalysis, and the artistic movements of decadence, expressionism, absurdism, surrealism, and DaDaism. To Berlin, romanticism was the greatest single shift affecting life and thought in the West (1999: 1–2).

For the Romantic, the self and one's life were to be a work of art, embodying principles of totality, unity, and individuality: a holistic view of the individual whose highest form was a full and unique development of human characteristics. And to the Romanticist, this required delving into the 'dark and unconscious forces which move within', in order to bring them to light and confront them (Berlin 1999: 98). In administrative and leadership terms, this means identifying and overcoming one's character and personality flaws, a misplaced desire for power and authority, and a scientised sensibility.

Romanticism plays virtually no role theoretically in educational administration and leadership even though many of its strong influences originated in the Romantic movement. Historically, Romanticism served a critical and formational role in the development of the Humboldt university model (see Clark 2006: 210–15, 226–30, 443–9) that established worldwide fundamental teaching and scholarship criteria for the modern research university. It is upon this foundation that many notions of higher education administration and leadership were built.

The elevation of emotion

German Romanticism arose from the confluence of philosophy, literature, art, and politics: inspired by Kant's notion of freedom, Fichte's lectures on individual freedom, Lessing's critique of art, and the French Revolution, early Romanticists promoted a view of the self guided by imagination, rather than rules or conventions, leading to an exploration of the self, emotions, and sensuality, and their expression in socio-cultural forms, often in ironic juxtaposition (Pinkard 2001: 99–100). Even though the early Romantic movement (or *Frühromantik*) had a very short duration, from 1797 to 1802, and whose meetings were informally held in literary salons, mostly in Jena and Berlin, its legacy extends through to the present day. Its proponents include some of the most important and renowned philosophical and literary figures: Schiller, Herder, Wieland, Goethe, Wilhelm von Humboldt (through the Humboldt university model), Schlegel, Novalis, Schleiermacher, and Hölderlin.

The Romanticists had a much stronger influence on the development of the modern university than is often thought. Ziolkowski (1990) outlines in some detail the chaotic and shallow nature of universities in the eighteenth century, which were so dysfunctional that there were calls to close down this medieval organisation for good. The Romantics, notably, Schiller, Goethe, Fichte, and Schelling, brought about a renaissance of learning at Jena, inspired also by their intellectual compatriots. Transformed were a unified curriculum, a truly scholarly professorial practice, and a set of regulations circumscribing errant student behaviour. While the Jena experiment was shortlived, partly due to the Jena–Auerstaedt battle in the Napoleonic wars, it provided a model for other universities and eventually the celebrated Humboldt model of the University of Berlin, the international archetype for the modern research university. One of the key documents was a proposal submitted by Schleiermacher defining a hermeneutical and dialectical relationship between the university and the state in a unified whole including the role of all other levels of education, particularly the Gymnasium, as well as the central role of faculty in university structure and governance, as well as academic freedom for faculty and students. It fell to Wilhelm von Humboldt, who had studied at Jena in the midst of the leading Romanticists, to implement this ideal, along with the Weimar notion of *Bildung*, in 1810 in Berlin.

Although a somewhat diverse and idiosyncratic movement, the Romantics subscribed to four related ideals: a unity of knowledge achieved through experience and imagination rather than logic; 'subjective inwardness' (*Innerlichkeit*) assuming an irreducibility and primacy of subjective experience while accepting a realist view of the external world; a re-enchantment of nature without returning to tradition or orthodox religion; and the primacy of imagination over intellect (Pinkard 2001: 101). Their common stylistic characteristics included eclecticism, the fantastic in the imaginative combining of materials, imitation in the sense of reproducing the fullness of life in its historical period, and sentimentality in the sense of 'revealing the spirit of love' (Beiser 2003: 12–13). In this way, emotion is a requisite capacity for creative imagination that is able to reveal deeper levels of reality and achieve a transcendent view (Richards 2002: 2). To Romanticists, all activity in life should be viewed as part of a creative and artistic process infused with morality, including politics and science, and especially the educational process of *Bildung*. To romanticise the world means to reintroduce 'meaning, magic and mystery' in modernised, technologised society (Beiser 2003: 19–20).

Hölderlin and Novalis argued for a primacy of Being as a foundation for subjectivity and as an existent that eludes introspection. For Hölderlin, Being consists in 'the all-desiring, all-subjugating dangerous side of man as well as the highest and most beautiful condition he can achieve' (in Larmore 2000: 145) and contains the problems of self-consciousness, an elusive pursuit with implications for the exercise of freedom. For Novalis, access to one's being, in even limited form, requires the development of intellectual intuition and reflection grounded in feeling, which themselves are grounded in Being (Larmore 2000: 153–4). The essence of Romanticism lay in the quality of poetic language to suggest more than it explicitly says in evoking this Absolute. In other words, the essence of knowledge and truth for Novalis are carried in implicit language: 'To the extent that I give to the lowly a high meaning, to the ordinary a mysterious air, and to the well-known the dignity of the unknown, I am romanticizing it' (in Larmore 2000: 155).

It is here in their exploration of Being that many seeds of phenomenology are sown, influencing Hegel's *Phenomenology of Spirit*, a not insignificant perspective from which administrative and leadership experience is explored. It also laid the foundation for an exploration of the unconscious, providing important sources for Freud's creation of psychoanalysis. While there were some significant differences between Romanticism and psychoanalysis (the latter emphasising subjectivity less and childhood experience more) (Kirschner 1996: 179–80), both regarded self-formation as a developmental spiral characterised by a 'trajectory of unity, rupture and division into contraries, higher unity' and interaction with the world that includes suffering producing individuation (Kirschner 1996: 180–3). The aim of both is authenticity and creativity, borne from the oftentimes painful range of experiences inherent to self-formation, producing the transformation of social and political experience as an art.

It is in the basic ideas of Romantic ethics and politics that a view of the proper place of emotion is found. Ethics was informed by a conception of aesthetic excellence in personal development, consisting of a totality of humanness, a unity of these powers into an organic whole, and individuality or uniqueness (Beiser 2005: 39). Their conception of ethics contrasted with their understanding of utilitarianism as consumer passivity and the ethics of duty as simply adhering to moral principles through a bifurcation of the human being into reason and sensibility. Instead, they followed an ethic of love allowing one to see oneself in others (Beiser 2005: 40). Their early conception of politics was that of the organic republican state (instead of the absolute monarchies with which they were familiar), consisting of the right to participate in public affairs, the right to equal protection of property and freedom of speech and the press, and the duty of the state to provide education for the development of its citizens (Beiser 2005: 41). Uniting all of this is a synthesis of reason and a sensibility grounded in emotion.

Many Romantic concepts were carried through Hegel's early philosophy, concepts upon which many notions of the state, authority, and political rights provide a foundation for administration and leadership, including 'Hegel's absolute idealism, his organic conception of nature, his critique of liberalism, his communitarian ideals, his vitalized Spinozism, his concept of dialectic, his attempt to synthesize communitarianism and liberalism' (Beiser 2005: 35). Drawn in part from Novalis' notion of the mystical state–individual informing all social structures, Hegel's conception of social institutions is a 'Spirit of the Times' that animates the state for which the

> *Volksgeist*, or national genius ... concretely manifested, expresses every aspect of its consciousness and will – the whole cycle of its realization. Its religion, its polity, its ethics, its legislation, and even its science, art, and mechanical skill, all bear its stamp.
>
> (Hegel 1956: 63–4)

Romanticism is also a reaction to societal modernisation which causes many divisions in human experience, from hiving off emotion for rationalisation to the division of labour and its attendant specialisations. They were confronted at that time with a mechanistic view of reality and society promoted by scientism ushered in by Descartes, and in full force by the late eighteenth century. For the Romanticists, only an organic and poetical transformation of the self and artistic modes of representation serving knowledge were possible antidotes. The malaise of modernity for them consisted of alienation, estrangement, division, separation, and reflection (Beiser 2003: 31). One inheritor of Romanticism is Weber, whose critique of bureaucratisation is reminiscent of Schiller's:

> Always chained to a single little fragment of the whole, man himself develops into only a fragment; always in his ear the monotonous sound of the wheel that he turns, he never develops the harmony of his being; and instead of putting the stamp of humanity upon his nature he becomes nothing more than the imprint of his business or science.
>
> (Schiller in Beiser 2005: 47)

Schiller's echo is clear in one of Weber's most celebrated comments on bureaucratisation:

> A lifeless machine is the materialization of mind. This fact alone gives it the power to force men into its service and to determine so coercively

> their everyday life in the factory ... Also a materialization of mind is that living machine which bureaucratic organization represents, with its trained, specialized labor, its delimitation of areas of competence, its regulations and its hierarchically stratified relations of obedience. In union with the dead machine, it is laboring to produce the cage of that bondage of the future to which one day powerless men will be forced to submit like the fellaheen of ancient Egypt. This will certainly be true if a purely technically good (i.e., rational) bureaucratic administration and welfare system is the ultimate and unique value, which is to decide the way their affairs are run ... a bureaucracy that has reached this advanced state [is among] the most difficult social creations to destroy.
>
> (Weber in Mommsen 1984: 166–7)

This type of rationalisation overcame even the university. Weber compared the relative fates of a world peopled by a rationalised professoriate with that of 'little cogs' of bureaucrats (1956: 127). Goethe's *Wilhelm Meister's Apprenticeship* describes the fate of these 'cogs':

> The middle class can acquire merit and, if driven to extremes, develop the mind; but in so doing it loses its personality ... the burgher must labor and create, developing some of his capabilities in order to be useful, but without it ever being assumed that there is or ever can be a harmonious interplay of qualities in him, because in order to make himself useful in one direction, he has to disregard everything else.
>
> (1989: 174–5)

From this perspective, education itself has become a technological site, so convincingly rationalised that self-awareness has been compromised. It is not a far step from there to the current conditions of corporatisation and commercialisation producing the market-model university.

The ills of modernity are overcome by pursuing the ideal of the beautiful soul, of community, the organic state, and an organic conception of nature. The Romantics' position was not 'post-modern', but advanced a reintegration and synthesis of Enlightenment values of reason, freedoms of civil society, and history. Their challenge was how to preserve individuality, critical rationality, and freedom while embracing feelings and desires that are necessary '*to inspire* the people, to touch their hearts and to arouse their imaginations, to get them to live by higher ideals' (Beiser 2003: 32, 94). And, as argued by Schiller in *Aesthetic Education*, it is art produced through this synthesis of reason and feeling and cultivation of the senses that can move people to higher moral and political ideals (1967: 17–23, Fourth Letter). Goethe's Wilhelm Meister represented for the Romantics 'an account of the self-formation of a man of genius – of how a man can take himself in hand and by the free exercise of his noble and unrestrained will make himself into something' (Berlin 1999: 111).

In Schlegel one finds a key conception of Romanticism for leadership resembling a closer proximity to Burns' complex and dynamic model than many simplistic ones that have arisen since: that the focus is on the subjective interest of the artist where conflicting elements are not resolved by a 'freely playing and ironic imagination' (Richards 2002: 21). A guiding principle for integrating these conflicts in the personality is to experience life through passion, including ecstasy and suffering which combined lead one both to one's absolute ego and to a deeper reality where creative force dwells (Richards 2002: 31–3). This includes heightened emotions that derive from pain and dejection that find a constructive expression in imagination, often in the form of a crisis resulting from disillusion and despair (Kirschner 1996: 171), experiences that became central to existentialism. This perspective affected 'political attitudes, aesthetic perceptions, philosophical considerations, and scientific ideas' (Richards 2002: 22–3). Such a complex view of reality and human development embracing authenticity, ambiguity, difference, transcendent states, and implicit meaning is best captured in the literary arts, an important form of expression carried up through existentialism and expressionism, and recently emerging in many qualitative and narrative forms of research. Their arguments also stress the need for a number of practical aspects in the training of those assuming authority roles: language, interpretation, apprehension, and intuition integrated with reason, judgement, and the analytic.

The construction of the (anti-)heroic

It was through Romanticism that the modern heroic ideal was formed as its highest expression of individual authenticity and the source of socio-political change, a figure who is both of his own time and able to transcend it, corresponding to many contemporary concepts of organisational change resulting from leadership through vision and the development of social relations operating at a higher moral level. The heroic encompasses the ability and position from which to achieve great feats of public expression, which for the relatively poor Romanticists lay primarily in the pastorate, despite its tendency at the time to remoteness and obscurity (La Vopa 2000: 206), essentially a public education role, or the law. One is reminded here of Aristotle's role as Alexander the Great's tutor and mentor. However, it is the Romantics who gave a psychological turn to passion and the heroic (Praz 1970: 108), that at times turned to a darker side of human nature.

Many of Romanticism's major figures were successful at administrative careers: Goethe was for three decades responsible for Weimar's mines, roads, and cultural institutions; Eichendorff was a minor functionary in the Prussian civil service for just as long; Novalis was a mining engineer and administrator for Saxony; and Hoffmann rose through the judicial administration to the Prussian Supreme Court. In this lies an important aspect of the tradition. Rather than a dichotomous view of the practical and intellectual, their perspective embraced a synthesis of 'mind and matter, rationalism and sentimentalism, reason and emotion', 'civilization and culture, of spirit and nature, of finitude and infinity', 'life and art, the bourgeois and the artist, the *vita activa* and the *vita contemplativa*' running against the popular image of the Romantic poet as isolated, when in fact most of them were more than capable professionals (see Ziolkowski 1990: 4–5). Given this heritage, it would seem apropos for an educational administrator to pursue their own and their charges' full humanity rather than succumb to 'cogness' however high in the hierarchy. For the Romanticist, the artist of genius can serve as the ideal regardless of one's occupation – intellectualism does not necessary exclude the administrative or vice versa, despite this incessant chorus in the dominant positivist and functional–structuralist character of educational administration and leadership. The traditional Anglo-Saxon administrative mandarin tradition of culturally and intellectually ept serving the highest strata of the public service reflects some of the Romantic view.

Romanticism also encompasses the tragic mode, carried through Hegel's complex conception of the dynamic of history, as a way of capturing and analysing crisis, and the unique confronting the universal – seen in his reading of Sophocles' *Antigone*, still a powerful representation of the abuse of organisational authority and a resistant heroism necessitating sacrifice yet achieving moral authority. In this way the tragic raises the question of law as a concrete instance rather than ethical abstraction, and a necessary component of the force of history, in other words societal and organisational change (see Schmidt 2001). For Hölderlin, tragedy represents on a most concrete level the complex interrelation of unity and conflict, and confronts us with the experience of the foreign and how well one embraces and accommodates it (Schmidt 2001: 123–4). It is in the tragic that the greatest tests of leadership lie, as one enters the domain of the unknown that is most feared in change and transformation. I would suggest here that *Antigone* is an unparalleled presentation and treatment of leadership, an instance of what Burns (1978) argued for in transforming leadership – his original model in which convention is questioned or overturned, where a strong ethic is central to leadership, where one is willing to risk reaching for a greater vision of humanity, and taking on resistance and conflict in order to pursue it with commitment.

Romanticism, however, is a Janus-figured movement. In addition to ideals infused with self-realisation, it can also lead to the pathologically heightened and ecstatic. It encouraged not only emotions associated with harmony and balance, internally and in social relations leading to cultural creation, but a broad range of emotions and passions associated with 'dark' Romanticism – self-destructive narcissism, a gothic irrationalism resulting in fantasy escapism, intense sensation producing horror and terror, and an excessive and self-indulgent abandonment to feeling subordinating reason. The imagination is not a force that submits to sentimentalism, and a sensibility for the infinite does not necessarily confine itself to convention or the benign. It is here that many of the preoccupations of existentialism are borne in the modern world: death, anxiety, nihilism, tragedy. In excessive form, Romanticism tipped into decadence, the 'demonic lure of the unfamiliar', tranquil death reflected a mystical side of nature, and 'sometimes teetered precariously on the line between reality and imagination' (Ziolkowski 1990: 3–4). Praz is most associated with a study of this side of Romanticism expressed in literature in his classic, *The Romantic Agony*. The range of experience explored on this side is the orgiastic, the ecstatic, the nostalgic, the melancholic, exciting, altered states of mind, horror, the macabre, corruption, what is often referred to as the 'mal du siècle' (1970: xix). Among its proponents were Wilde, Poe, de Sade, Byron, Baudelaire, and the gothic writers. Romanticism did not just embrace the notion of death as part of life's totality, but developed a fascination with it (Pinkard 2001: 102), an important caution for those overly enthused with charismatic leadership models or who too quickly embrace models that refrain from dealing with the more destructive capacities in the human being wielding authority and power.

The archetype of the Romantic hero, or more properly anti-hero, can be found in Goethe's Werther and Mephistopheles (in *Faust*), often referred to as the Byronic hero, who embodied a more unconventional approach to social roles, rules, and mores ultimately marginalising the hero into cynicism, alienation, and anomie, all phenomena associated with the darker side of charisma. In the Mephistophelean hero, one finds the 'mysterious ... traces of burnt-out passions, suspicion of a ghastly guilt, melancholy habits, pale face, unforgettable eyes' (Praz 1970: 61). And women also share in this Romantic tradition, for whom Cleopatra and Lucrezia Borgia were illustrations (see Praz 1970: Chapter IV).

In perverted political form, Romanticism produces fascism. Its correlation in administration is the bureaupathological, and in leadership the cult of personality, forces that worldwide have cost tens of millions of lives in the twentieth century alone. The Rousseau of the *Social Contract* is the same Rousseau inspiring Robespierre and St. Just, who effectively and efficiently institutionalised violence during the French Revolution.

Conclusion

Romanticism is much more often used for curriculum and teaching theory in the Anglo-Saxon world, primarily through Rousseau, than for administration and leadership studies. It is often used in an idealised and sanitised form excluding the strong socio-political critique and birth out of rebellion and revolution that unleash destructive and tyrannical powers, evident in Napoleon, who served as a model of the heroic. It requires self-discipline, self-knowledge, discernment, and judgement in order to wield such a powerful weapon morally and humanely. In its most positive form, those rising to the Romantic ideal are cultivated in community, which in the Romantic sense of the lives of those who made up the movement, meant a 'magical circle of friends' who studied, learned, experienced together through philosophical and political enthusiasms, 'through longings and desires, loves and passions, the sorrows and hatreds that swirled around them' (Richards 2002: 200). Theirs was a non-simplistic model of collaboration and cooperation that did not sacrifice individuality and conflicting views, in other words intellectual freedom, through demands for conforming consensus.

The essence of Romanticism is the pursuit of a higher potential, captured by Hardenberg, a man born from the Romantic movement and creating for himself a distinguished administrative and diplomatic career that led him to a critical role in implementing pioneering liberal reforms, and through this, an exemplar of leadership:

> The world must be romanticized. In this way one finds again its original meaning. Romanticizing is nothing other than a qualitative potentializing. The lower self becomes identified with a better self in this operation. Thus we ourselves are such a qualitative potentialized series. This operation is yet completely unknown. Insofar as I give the common an elevated meaning, the usual a secret perspective, the known the value of the unknown, the finite an infinite appearance – I thus romanticize.
>
> (Translation in Richards 2002: 200)

References

Beiser, F. (2003) *The Romantic Imperative: The Concept of Early German Romanticism*, Cambridge: Harvard University Press.

—— (2005) *Hegel*, New York: Routledge.

Berlin, I. (1999) *The Roots of Romanticism*, Princeton: Princeton University Press.

Burns, J.M. (1978) *Leadership*, New York: Harper & Row.

Clark, W. (2006) *Academic Charisma and the Origins of the Research University*, Chicago: University of Chicago Press.

Goethe, J.W. von (1989) *Wilhelm Meister's Apprenticeship*, trans. E. Blackall, Princeton: Princeton University Press.

Hegel, G.W.F. (1956) *The Philosophy of History*, trans. J. Sibree, New York: Dover.

Kirschner, S. (1996) *The Religious and Romantic Origins of Psychoanalysis: Individuation and Integration in Post-Freudian Theory*, Cambridge: Cambridge University Press.

Larmore, C. (2000) 'Hölderline and Novalis', in K. Ameriks (ed.) *The Cambridge Companion to German Idealism*, Cambridge: Cambridge University Press.

La Vopa, A. (2000) 'Fichte's road to Kant', in P. Coleman, J. Lewis, and J. Kowalik (eds) *Representations of the Self from the Renaissance to Romanticism*, Cambridge: Cambridge University Press.

Mommsen, W. (1984) *Max Weber and German Politics, 1890–1920*, Chicago: University of Chicago Press.

Pinkard, T. (2001) *Hegel: A Biography*, Cambridge: Cambridge University Press.

Praz, M. (1970) *The Romantic Agony*, London: Oxford University Press.

Richards, R. (2002) *The Romantic Conception of Life: Science and Philosophy in the Age of Goethe*, Chicago: University of Chicago Press.

Schiller, F. (1967) *On the Aesthetic Education of Man*, trans. E. Wilkinson and L. Willoughby, Oxford: Oxford University Press.

Schmidt, D. (2001) *On Germans and Other Greeks: Tragedy and Ethical Life*, Bloomington: Indiana University Press.

Weber, M. (1956) 'Max Weber on bureaucratization in 1909', in J. P. Mayer, *Max Weber and German Politics: A Study in Political Sociology*, London: Faber & Faber.

Ziolkowski, T. (1990) *German Romanticism and Its Institutions*, Princeton: Princeton University Press.

2 Philosophy and authority

Passion in ambivalence

Nigel Tubbs

Psalm 111: 10 states that 'the fear of the Lord is the beginning of wisdom'.[1] The German philosopher G.W.F. Hegel (1770–1831) reworks the negative and religious overtones of this statement around an experience of philosophical learning that brings power, mastery, and authority face-to-face with their opposites. In doing so, Hegel offers those charged with leadership in education an education in the philosophy of leadership. Specifically he offers a way of learning from and about the ambivalence of authority on its journey to-and-fro between certainty and doubt, conviction and pragmatism, and between the formal and the personal. In sum, I argue that this philosophical education commends one not to seek to resolve this ambivalence but rather to embrace its truth.

Hegel's master and slave

Hegel explores the dialectic of authority and its accompanying emotions in the master/slave section of his *Phenomenology of Spirit* (1807). He shows us a master who enjoys independence and autonomy. He is his own man.[2] At an abstract level, his authority can be seen as institutional, hierarchical, and role-governed. But this is no guarantee that his authority will be respected by others. Formal authority requires to be complemented by inner qualities deserving of respect. 'Robust' leadership is often the refuge of those lacking any such graceful relation of inner and outer authority. Proving one has authority is not the same as having it. Hegel draws attention to a similar ambiguity in the identity of the master. He notes that the independent identity of the master undermines itself or, as Derrida would say, is autoimmune. At face value the independence of this modern western master seems legally and financially secure in his freedom. But this hides the fundamental dependence that the master has upon those who are not free. This was easier to see when the land-owner needed his serfs or the mill-owner needed his workers. Marxism, and with it part of the recent shape of European history, was grounded in the truth of this political fact: the master needed his slaves but the slaves, under different economic and social relations, would not need their masters. The trembling of the ruling class, predicted by Marx, would be the inner truth of this external political fact. But times have changed. Now, in a modern democracy all men are deemed to be legally independent. We are all masters now. But the fundamental ambivalence of the master's authority and independence has not been overcome, even though it is presently better hidden, as we will see below.

Thus far, then, for Hegel the master's identity is really the opposite of itself. The truth of the master is not independence but dependence. He lives in this broken life where his identity is fundamentally ambivalent. For the educational leader this is to learn that he is really led by those who follow him. But we have only looked at this negation and uncertainty from the point of view of the master. What of the slave?

Hegel argues that there are two related characteristics that constitute the truth of the identity of the slave. First, legally and financially the slave is utterly without rights or security of any kind. The slave existed only in so far as he was the property of another. His whole being was not his own but someone else's. Hegel says of this that the slave experiences a vulnerability here that goes all the way to the very core of his being. His experience of himself is of nothing. Legally he is nothing. Everything that he might claim for or as himself is the property of another. He is nothing of his own. He is not his own person. Indeed, he is not a person at all, only an object. This nothingness, says Hegel, is experienced by the slave as absolute fear and dread. Here the slave is 'unmanned, has trembled in every fibre of its being, and everything solid and stable has been shaken to its foundations' (1977: 117). It is an experience in which the being of the slave simply melts away, and he is left touching the void of non-being. His life is in this sense only a living death.

Second, however, this fear and trembling has significance for the slave that is as surprising as it is profound. Hegel says that when the slave actually does the work required of him, he is experiencing in his service to another the truth of his fear and trembling. Hegel's case here is that the work of service has its truth in the same nothingness that the slave experiences in his non-being. Here, remarkably, the slave – unlike the master – achieves a mind of his own. The tables are truly turned. The master who assumed he had a mind of his own in fact experiences the opposite, that his mind has its true nature only in someone else. The slave, who seems unable to have a mind or indeed a body of his own, in fact, is the one who experiences his own truth in the work that he does. We will see below how the modern individual master is both master and slave within this ambivalent identity.

However, we must be cautious here with this truth of the slave for there have been some absolutely false and indeed murderous misappropriations of it. I mention only one such example. The Nazis placed at the entrance to Auschwitz the slogan *Arbeit macht Freiheit*, or, 'in work is freedom'. Here work meant slavery, and freedom meant death. The fear and trembling of the prisoners reduced slaves here to what Agamben (1998) calls 'bare life', or *homo sacer*, a reduction made absolute because the work is unfree and the freedom spoken of at the gates is only for the masters. Without the difficult freedom of being master *and* slave the fear and trembling is not able to determine its own truth, but only that of another, in this case, the genocidal truths of the camp masters. It has to be noted that these camp masters also believed their own truth to be in service. But this notion of service is only a self-deception. They did not learn the truth of service from the vulnerability of the identity of the master to its contrary. Rather, these masters exported such vulnerability to those deemed other than the masters, primarily European Jews. To export fear and trembling is to eschew that which holds the master to humanity. These masters served only themselves. They refused the lesson of the master/slave relation that the truth of the master lies precisely in the other, that is, in having an other outside of oneself and in being other to oneself (see Tubbs 2008 on this relation as Hegel's theory of the other).

The history of western anxiety

One can read the history of western philosophy and theology as the struggle for and against relief from the emotions that register the truth and untruth of this finite and earthly master. I rehearse such a reading briefly now in this section.

In regard to the search *for* relief, the untruth of western man has been set against the calm and tranquillity that pertains to the truth of God. Where God is eternal and unchangeable, man is finite and held captive in turbulent contradictions. Where the natural world obeys God's laws, the social is corrupted and sinful. Where God's knowledge is infinite, human knowledge is temporary and unstable. This division between a calm infinite being and an agitated human being is set out as a principle by Aristotle in his idea of the unmoved mover. For Aristotle, what could not be otherwise than it is must be itself necessarily. Against truth as eternal and necessary, human being was thus cast in a storm of change and impermanence.

The Stoics and Sceptics who followed Aristotle in the ancient world based their philosophy on the search for tranquillity in life, which meant, in essence, to be like God. They based this on the idea that there is no distinction between thought and the true nature of the universe because the universe is God thinking Himself. As such, the Stoic aimed for purity in thought, and held the highest value to being indifferent to all that is turbulent and changeable in the world. This indifference has its nobility in Stoic ethics which refuses attraction or seduction by the desire for wealth, fame and honour, as it does by life's events. Only when the mind is aimed at the inner world of the soul will it achieve control over the passions, a control that will, through reason, bring happiness and the virtuous life. External events, therefore, including death, are outside of human control and should produce in us no frustration, anger or disappointment. Marcus Aurelius (CE 121–80) stated that one must accept one's own death with equanimity and 'with good grace' (1964: 51) while Seneca (*c.*4 BCE – CE 65) argued that 'the breast from which you have banished the dread of death no fear will dare to enter' (1997: 55). The Epicurean philosophy had a similarly stoical outlook. Epicurus (BCE 341–270), noted that death cannot be a source of fear or anxiety to the rational mind, since death is not present to the man who is alive, and is only present to the man who is not alive. Stoicism and Epicureanism both offered an antidote in the soul to the man, and particularly the leader, who felt mastered by events in the external world.

The Sceptics took this stoicism one step further. Sextus Empiricus (*c.* end of second century CE), for example, argued that true tranquillity in the soul requires the intellect to make a 'suspension of judgement' (2000: 5) in facing the fact that one person's judgement is about as good as any other's. Their maxim was that 'opposed to every account there is an equal account' (2000: 51). Tranquillity here, then, is achieved in freedom from judgements and decisions. It is perhaps hard to see how the epithet 'successful educational leader' would be attached to such a freedom and tranquillity, but this may obscure the importance of scepticism as a criticism of existing dogmas and practices.

This search for tranquillity on earth soon became a more sober realisation that such tranquillity may belong not to this world but to the next. The collapse of the Ancient Empires of Greece and Rome saw philosophy migrate east to the Alexandrian Empire. This saw work emerge in a phase of western philosophy known as 'neo-Platonic' and was both Christian and non-Christian. The agitation of man's untruth here was grounded in the unknowability of God by man. Man can know *that* God exists, but not *what* God is. His existence touches the soul but the intellect cannot comprehend Him, with the resulting anxiety as to whether or not a man's soul will be saved from his untruth after his death. The anxiety manifested itself in a set of strictures that the good man should adopt in order to prevent his soul from being corrupted in this earthly life. The body and its desires were held to be the main culprit for this corruption, beginning a war on behalf of the soul against the body. In this constant struggle no peace is to be found unless, very rarely, a man is blessed with prophetic visions and ecstatic experiences of God. Philo of Alexandria (*c.*20 BCE – CE 50) lists some 152 vices that attend the body and cites education and learning in a disciplined and sober fashion as the way to combat these vices. The man who puts pleasure above the education of his soul is 'foolish [and] full of evil acts' (1993: 98).

Plotinus (CE 204–70), writing after Philo, deepened this separation of soul and body arguing for a philosophical journey in man upwards from the body to God or to the intellectual principle. Mind and body are separated and thus so are tranquillity and anxiety. On earth, and in the body, each particular soul is lonely and isolated, partial, incomplete, and self-centred. The soul here is 'a deserter from the totality' (Plotinus 1991, IV, 8.4: 338) fallen into sin and evil. This soul yearns for what is lost, for completion and unity with the Oneness of God. When Plotinus says famously that this return to God requires one to 'withdraw into yourself and look' (1991, I, 6.9: 54), he might have added, and know instability and untruth as the evil of incompletion.

Neo-Platonic Christianity shared the anxiety that man on earth was sinful and that true peace and tranquillity of the soul would only be possible in the next world. Thus, whereas the Stoics sought to avoid agitation in the mind, Christianity saw it serving a pedagogical function. Origen (CE 185–254), for example, believed that difficulties and contradictions experienced in reading the holy texts were deliberately designed to encourage the mind away from the corporeal towards the metaphysical idea of tranquillity, or towards God. The anxiety associated with untruth here in the *vita negativa* or the negative life was precisely the means by which one could relate to God.

Augustine (CE 354–430) made a similar case regarding the anxiety and unhappiness brought about by evil. He distinguished the earthly city, ruled by the desires of the flesh, from the city of God, which was at best only ever on pilgrimage on earth and in opposition to it. He was clear, though, that 'God enriches the course of world history by the [use of] antithesis' (1972: 449). Sin and its consequent turbulence in life on earth is the means by which God educates man about that which lies beyond man. The sufferer knows – because he suffers – that there is a future in which 'he will share with the angels the endless enjoyment of God most High' (1972: 444), a future life in which man's nature will 'be healed by immortality and incorruption' (1972: 893) and will enjoy the most blessed peace. This relationship of present untruth to a desired peace in truth characterised much of Augustine's own life until (and after) his conversion to Christianity.

Aquinas (*c.*1225–74), over 600 years after Augustine, rehearsed similar themes. For him, man is always inferior to God, which serves to teach man humility on earth. It is only in paradise that man will be in the eternally peaceful state of being unable to sin because he will be united with God. After the resurrection the body will be spiritual, requiring no food, and having no desires associated with the body on earth. Again earthly life is characterised by struggle, disharmony and anxiety, as man is taught that the more he abandons the material world the nearer he will move to eternal happiness, although Aquinas does note that the material world does not have to be completely abandoned – how could it? – since the things of this world can be used to attain eternal happiness provided that man does not place his end in them (1920, vol. 8, I, 6.9: 318).

Later still, one can see in Descartes (1596–1650) the desire to overcome the anxiety and agitation of doubt, this time in an indisputable rationalism. In the *Discourse on Method* he states 'I found myself beset by so many doubts and errors that I came to think I had gained nothing from my attempts to become educated but increasing recognition of my own ignorance' (1985: 113), whereas, in mathematics, he found a peace 'because of the certainty and self-evidence of its reasonings' (1985: 114). Famously he set out to discover and to accept only that which cannot be doubted. He observed that whilst doubting he was, nevertheless, existing as the one who doubts. Thus, he reasoned 'I am thinking, therefore I exist' (1985: 127), and this became the self-evident truth and the first principle of his philosophical method.

From this he was able to enjoy the certainty that God exists with the same confidence that truths have in mathematics and geometry. In taking this doubt further than anyone else Descartes believed he had established the true knowledge 'of all other things to be found in the world' (1985: 184).

We must draw attention now to an altogether different interpretation of the search for relief from the unrest of man's untruth as it appears in the history of western philosophy. Most famously, perhaps, Nietzsche (1844–1900) has argued that the war on the body and on its emotions was endemic in the decay of western man, and that the idea of seeking a rational peace in the truth of God set man against his true passions and emotions. Tranquillity is seen as nothing more than an idea by which philosophy and theology can exercise control over man, and God here becomes 'an enemy of life' (1998: 23), which is why, through his character Zarathustra, Nietzsche proclaims to mankind that God is dead. In the *Twilight of the Idols*, he argues that the history of western philosophy as presented above is based on an error in regard to what it is to be human. Human emotion has been stifled under the weight of rationalism, dialectic, and the relation of cause and effect. Equally, spontaneity has been healed of its irrationality by morality, religion, and philosophy. What he finds in the history of this suppression of emotions is a decline of the strengths of the man who is prepared to live without calculation and rational justification. Indeed, those who set themselves up as critics of decline are really the decadent protagonists of just such a decline, beginning, says, Nietzsche, with Socrates and Plato. Their critiques of decay are symptoms of that decay. Thus, he states that while the philosophers and the moralists have claimed to be improving mankind, in fact their demand for 'rationality at any price; life, bright, cold, cautious, conscious, without instinct, in opposition to the instincts' (1982: 15) marks the decline of mankind. Against them is the man who obeys himself and refuses to let impulse be corrupted by rational systems of thought. For this man of the future, 'all that is good is instinct' (1968: 48).

But Nietzsche is not alone here. The idea of a universe that is not ordered by some rational system, nor should be so ordered, was also present in the ancient world. The illogicality of motion in the universe was argued for by Zeno of Elea (*c.*490–425 BCE), following the atomistic theory of Leucippus and Democritus (both *c.* fifth century BCE), who argued for the truth of the world as composed of an infinity of invisible atoms. The idea of the universe in flux and constantly changing is credited to Heraclitus (*c.* late sixth and early fifth centuries BCE). Here the emphasis is on the truth of agitation and not in its resolution.

More recently, part of the European philosophical tradition, particularly in France, has returned to the idea that the universe cannot be tranquilised by rational systems of thought, and that it must always exceed attempts to do so. Deleuze (1925–95), for example, has argued that a subjective identity is nothing more than a wall against which man is pinned so that he may be fixed and identified. This subjectivity is 'a hole where we deposit – together with our consciousness – our feelings, our passions, our little secrets' (2002: 45). Against such a fixing, Deleuze argues for man to comprehend himself as a process of becoming constituted by what can be called multiplicities. These are not related as cause and effect, but rather are as grass that grows between paving stones while remaining unrelated to them. Such a philosophy has a very different character to that which sought to resolve the anxiety of untruth. Deleuze is arguing for life as experimentation, uncertainty, and flying across borders and territories. The multiplicity of identity – no longer subjective – is found only in lines of flight that are nomadic, having no roots in anything permanent. This is where desire meets proper names and where multiplicities grow in the space between them. This is not the search for tranquillity, then, for desire is the raw material that experiments without resentment or self-hatred, and where there is only risk and peril. Tranquillity is no longer the goal of philosophy, seeking now not peace or rest, but events and intensities, and combinations of movements and fluxes. With Nietzsche, so for Deleuze, 'desire never needs interpreting, it is it which experiments' (2002: 95). Such becomings 'are acts which can only be contained in a life and expressed in a style' (2002: 3). For Nietzsche, this philosophical reworking of ancient ideas commends one to follow the example of the tightrope walker and to make danger one's vocation.

We have, then, two distinct responses in the western philosophical tradition to the emotion surrounding the instability of the identity of the master. The one damns anxiety and agitation, the other praises it. It is common for theorising in a range of different specialist areas to divide along these familiar lines of systems versus flux. In the classroom it is the carefully planned lesson opposed to unstructured creative and spontaneous activity. In educational leadership it is management by conformity to robust systems opposed to the vagaries of arbitrary and un-standardised and perhaps more spontaneous practices. So often it is characterised as the formal heartless bureaucratic machine of administration and procedure opposed to the informal human engagement in untrammelled relationships and activities. But these dualisms make life easy for both camps, for they defend their own stance in reference to the other. Such dualism constitutes the cosy consensus of the power-brokers on each side who know that it is vital for them that the game continues to be played. But is there another way in which one can understand this opposition, one that does not just repeat the dualism but learns something from it that has value-added significance? There is, and it requires us to return to the relationship between anxiety and authority in the identity and non-identity of the master and slave.

Anxiety in authority

We could rest here in another comfortable dualism, by arguing that the figure of the master in Hegel embodies the tradition that would resolve anxiety and doubt through the command of the certain and the autonomous, and that the slave is the tradition that commends instability and emotion, including fear and trembling of non-identity. But we must resist such comfort for the sake of something much more interesting about the nature of the relationship.

We saw above how, when the master and slave are two persons, the truth of the master collapses into that of the slave, and the truth of the slave unites with itself. What concerns us now is how this whole relationship of master and slave is embodied by the modern individual. We can make the legal presupposition here that slavery, in its formal sense, has been abolished, and that men, women, and children (and to a very limited extent animals and nature) have their rights guaranteed. But we must also make the political observation that at the very least *economic* slavery persists. In the European tradition of social and political theory there are many warnings about the dehumanising effects of mechanical and bureaucratic work. This economic slavery of the free man is making itself felt currently in debates about quality of life and work/life balance. The slave, in this sense, persists in the free labourer.

Perhaps of greater significance, the modern master cannot easily see his dependence on others because this dependence is being 'outsourced' to poorer and less visible parts of the world. Slavery has been abolished and yet modern western societies are increasingly dependent on eastern manufacturing economies for their financial autonomy and freedom to have access to cheap goods. The truth of the free economic master is now just as it always was: self-opposed or autoimmune. His independence is grounded in dependence, but this time in addition to knowing the slave who is other, there is the modern experience of the contradiction of the modern master who is also slave, or is self-opposed in his identity. We cannot pursue here the relation of both experiences to each other, although the relation holds within it the possibility for learning how to re-conceive of the idea of humanity (see Tubbs 2008: Chapters 1 and 2).

For our purposes we note that the western individual experiences himself as both master and slave. As master, he is not master, for he is dependent, and in experiencing himself as dependent he is also finding in himself the truth of the slave. Fundamentally the identity of the modern master consists of this ambivalence, and we have to begin to refer to this person in a way that recognises this. The modern master is sovereign and subject, independent and dependent, free and not free, identity and non-identity. We have to refer to him as both parts of a contradictory totality which together don't add up to the totality because it, too, is total and non-total.

Passion in ambivalence

If we return now to seeing the instability of the identities of the master and slave and the emotions accompanying this instability, we begin to see how philosophy can comprehend the contradiction of the person with authority and who is charged with leadership. The identity of this master has its truth only in uncertainty and anxiety. It is this uncertainty and anxiety that relieves him from the illusion that his identity is somehow immune to the agitation of doubt and untruth. To seek to resolve this uncertainty is to seek an identity of master and leader free from its ambiguity. The effect of such resolutions is always a turn away from truth and towards terror and tyranny. Authoritarianism is precisely the refusal of the ambivalent truth of authority. On the other hand, to work with anxiety, doubt, and uncertainty as the truth of one's work in the world does not mean giving up authority or leadership. Quite the reverse. It is the courage needed to work with and not against their truth.

It might come as a surprise to know that truth in anxiety and uncertainty is part of the western philosophical tradition. It can be found, however, in those philosophers that do not fall into the either/or of master *or* slave, leader *or* led, independence *or* dependence, or authority *or* heteronomy. It is found in philosophies that are able to acknowledge a third party that is present in such dualisms, a third party which we could call the middle were it not for the fact that the very idea of a middle settles the difficult relation of its two components. The best we can say of the middle is that it is the truth of contradictions because it too is present only in being self-opposed. *But* this kind of truth is known very clearly by us, for it is real, or actual, in our struggles and our dilemmas, and is known to us as difficulty and in the emotions that carry such difficulty. What it comes down to is this. If you think that difficulty is only an error to be resolved, then you find difficulty and its anxiety to be nothing in itself. If, on the other hand, you are open to the philosophical education that difficulty is substantial, is something in its own right and carries its own truths and meaning, then you will come to comprehend ambivalence as a way of life. The eternal movement from certainty to uncertainty and from uncertainty to certainty is a truth of the modern human condition. Indeed, to be passionate about ambivalence is to be passionate about the difficult truth of authority and leadership. If one is open to this then there are major philosophical thinkers in the western tradition who have made this passion in ambivalence the content of their work. This list includes Plato, Aristotle, Augustine, Eriugena, Kant, Hegel, Kierkegaard, Nietzsche, Weil, Adorno, and Derrida. If you wish to understand better the ambiguities of authority and leadership you will find its voice in these writers and thinkers.

Let us end with a provocative thought. The history of western philosophy has always been in relation to an idea of the soul. The soul is perhaps understood as the site where God or truth meets man. The soul is therefore permanently without peace and rest for it is where peace meets unrest. It is in the soul that one finds one's humanity, for the soul knows its instability to be significant and meaningful. It knows that it is both master and slave, known and unknown. It is the substance of the ambivalence of the modern human condition. If the leader or the one with authority does not know his own soul in this way then he does not know himself; and if he does not know himself how can he ever understand those for whom he is charged with responsibility? The urgency in the west, in schools and universities as much as in international relations and economics, is that the master take the advice of the oracle at Delphi in Ancient Greece to 'know thyself' so that he can learn to find his own truth in those who are served by him.

Notes

1 Aquinas discusses this Psalm in the *Summa Theologica* (1920: 229; vol. 9, Part II, 2nd Part, 19.7) and, with Ecclesiasticus (1916: Book I and Book XXV. 12), argues that although fear is appropriate in knowing God, faith is the beginning of wisdom regarding first principles and essence. Descartes' earliest known notebook, since lost, begins with the quotation that 'fear of the Lord is the beginning of wisdom' (1985: 1). The Islamic scholar al-Ghazali also refers to the fear of God being the beginning of wisdom in his autobiographical *Deliverance from Error* (1980: 36).

2 Since the relation of man and woman can also be seen to be one of master/slave, it would not be consistent to suppress the difficulty of this relation within *he/she*. The question of authority and leadership can have distinctive gendered characteristics. This is further complicated when the leader or the one with authority is a woman.

References

Agamben, G. (1998) *Homo Sacer*, trans. D. Heller-Rouzen, Stanford: Stanford University Press.

Al-Ghazali (1980) *Deliverance From Error*, trans. R.J. McCarthy, Louisville: Fons Vitae.

Aquinas, T. (1920) *Summa Theologica*, trans. Fathers of the English Dominican Province, London: Burns Oates and Washbourne.

Augustine (1972) *City Of God*, trans. H. Bettenson, Harmondsworth: Penguin.

Aurelius, M. (1964) *Meditations*, trans. M. Staniforth, Harmondsworth: Penguin.

Deleuze, G. (2002) *Dialogues II*, London: Continuum.

Descartes, R. (1985) *The Philosophical Writings of Descartes*, vol. 1, trans. J. Cottingham *et al.*, Cambridge: Cambridge University Press.

Ecclesiasticus (1916) *The Wisdom Of Ben-Sira*, trans. W.O.E. Oesterley, London: SPCK.

Empiricus, S. (2000) *Outlines of Scepticism*, trans. J. Annas and J. Barnes, Cambridge: Cambridge University Press.

Hegel, G.W.F. (1977 [1807]) *Phenomenology of Spirit*, trans. A.V. Miller, Oxford: Oxford University Press.

Nietzsche, F. (1968) *Twilight of the Idols*, trans. R.J. Hollingdale, Harmondsworth: Penguin.

—— (1982) *The Portable Nietzsche*, trans. W. Kaufmann, New York: Viking.

—— (1998) *Twilight of the Idols*, trans. D. Large, Oxford: Oxford University Press.

Philo (1993) *The Works Of Philo*, trans. C.D. Yonge, Massachusetts: Hendrickson.

Plotinus (1991) *The Enneads*, trans. S. MacKenna, London: Penguin.

Seneca (1997) *On The Shortness Of Life*, trans. C.D.N. Costa, London: Penguin.

Tubbs, N. (2008) *Education in Hegel*, London: Continuum.

3 Kierkegaard, emotion, and the individual

Passion of the infinite as the truth for educational leadership

Yaroslav Senyshyn

There are many ways that Kierkegaard can be approached in terms of educational leadership and emotion in higher education. Given the obvious space limitations of this chapter, I have decided to focus on the passionate individual as educational leader. But such a discussion cannot be successful unless it incorporates Kierkegaard's notion of passion as truth that is unavoidably related to both a discussion of subjectivity (feeling) and, in turn, its relatedness to objectivity. Kierkegaard's great work on the shared emotion of anxiety, and its corollary despair, cannot be dealt with in this chapter except in a very brief cursory manner and only as it relates to the aforementioned topics (for a more detailed discussion see Kierkegaard 1980; Senyshyn 1999; Senyshyn and O'Neill 2001). No one can be surprised to learn that Kierkegaard's thinking is labyrinthine in nature and inextricably linked and inseparably fused to the total summation of his thought. It is in this remarkable complexity that Kierkegaard's thought is so highly valued for all individuals working in the field of educational leadership.

Kierkegaard's treatment of the notion of subjectivity as truth is found in his book entitled *Concluding Unscientific Postscript*. For Kierkegaard, there is no authenticity in individuals' actions if these are not grounded in a thorough understanding of one's feelings or emotions in subjectivity and the concomitant and related notions of objectivity. Certainly, the topic of emotion in Kierkegaard's oeuvre is worthy of a voluminous book that would encompass topics such as a concept of anxiety and its relatedness to despair and the demonic, notions of the individual and the problems of conformity and levelling, and religious feeling and its relationship to the irrationality of faith. These I can only allude to in a passing way as they are related to some degree to the problem of subjectivity and objectivity because everything else in Kierkegaard proceeds from these seemingly dichotomous but ultimately related notions that are invaluable for educational leadership studies in higher education.

The Preface to his *Concluding Unscientific Postscript* is especially important in that he presents his intentions, contradictions, and unconscious assumptions. For example, he announces in his first two sentences that in this work he does not intend to raise the issue of truth and Christianity; rather, the focus is on the individual and a relationship to Christianity. First and foremost, subjectivity would appear to be an attack on Hegel's systematisation of religious thought. This approach Kierkegaard views as one of personal indifference. In an intolerant tone, the pseudonymous Johannes Climacus (Kierkegaard actually added his own name as editor) writes that the concept, or as he calls it the 'problem', of truth as subjectivity

> ... has nothing whatever to do with the systematic zeal of the personally indifferent individual to arrange the truths of Christianity in paragraphs; it deals with the concern of the infinitely interested individual for his own relationship to such a doctrine.
>
> (1968: 19)

In spite of Kierkegaard's intentions not to raise the issue of the truth of Christianity, he nevertheless does just that in that he assumes that there is a higher good that awaits all of humankind. He writes:

> I Johannes Climacus ... like most people assume that there awaits me a highest good, an eternal happiness, in the same sense that such a good awaits a servant-girl or a professor. I have heard that Christianity proposes itself as a condition for the acquirement of this good, and now I ask how I may establish a proper relationship to this doctrine.
>
> (1968: 19)

Kierkegaard is aware of the irony of his inquiry in that it defies the Hegelian universal of the collective 'we' and instead focuses on the individual 'I'. But, he feels compelled to defy collective consciousness on the basis that Christianity, in its very nature, elicits emphasis on the self in that it provides each with eternal happiness on the condition that an individual can create a proper relationship with Christianity. Also, Christianity is viewed as having an infinite interest in our eternal happiness: '...an interest by virtue of which the individual hates father and mother, and thus doubtless also snaps his fingers at speculative systems and outlines of universal history' (1968: 19). As we can see from this quotation, this interest of Christianity is never too far away from Kierkegaard's scorn of Hegelianism in terms of its speculative and universal systems of thought; he also shows his well-known contempt for a 'comfortable' Christian bourgeois morality in that he purposely brings up an uncomfortable relationship between the demands of Christianity and an individual's relationship to her parents and loved ones.

Kierkegaard believes that the only unpardonable offence against the 'majesty of Christianity' is the taking for granted of an individual the personal relationship that purportedly exists between Christianity and the human being. The theologians and philosophers of Kierkegaard's time were opposed to this personal relationship between the individual and Christianity. Thus, in his defence he writes:

> However unassuming it may seem to permit oneself this kind of a relationship to Christianity, Christianity judges it as insolence. I must therefore respectfully decline the assistance of all the theocentric helpers and helpers' helpers, in so far as they propose to help me into Christianity on such a basis. Then I rather prefer to remain where I am, with my infinite interest, with the problem, with the possibility.
>
> (1968: 19–20)

Typically, Kierkegaard contradicts his original intention in his Preface to the *Concluding Unscientific Postscript*. I refer to the opening statement in which he writes that he does not intend to raise the issue of truth and Christianity. Yet, he seems to do just that in his Preface in that he begins to discuss the 'possibility' of an eternal happiness that may not be attainable after all if an individual loses a 'sensibility' for eternal happiness. This possibility happens to be very much an issue of truth and Christianity. Kierkegaard expresses this doubt and contradiction of his original intention in this quotation:

> It is not entirely impossible that one who is infinitely interested in his eternal happiness may sometime come into possession of it. But it is surely quite impossible for one who has lost a sensibility for it (and this can scarcely be anything else than the infinite interest), ever to enjoy an eternal happiness. If the sense for it is once lost, it may perhaps be impossible to recover it.
>
> (1968: 20)

In the second last paragraph of his Preface, Kierkegaard attempts to clarify the issue in that he defines the objective problem as consisting of 'an inquiry into the truth of Christianity. The subjective problem concerns the relationship of the individual to Christianity' (1968: 20). His assumption or presupposition is that the subjective problem will concern everyone else in the same manner if properly posed. He concludes the Preface with the irrational remark that 'the posing of the [subjective] problem cannot be regarded as presumption on my part, but only as a special kind of madness' (1968: 20).

Kierkegaard believed that when Christianity is approached in any historical documental approach, it can only lead to despair because 'the greatest attainable certainty with respect to anything historical is merely an *approximation*' (1968: 25). He considered approximation to be incommensurable with the notion of eternal happiness because a 'result' could not be possible. In other words, approximation cannot justify the reality or guarantee argumentatively an eternal happiness. On the other hand, Kierkegaard scorns those who do not respect the findings of philological scholarship so long as the scholar realises the limitations of such study in terms of approximation. He has other reservations as well but these pertain to what he specifically calls 'scholarly critical theology'. It would be useful to contrast Kierkegaard's understanding of the end results of scholarship between the disciplines of philology and critical theology.

According to Kierkegaard, the philologist's activity is bounded by his familiarity and ingenuity with the period in which he prepares his edition; the result of his labours can only be admirable because his scholarship provides us with a finished product in its most accurate form. Also, the philologist does not pretend that the finished product of his scholarship is based on some connection with the individual and eternal happiness. Unfortunately, for the theologians, no such praise is reserved for them because, according to Kierkegaard, they always assume that we can base our eternal happiness on their completed product. What then can a theologian ultimately attain in his scholarly criticisms of the Bible? Kierkegaard answers: 'I assume, accordingly, that the critics have succeeded in proving about the Bible everything that any learned theologian in his happiest moment has ever wished to prove about the Bible' (1968: 29). This is a very caustic remark that makes me wonder if the same accusation could not in all fairness be hurled to some degree at Kierkegaard himself concerning his 'critical' assumptions of eternal happiness that he must ultimately derive from Scriptures. But, he might answer that I have a short memory and would remind me that eternal happiness and the individual is not a critical objective problem but a subjective one that derives not from his presumption but from 'a special kind of madness'!

Thus, for Kierkegaard, faith can never be directly attained by a scientific enquiry. Critical proof as a basis for faith is not needed by faith; rather it is the enemy of faith. How is one then to view his understanding of the nature of subjectivity *in itself* and its connection with objective understanding?

Kierkegaard approaches this problem indirectly by focusing his ideas on 'passion'. Stephen Evans writes that

> it is passion ... that makes existence in the strongest sense possible. Only through passion can a person begin to collect herself and give her life a unified direction so that she actually becomes something – and in so doing becomes a self. This process has something in common with what contemporary psychologists call, again rather colorlessly, personal integration.
>
> (1983: 40)

Nevertheless, this is just a step toward subjectivity:

> Human existence is thus a synthesis of the temporal and the eternal, finite and infinite. It is a successive process in which the individual can recognize and attempt to actualize 'the eternal' (ethical values). The recognition and realization is made possible in and through the passion the individual develops in the course of living. This passion then makes up the inwardness or subjectivity that is the actual content of a person's existence.
>
> (Evans 1983: 72)

To make this quotation more relevant, it is necessary to clarify what Kierkegaard meant by objectivity as an opposite of subjectivity. First, he was convinced that objectivity was an illusion and that in the blind pursuit of objectivity individuals lost their capacity for subjectivity. For Mary Warnock,

> The myth which Kierkegaard aims to destroy is the scientific myth that everything is causally determined, and that therefore in principle a complete and objectively true account of the behaviour of everything could be provided, if only we took trouble and observed enough.
>
> (1988: 8)

Of course this does not mean that Kierkegaard wanted to disregard objective knowledge. Far from it. He simply wanted people to recognise the limitations and myths of objectivity. Instead, he wanted us to preserve our individuality through subjective reflection. Warnock clearly defines three essential characteristics of subjective knowledge:

> First it cannot be passed on from one person to the next, nor added to by different researchers. It cannot be taught in the classroom. Second, what is known subjectively always has the nature of a paradox. Therefore, subjective knowledge is identical with faith. For faith alone, and not reason, can induce us to accept paradox. Faith is not an intellectual, but an emotional attribute.
>
> (1988: 16)

Kierkegaard says: 'Christianity wishes to intensify passion to the highest pitch; but *passion is subjectivity*, and does not exist objectively' (1968: 116, italics added). Third, subjective knowledge is concrete, not abstract. This is because it must necessarily be related to the actual concrete existence of a living individual (Warnock 1988: 9–10). Thus, on the subjective level, an individual would not evade the actual content of his or her existence. In this sense one cannot evade or escape one's subjective inner self. Evans writes:

> The answer in general is that such communication must be artful or 'indirect', since the communication to be understood must eventuate in a double reflection on the part of the recipient. The receiver must personally appropriate the content, and he is free to do this or to refrain. Hence the success of the communication cannot be guaranteed. The true subjective communicator practices the maieutic art, as did Socrates ... The paradox of the maieutic life is that 'the recipient by the help of another comes to stand by himself.' But if this is to be possible the communicator must find a way to reduce his own significance to the recipient to a vanishing nothingness.
>
> (1983: 102, 103)

The next step in our enquiry will take into consideration Kierkegaard's concept of subjective understanding and how it relates to the individual as leader. Mullen succinctly expresses this opposing Kierkegaardian dichotomy:

> To be committed is to be subjective, to be detached is to be objective. A person must be both a subject (a center of commitment) and an object (an item of analysis) to himself. Yet these are opposing tendencies. They can never be made to live harmoniously together. They will always cause you trouble (anxiety) in so far as you attempt to satisfy both, and yet this is exactly what you must do. This is therefore a problem which is built into the requirements of being a person. That is what an existential paradox is, a problem (source of anxiety) which goes away only when you cease to be a complete person – in death, in insanity, in self-deception.
>
> (1988: 46–7)

What, then, is the nature of objective knowledge as the opposing tendency of subjective understanding? According to Kierkegaard, when an individual's reflection is directed to objective truth, then she becomes related to an object of truth. Thought or reflection in this relation between the individual and the known object does not result in a focus on the nature of the relationship per se, but rather on the question of verifiability of the truth of the object to the knower. In Kierkegaard's view it is possible to state categorically that 'if only the object to which he is related is the truth, the subject is accounted to be in the truth' (1968: 178). When an individual's reflection is directed to truth subjectively, then the reflection is directed subjectively to the relation between the individual and the question of truth raised in a subjective manner. 'If only the mode of this relationship is in the truth, the individual is in the truth even if he should happen to be thus related to what is not true' (1968: 178). Kierkegaard gives an example in the form of the knowledge of God to clarify his line of reasoning. He posits the problem in this way:

> Objectively, reflection is directed to the problem of whether this object is the true God; subjectively, reflection is directed to the question whether the individual is related to a something in such a manner that his relationship is in truth a God-relationship. On which side is the truth now to be found?
>
> (1968: 178)

Obviously, the answer is on the side of subjectivity. But how does he get there? Kierkegaard begins with the mediational point of view; that is, that the truth is on neither side. He rejects this argument on the basis that the individual is in the state of existence and thus by definition in order to take a mediational approach must be in a 'finished' state; but this is not possible because the individual exists and therefore is 'becoming' and not 'finished'. Thus, according to Kierkegaard's logic, an individual cannot be in a state of mediation because a human being exists.

Kierkegaard offers another argument; he says that the mediational state is also impossible because an existing individual cannot be ubiquitously identifying herself as subject and object. 'When he is nearest to being in two places at the same time he is in passion; but passion is momentary, and passion is also the highest expression of subjectivity' (1968: 178). In other words, passion can only sustain the individual's ubiquitous relationship of subject and object for the moment only.

The objective process is impossible because God, according to Kierkegaard, exists only in the inwardness of subjectivity. I need not point out to my reader that this is his a priori presupposition and thus cannot be entertained as a fallacy of the objective approach. He writes that the objective search for a relationship with God

> ... is marked by the fact that while objective knowledge rambles comfortably on by way of the long road of approximation without being impelled by the urge of passion, subjective knowledge counts every delay a deadly peril, and the decision so infinitely important and so instantly pressing that it is as if the opportunity had already passed.
> (1968: 179)

But can the urgency of the subjective seeker of God truly constitute an argument against an objective approach? Could one not argue that the fanaticism of a fascist is also based on the urgency of a passionate, subjective approach? Surely the means cannot justify the end! Kierkegaard would have to answer that it is precisely the end as the 'majesty of God' that justifies the passionate approach; thus, he makes assumptions that cannot be philosophically contained. These are, according to Kaufmann: first, belief as defined by Scriptures is assumed to be true – even objectively true; second, his focus on 'eternal happiness' is based on one religion only – Christianity – and thus does not acknowledge the points of view of other religions; third, Kierkegaard goes through great pains to discredit the 'approximation-process' of the objective approach and to show that scholarship cannot firmly establish faith. Kaufmann asks, 'Why does he ignore the no less obvious fact that it can and often does, undermine faith' (1975: 85)? This latter criticism is unfair because the whole notion of subjectivity was constructed by Kierkegaard precisely because he was all too aware of this influence and was certainly not afraid to admit it in affirming the objective absurdity of faith in the first place, as we shall see later. It is clear that Kierkegaard was not one of Kaufmann's favourite philosophers – given the invective and scorn included in his chapter on Kierkegaard in *From Shakespeare to Existentialism* (1980: 184, 186, 190).

In the famous passage on the idolater and the Christian, Kierkegaard redeems himself and reveals the type of universality that has attracted to him thinkers of other world religions who believe his message is universally applicable from the standpoint of world faith. This is the famous quotation that reveals that he is not a narrow Christian bigot:

> If one who lives in the midst of Christendom goes up to the house of God, the house of the true God, with the true conception of God in his knowledge, and prays, but prays in a false spirit; and one who lives in an idolatrous community prays with the entire passion of the infinite, although his eyes rest upon the image of an idol: where is there most truth? The one prays in truth to God though he worships an idol; the other prays falsely to the true God, and hence worships in fact an idol.
> (1968: 179–80)

Kierkegaard's intention is also to contrast the objective approach to the problem of immortality with that of the subjective believer who embraces 'uncertainty' with infinite passion. He leans with the subjective believer and with the same parallel line of reasoning he used with the problem of the knowledge of God; that is, immortality cannot be approached by the 'never-ending approximation' of the objective approach because the truth or certainty of immortality can only be found in the subjective sphere of the individual; thus, his assumption is that the individual who struggles with uncertainty in the subjective mode is immortal and 'fights for his immortality'. Kierkegaard has nothing but scorn for those who believe they have the 'proofs' for immortality. He contrasts these 'proof-mongers' (he does not name them) with the heroic example of Socrates who embraces the uncertainty of the issue of 'if there is an immortality', with 'the passion of the infinite'.

Kierkegaard sums up his argument by referring to what he calls objective and subjective 'accents'. He writes that these accents are related to the 'what' of a statement and to the 'how' of a statement respectively. The 'what' of a statement is relative to the person speaking in those terms; thus, the truth of what is being said is relative to the person or persons speaking. In other words, the 'what' of a statement only has relative truth. I quote Kierkegaard for the sake of clarity:

> *The objective accent falls on WHAT is said, the subjective accent on HOW it is said....* Objectively the interest is focused merely on the thought-content, subjectively on the inwardness. At its maximum this inward 'how' is the passion of the infinite, and the passion of the infinite is the truth. But the passion of the infinite is precisely subjectivity, and thus subjectivity becomes the truth. Objectively there is infinite decisiveness, and hence it is objectively in order to annul the difference between good and evil, together with the principle of contradiction, and therewith also the infinite difference between the true and the false. [It is here that we see the relativity of truth in the objective mode in the example of good and evil and the true and the false.] Only in subjectivity is there

> decisiveness, to seek objectivity is to be in error. It is the passion of the infinite that is the decisive factor and not its content, for its content is precisely itself. In this manner subjectivity and the subjective 'how' constitute the truth.
>
> (1968: 181)

Although this quotation is very useful for our understanding of the differentiation of objective and subjective truths, it nevertheless still leaves us with the legitimate question of truth in itself; that is, *what is truth?* Surely, it is not enough to say that truth is subjectivity. Kierkegaard does not shirk in providing an answer – his definition is quite succinct: '*An objective uncertainty held fast in an appropriation-process of the most passionate inwardness is the truth*, the highest truth attainable for an *existing* individual' (1968: 182).

But such a definition is not passive or abstract in nature; Kierkegaard refers to the 'appropriation-process' as a 'venture' by which an individual actively 'embraces' uncertainty 'with the passion of the infinite' in order to gain this truth. It is apparent that this truth is faith and Kierkegaard admits to this; he claims that his definition of truth is an 'equivalent expression for faith'. All of this is quite acceptable, but what about the possibility of an objective certainty? Can we dismiss this notion altogether? Kierkegaard addresses it with a brief dismissal. In a curt way he admits to the objective truth of a 'mathematical proposition', but dismisses this by labelling the propositional truth as one that is an 'indifferent truth'. Thus, this kind of truth is irrelevant to the more important issue of objective uncertainty and its relation to the faith of Christianity. How is one to acquire this faith? He answers that this kind of faith is acquired through risk: 'Without risk there is no faith. Faith is precisely the contradiction between the infinite passion of the individual's inwardness and the objective uncertainty' (1968: 182).

In order for an individual to have faith, risk must be involved. Faith is in direct incremental proportion to the risk involved. The greatest risk of all is the belief in the absurd; the absurd is the 'eternal truth' of God's reincarnation and his coming into being and into temporal time. The only object of faith is the absurd and only this object can be believed. Thus, objective scholarship cannot aid in this interaction between faith and the absurd.

If the maximum of understanding of Christianity is that it refuses to be understood, then one can only understand that it cannot be understood. To do otherwise is not only a paradox, but a self-defeating process by which Christianity becomes attributed with a knowledge that leads to the confusion of viewing it as a 'matter of knowledge' and thus a kind of objective faith which is a contradiction in terms, that is, a paradox that is objectively conceived and therefore inaccurate and ultimately a disservice to Christianity.

In summation, I would say that Kierkegaard's greatest weakness in his notion of subjectivity is the fact that it is so closely related to the doctrine of Christianity as the one and only religion. Although he does not really say this, he does imply it strongly by not actually referring to other world views. I believe that the concept becomes very meaningful when it is applied universally to all religious views in which the 'absurd' as understood by Kierkegaard plays a pivotal role or when subjectivity is displaced from a sacred context to a secular one and then applied to other human creative efforts, for example, educational leadership.

In conclusion, without a greater shift toward subjectivity and passion the educational leader may very well become a fossil in a museum that is replaced by a robotic technology. Any notion of the merely objective as a conceptualisation of rigidity and determinacy based on a false sense of objectivity and efficiency, in a spirit of authoritarian prejudice, does not allow for perceptions of conceptualisations of subjectivity and the possibility for transformative creativity. Why espouse a conformative determinacy in knowledge that is incompatible with transformative creativity? Educational leaders should take advantage of subjectivity and objectivity as transformative, decentralising strategies and tendencies as essential ingredients of creativity. At all cost conformative–uniformative ends at the expendability of imagination and creativity are to be avoided. To do this one must be an authentic individual.

The term 'individual' for Kierkegaard is more than just another person in the generic sense of the word. For him an individual is a specific human being – a leader – who must struggle to resist the levelling of the masses. In order to gain a more specific understanding of this concept of a leader as individual, we should consider educational leaders and that which constitutes their public. Such leaders do not work in a vacuum for that would deny the definition of the very word 'leader'. Leadership depends and relies very much on the fabric of society in order to function in its capacity.

Recent scholarship, the work of Merold Westphal (1987) and, in particular, the philosophical interpretations of the late Gregor Malantschuk (1987) has made important contributions to our understanding of Kierkegaard's philosophy of the individual and society. For example, Westphal writes that his

> ... first discovery was that the concepts of ideology and the sociology of knowledge were first worked out in the 1840's, not just by Marx but also by Kierkegaard ... At the same time I was not comfortable with Kierkegaard's individualism. On the basis of Hegel [and] Marx ... it seemed to me that human existence was more fundamentally social than Kierkegaard's thought permitted ... Kierkegaard's individualism, I have become increasingly persuaded, expresses a radical politics and is anything but a form of apolitical or antisocial indifference or withdrawal.
>
> (1987: vii–viii)

Westphal attributes his misconception to what he believes is a tendency on the part of scholars to forget that the terminology of Marxist tradition, vis-à-vis the concepts of ideology and sociology, essentially was also worked out by Kierkegaard. Also, a closer reading of the text reveals that 'Kierkegaard's critique of reason was all too frequently misinterpreted in "existentialist" and "irrationalist" terms … the "individualist" interpretation was as fundamentally misleading as the "irrationalist" interpretation, reflecting more an a priori "existentialist" stereotype' (1987: vii–viii).

The erosion of individuality and the ever-increasing encroachment of individual civil liberty and academic freedom in our society is an ongoing concern for many educators in our difficult times since 9/11. There is a general malaise in our time that goes back to at least the time of Kierkegaard, who very accurately prognosticated and even prophesied our devastating uniformity and distaste for individuality and painstakingly with great integrity attempted to provide a philosophical explanation for this situation. It is well known that in the hierarchy of his thought, 'the individual' and individuality received a good deal of Kierkegaard's attention and analysis. In his *Journals* he wrote that, had he to carve an inscription on his tombstone, it would be none other than 'the individual'. For our purposes, we are especially fortunate that Kierkegaard left his ideas on this subject in his *Two Ages* (1846) under the subtitle of 'The Individual' and 'The Public'.

The individual as the ideal educational leader is someone that is empowered by the ability to resist the conformity and levelling of the public. Such an individual has mastered the ability to study issues in their entirety by embracing both objectivity and subjectivity as relational and non-dichotomous entities that are dependent upon each another and are not precluded by the irrationality of faith. Such an individual will seek out the good and find moral truth because *the* individual as leader is passionate and thus responsibly cognizant of truth *in this way*.

References

Evans, C.S. (1983) *Kierkegaard's 'Fragments' and 'Postscript': The Religious Philosophy of Johannes Climacus*, Atlantic Highlands: Humanities Press.

Kaufmann, W.A. (1975) *Existentialism from Dostoevsky to Sartre*, New York: New American Library.

—— (1980) *From Shakespeare to Existentialism: An Original Study*, Princeton: Princeton University Press.

Kierkegaard, S. (1968) *Concluding Unscientific Postscript*, trans. D. Swenson and W. Lowrie, Princeton: Princeton University Press.

—— (1978 [1846]) *Two Ages: The Age of Revolution and the Present Age*, trans. H. Hong and E. Hong, Princeton: Princeton University Press.

—— (1980) *The Concept of Anxiety: A Simple Psychologically Orienting Deliberation on the Dogmatic Issue of Hereditary Sin*, trans. A. Anderson and R. Thomte, Princeton: Princeton University Press.

Malantschuk, G. (1987) *Kierkegaard's Way to the Truth: An Introduction to the Authorship of Søren Kierkegaard*, Montreal: Inter Editions.

Mullen, J.D. (1988) *Kierkegaard's Philosophy: Self-Deception and Cowardice in the Present Age*, New York: New American Library.

Senyshyn, Y. (1999) 'Perspectives on performance and anxiety and their implications for creative teaching', *The Canadian Journal of Education*, 24: 30–41.

Senyshyn, Y. and O'Neill, S.A. (2001) 'Subjective experience of anxiety and musical performance: a relational perspective', *Philosophy of Music Education Review*, 9: 42–53.

Warnock, M. (1988) *Existentialism*, Oxford: Oxford University Press.

Westphal, M. (1987) *Kierkegaard's Critique of Reason and Society*, Macon: Mercer University Press.

4 Unconscious dynamics in the educational organisation

Psychoanalytic contributions to administration and leadership studies

Eugenie A. Samier

Psychoanalytic theory has always played a role in administrative and leadership studies, enjoying periods of popularity and decline. Kets de Vries' extensive work in this area over the last 20 years, since the appearance of *The Neurotic Organisation* in 1984, has renewed interest in psychoanalysis, as well as the recent spate of books and articles on narcissism and psychopathy in management studies, most from a psychoanalytic perspective. In the field's earlier history, Horney, Bettelheim, Fromm, and Klein led theorists like Baum, Hirschhorn, and Argyris to incorporate fundamental psychoanalytic concepts in their work as it offered an explanation for the more hidden yet tacitly perceived aspects of organisational experience arising from preconscious and unconscious dynamics. This includes the undisclosed, avoided, and often denied fears and anxieties of individuals affecting culture and politics by examining unconscious meaning of 'behaviors, psychological processes, social actions, and life situations' (Cartwright 2004: 211). Most educational leadership underestimates those interrelations of an individual's internal and external worlds central to psychoanalysis that contribute to healthy relationships and environments as well as conflict resulting in bureaupathologies, toxic cultures, and destructive micropolitics. It is part of the 90 per cent of the tacit and informal organisation that lies beneath rational structures and functions.

The purpose of this chapter is to review important contributions psychoanalysis can make in uncovering unconscious processes affecting personality and behaviour, and explore selective aspects of neo-Freudianism for their potential in creating an interpretive approach to emotions. These include: ego and superego development informing morality, just action, and self-respect; transference and counter-transference; defence mechanisms, particularly projection, denial, resistance, and sublimation in both positive and negative forms (one cause of sabotage); and neurotic dispositions. These can be used to explain a number of phenomena such as abuse of authority, excessive management control, the ambiguous role of leadership, groupthink, and counter-transference reactions of emotions onto colleagues and superordinates leading to idealisation in positive or demonisation in negative forms. All of these are important considerations when examining how individuals influence each other, accept authority, and exercise power, serving as an important approach for accessing unconscious processes complementary to other forms of research.

Foundational writings

Psychoanalysis is probably the most controversial school of psychology after behaviourism, generating a considerable contrary literature. Some of this is unwarranted, omitting many variants and later developments, not all of which are subject to the same critiques. Freud's writings exhibited the constraints of his time, being a member of bourgeois Viennese society and a pioneer in a new discipline. But he also has many defenders like Bettelheim (1982), who critiques many English translations that have replaced humanistic with mechanistic language, and Fromm (1979), the naïve positivism of Freud's 'scientific' detractors and for whom Freud's greatness still lies in his investigation of the unconscious, the Oedipus complex, transference, the concept of narcissism, a dynamic concept of character with four types of developmental structure (oral–receptive, oral–sadistic, anal–sadistic, genital), and the significance of childhood experience. Probably of most importance in organisational culture and politics are the defence mechanisms (e.g. repression, denial, displacement, projection, rationalisation) and unconscious conflicts (e.g. suggestibility, powerlessness, cynicism, passivity). Psychoanalysis as a treatment has also been subjected to competitive critique in the marketplace, as much a problem for it as for educational organisations currently subjected to commercialisation dependent upon quick fixes and panaceas.

While its clinical applications have limited professional use in administration, psychoanalysis has been developed for broader scholarly purpose aimed at both individual self-knowledge and meaning and social expression. Freudian analysis did not develop solely from an observation of individuals, but from a broad interdisciplinary exploration into art, literature, philosophy, mythology, religion, anthropology, and history (see Essman 1998), suggesting its application to many levels of social analysis. For Elliott, who has examined psychoanalysis for social theory, its value lies primarily in the 'problems concerning self-identity, power, and ideological domination; sexual difference and gender; and the question of human subjectivity' (1992: 234). Dauphin (2000), in typical classical psychoanalytic use of mythological metaphor examines our re-enactment of the myth of Tantalus whose punishment for attempting to 'tantalise' the gods was cursed to never be satisfied, but rather was excited by omnipotent wishes always out of reach, a theme applied to the modern belief in science and technology, including the desire for a 'science' of management, or, currently, a belief in leadership, that will realise all of our wishes. The psychoanalysis of politics was explored by Freud, beginning with 'Group Psychology and the Analysis of the Ego' (1921) and *Civilization and Its Discontents* (1930) aimed at understanding social institutions, intra- and inter-state relations, large-group psychology, government and leadership, the rights of individuals, large-scale political conflict, and political biography. Freud also addressed work inhibition caused by hysteria or obsessional disorder (see 1926: 89).

On an individual level, psychoanalysis lends itself well to biographical work, an application that Freud established in 'Leonardo da Vinci' (1910) and 'Moses and Monotheism' (1939), ushering in the disciplines of psychobiography and psychohistory. Biography occupies a significant position in the study of leadership outside of education, exploring both psychopathology and normality in societal context, and in the construction of leadership between leader and the led, covering loves and hates, unconscious fantasies, and symbolic interactions that characterise the individual and group self found in shared ideals (Offer and Strozier 1985: 7, 75).

Many psychobiographies have focused on political figures, exploring conflicting motivations and other aspects of the 'inner theatre' that result in leadership roles. Erickson's (1962) biography of Luther is exceptional in its perspicacity, exploring the importance of Luther's identity conflicts in adolescence that in part contributed to his originality as a theologian and the radical innovations he brought about. It exemplifies the importance of inner conflicts to our construction of identity, organisational and cultural roles, and the ability to put to constructive use the suffering of these conflicts. Luther himself was aware of this to some degree: 'I did not learn my theology all at once, but I had to search deeper for it, where my temptations took me' (1962: 251). Erickson, whose psychosocial stages of development are important in educational developmental psychology, argued for the importance of adolescent identity crises for biography (1962). This complements the emphasis placed in psychoanalysis on formative childhood experiences when interactions with others play a strong role in creating a psychic foundation to the personality and the seeds of neuroses creating interactional patterns carried through later life. Adult recollections may be realistic, distorted, or fantasised, all of which may change with an understanding of the inner world and the meaning of formation experience. An example is Marvick's study of Richelieu (1983) examining how political leaders' personality in organisations develop, or Volkan *et al.*'s biography of Nixon (1997) and Volkan and Itzkowitz's biography of Ataturk (1984) that draw on ego psychology and object relations theory in examining personality formation from childhood, the development of self, and representations of others.

Psychobiography has developed over time from an analysis of symbols employed in social life to a broad range of conscious and unconscious meanings to an individual's decisions and actions, producing what Volkan calls a 'total history' of the individual since it unites a study of the inner reality and external world (2008: 259, 261), in the case of political leaders taking note of culture and conditions, as well as the leader's ethnic, religious, or sectoral group identity (2008: 261–2). The same contextualisation principle applies to administrators and leaders in educational fields. Guidelines for psychobiography are also important in the life of administrators and leaders: all organisational actors construct 'biographies' of each other that are subject to the same problems as academic biographers: projecting wishes, fantasies, and expectations of, or defences against, the leader figure (Volkan 2008: 260; Freud 1910).

In larger-scale group analysis psychoanalysis has an established application, inspired by Freud's *Civilization and Its Discontents* (1930), examining the psychic costs to humanity of a technologised and overly managed (or bureaucratised) life, creating neurotic dispositions that eventually undermine society. Hughes, in *History as Art and as Science*, argued that psychoanalysis brings to history insight into the comparative study of groups of emotional common denominators and 'valid generalizations about the deep-seated fears and ideal strivings' (1964: 62). He sees in both history (including biography) and psychoanalysis a common interpretive methodology taking as the primary datum the mind and 'radical subjectivity of human understanding' (1964: 63). It has also been used for some time in examining more significant societal changes that influence educational organisations. Fromm's *Escape from Freedom* (1941) explores similar societal themes, but argues that most people will retreat from freedom, even if into authoritarian or totalitarian systems. Mitscherlich, in *Society without the Father* (1993), interprets the impact of industrial society on authority structures based on the father leading to greater impersonalism. Psychoanalysis has also been adapted to analysing large-scale political conflict, for example, Falk's *Fratricide in the Holy Land: A Psychoanalytic View of the Arab–Israeli Conflict* (2004) and *Antisemitism: A History and Psychoanalysis of Hatred* (2008).

Organisation, management, administration, and leadership theory

One of the most prominent psychoanalytic approaches to organisations is that of the Tavistock Institute, having developed in the 1960s 'systems psychodynamics', a synthesis of open systems theory and psychoanalysis derived from Freud's 'Group Psychology and the Analysis of the Ego' (1921) and Kleinian object relations theory, initially by Bion in *Experiences in Groups* (1961). Core concepts include transference, resistance, object relations, fantasies, anxieties, and defences, applied to group and social unconscious processes. From this perspective, one can study the interrelationships between organisational structures and individual and group experience such as exercising 'one's authority, to manage oneself in a role and to become less of a captive of group and organizational process' (Miller 1989: 8), and how unconscious anxieties are reflected in structure, design, and task management. Critical to leadership is the examination of dependency on power and authority, the role of paranoia and enmity, psychic challenges of and resistances to organisational change, the psychodynamics of, and role in, organisational culture, and conditions conducive to creativity that reflect various psychoanalytically recognised processes as projective identification, splitting, psychotic anxiety, symbol formation, schizoid mechanisms, and part-objects (see Gould *et al.* 2001).

A central task for leadership is overcoming staff resistance, which to Freud was an indication of past methods of adaptation in childhood (1954: 226). He identified five types of resistance, all of which may play a role in organisational culture and micropolitics:

1. repression, arising from remembering a significant life experience, such as trauma;
2. secondary-gain, expressing reluctance to surrender advantages from illness or stress;
3. superego, characterised by guilt and a need for punishment produced by feelings of unworthiness;
4. repetition compulsion in which unconscious prototypes exert attraction on repressed instinctual processes resulting in a powerful craving for gratification of aggressive and other libidinal impulses; and
5. transference, produced when frustration and resentment are created by not getting expected responses from the analyst [or leader in an organisational context] as representative of an earlier figure in the person's life (Freud 1926: 154; see Rosenthal 2005)

Psychoanalysis has lent itself well to multiple subject studies, an important approach in organisation studies, particularly for questions of culture and politics where interactions among individuals are significant (Isaacson 2005). This includes explaining how public persona are created, how impression management works, what motivates styles of decision-making, the desire for control, denial of responsibility, scapegoating, and acceptance of another's dominance (see Elms and Song 2005). It is equally important in cases of the malignant exercise of power and influence: psychobiography can reveal the inner workings of tyranny or authoritarianism in those granted too much power. Psychoanalysis is used most recently in examining those who have narcissistic traits, driven by insecurity and rage to exhibit unwarranted defensiveness and vindictiveness, and able in positions of authority to act out power fantasies that violate boundaries demarcating societal constraints (Glad 2005), and organisational policies and regulations.

One early administrative piece is Sperling's 'Psychoanalytic Aspects of Bureaucracy', tracing many of what we now call bureaupathologies to psychodynamic processes. In contrast to the more common explanation of goal displacement (instrumental values replacing terminal values) or the 'structural generalization of goals', he proffers deeper personality explanations. One is pedantry – the limitation of one's authority and specialisation by themselves do not produce problems, but instead are symptomatic of anal–sadistic character or 'compulsion neurosis: indecision, avoidance of responsibility, waste of time, rigid adherence to rituals which make no sense, and the compulsion to make others conform to them' (1950: 91). Two other disorders prominent in the bureaucratic world are the fanatic and the idiopathic–psychopathic, both of which differ from compulsive neurotics by practising conscious sadism (1950: 92–3). Part of his argument for their frequent occurrences is that culturally, officialism provides opportunities to 'vent' sadism under the guise of bureaucratic rationalism (1950: 93). Sperling's argument is also prophylactic: organisations should use personality tests to eliminate from applicant pools those who have potentially damaging disorders, a concern that has recently reemerged in management literature examining the destructive effects of psychopaths and narcissists. The unchecked effects of such personnel, he argues, lies largely with those in leadership positions.

From a psychoanalytical perspective, leadership is a complex phenomenon, exemplified in James MacGregor Burns' seminal *Leadership* (1978). Despite its misrepresentation and simplification in much of the transformational leadership literature that hives off Burns' moral dimension, it is instructive in its psychobiographical case studies demonstrating how early formative experiences influenced their alliances, how they handled conflict, and overcame resistance, sometimes in tyrannical form. Offer and Strozier pursue a similar approach, arguing the importance of the interaction of personality, follower aspirations, and socio-cultural–historical context in determining 'good' leadership. In other words, it varies considerably depending upon contextual factors. At the centre is personality, structurally composed of id, ego, superego, and ego ideal, and the self consisting of the 'sum total of perceptions, thoughts, and feelings held by a person in reference to himself or herself' (1985: 307), and consisting of six parts – physical, sexual, familial, social, psychological, and coping – with the last four of most importance to successful leadership (1985: 308). Obholzer draws upon early experience of individuals in their later capacity to assume responsibility rather than blaming others for failures and being able to adjust to organisational structures. He highlights a major problem of leadership envy that can produce 'blocking, bureaucratic, non-facilitating responses to creative ideas that at heart are envious attacks by the leader' (1996: 55). Perhaps an equally important problem in periods of organisational crisis, or instability, is the need people may express, at least unconsciously, for a saviour, allowing their perception to be distorted by seeing omnipotent characteristics in leadership candidates and incumbents.

Kernberg is probably one of the most notable who has turned a psychoanalytic eye to leadership studies. His work is derived in part from the study of group processes by Freud (1921), object relations, Bion (1961), and others following their lead, which focus on ego psychology, the projection of ego ideals onto leaders, and various regressions that can occur in small unstructured groups, threats to internal group cohesion, and the loss of identity and fears of internal aggression that can be experienced in large unstructured groups (1998: 40–4) (roughly characteristic of academic environments). Of particular interest for the study of leadership styles, are a number of more pathological forms: the leader who can't say no, those who require love and admiration, those who need complete control, the absentee leader, those with unavailable or unstable affect, and the corrupt (1998: 143–53).

More recently neo-Freudian theory has emerged again as a powerful interpretive approach characterising social dynamics as the product of underlying personality dynamics and their interpersonal relationships (unconscious motivations, etc.). Diamond's *The Unconscious Life of Organizations* (1993) examines how aspects of the mind (ego, id, superego), neuroses, and defence mechanisms create organisational culture and identity in functional and dysfunctional forms from feelings, emotions, and experience, such as repression causing resistance to change and neurotic dispositions inhibiting organisational change and renewal. Possibly of most relevance currently is his thesis that leadership transitions are disorienting for organisational members, creating an absence of object constancy and leaving feelings about the departing leader unresolved. Gabriel, in the collective work of a number of colleagues in *Organizations in Depth* (1999), explores psychoanalytic theory and its possible applications to the individual, work groups, culture (including images, symbols, and myths), ethics, and a new conception of management.

Manfred Kets de Vries is perhaps the most successful proponent of a neo-Freudian organisation and administration theory, having authored 24 books and over 250 chapters and articles, on the 'inner' theatre of the mind of those in senior management and leadership positions. From his early *Organizational Paradoxes* (1980), he has argued for a less simplistic and more emotionally informed understanding of organisations and leadership. Kets de Vries (1989) has explored the darker side of the entrepreneurial, increasingly important in an age of commercialised education in which the need for control, distrust, the need for applause, and defensive behaviour in reaction to power relationships and structure (including policies and procedures) can become destructive to an organisation. It is from this perspective that he also has demonstrated in 'Beyond the Quick Fix' (1998) that organisational change is not simply the function of a rational process but that it requires significant individual and personality change, accompanied by anxiety, resistance, and fear that easily contributes to failure in contrast to most of the change literature in educational administration.

Twemlow and colleagues have recently applied psychoanalysis to work settings with various types of communities in bringing about healthier personal relations and work lives, in reducing criminal violence in a community with a corrupt and unstable infrastructure and narcissistic leadership, by using a model of training aimed at increasing altruism and self-observation (Twemlow and Sacco 1999). They also applied these techniques to a 'chaotically disorganised elementary school where a sado-masochistic ritual of humiliation prevailed through bullying, using a dialectical social systems psychoanalytic intervention aimed at engaging the by-standing audience requisite for bullying' (Twemlow *et al.* 2000: 321). These examples are relevant also in university units where narcissism or bullying has taken over the organisational culture. The main aim of psychoanalysis applied at this level is to regard everyone as involved in the process, particularly those members of the community who adopt passivity. Some of these principles have also been successfully applied in resolving labour disputes involving focusing attention on the personalities involved rather than using the typical quid pro quo or rational actor mediation process, intervening in the actions of the narcissistic senior administrator, and infusing compassion and empathy into the authoritative style.

Abraham Zaleznik is notable in leadership studies for examining the unconscious psychodynamics of managers and leaders, attributing to Freud revolutionary status in transforming the sixteenth- and seventeenth-century rationalist view of people into a much more complex and multifaceted approach that captures the many internal and external forces acting on personality and behaviour. His *Executive's Guide to Motivating People: How Freudian Theory Can Turn Good Executives into Better Leaders* (1990) provides a relevant treatment of the unconscious, neuroses, defence mechanisms and group psychology as it applies to organisational experience for both leaders and followers. This work has been supplemented more recently with *Learning Leadership: Cases and Commentaries on Abuse of Power in Organizations* (2006) which provides illustrative cases relevant to the current issues of bullying and mobbing in educational organisations, organised into sections dealing with various aspects of problematic power: the conscious and unconscious fantasies of power and the expectations of authority; the relationship between dependency and ambition; drives that lie behind leadership; and problematic forms of power in organisations experiencing crisis.

A number of other authors in the leadership field have found psychoanalysis insightful in determining various ways in which personality functions, such as the proper formation of defences to withstand ambiguity, uncertainty, stress, and one's own aggressive feelings, as well as using 'integrative' defences leading to greater team orientation (Khaleelee and Woolf 1996). Rudden explores the role of regressive group phenomena in inter-group rivalry, drawing on Freud's theory of individual regression in groups (1921). The politics of psychoanalysis itself provides a valuable illustration of the psychodynamics of intellectual movements and educational organisations, for example, Douglas Kirsner's *Unfree Associations* (2000) examining the inner conflicts in psychoanalytic institutes.

Conclusion: research implications

Psychoanalysis is also a research method that provides a range of approaches and techniques: its traditional form of the case method, and later interview methods, intended to 'explore intrapsychic processes and unconscious meaning associated with situations, phenomena, or behavioral acts not necessarily linked to the clinical setting' (Cartwright 2004: 210). Diamond (1993) compares psychoanalytic organisation theory to action research, sharing traits such as causing organisational change using interpretive and critical techniques and interventions.

The psychoanalytic interview is rooted in the narrative tradition aimed at understanding and interpreting the context of meaning and its construction, centred on 'unconscious processes, self- and object representations, defenses and so forth through the analysis of narratives' attempting to uncover 'unconscious fantasy, object relations, predominant defenses, symbolic meaning, and the slippages and transformations of meaning' (Cartwright 2004: 212, 213). Aspects of the psychoanalytic interview that are not as acute a problem in other forms of research are transference and resistance, which in themselves also indicate interesting aspects of relationship in administration and leadership. These aspects of the psychoanalytic interview can best be understood from a hermeneutic perspective in which understanding and meaning construction occur in a 'hermeneutic circle', as an iterative process, and differentiate this research method from those such as free association used in psychoanalytic therapy where both context and motivation differ. One approach emphasising the hermeneutic, which could inform administration and leadership, and one most appropriate to an educational organisation, is Viktor Frankl's logotherapy practice first outlined in *Man's Search for Meaning* (1963).

Four epistemological assumptions of the psychoanalytic interview relevant to the study of leadership are:

1 the construction of meaning focused on how the self reconstructs events, so it is the way a narrative forms that is important as well as the narrative content, and the metaphorical nature of the narrative in representing the self;
2 the associative nature of communicating meaning, particularly implicit forms of association created by unconscious forms of psychic determinism;
3 the critical relevance of internal (intrapsychic) and external contextual influences on meaning, its construction and communication that inform interpretation;
4 the use of inchoate transference–countertransference in evaluating and understanding the interviewer, interviewee and their interactions, particularly observer bias transferred onto the research situation and the transference–countertransference interactions during the interview process itself (including analysis). For the researcher this requires taking one's own subjectivity into account to achieve some measure of objectivity, and identifying one's own motivations, perceptions, and conflicts related to the research subject. To not do so can result in a self-fulfilling prophecy where the researcher uses the interview as an 'arena in which conflicts and fantasies are subtly acted out' (Cartwright 2004: 217–25).

The analysis and interpretation of such interviews involves three aspects that have clear implications for educational administration and leadership: '(1) the search for core narratives while exploring the interview text in its entirety; (2) matching narratives with initial transference–countertransference impressions; and (3) tracking key identifications and object relations within dominant interview narratives' (Cartwright 2004: 211).

In keeping with Volkan *et al.*'s notion of a 'total history', psychobiography requires the use of a broad range of sources, and is interdisciplinary in nature, similar to the practice of Gadamerian hermeneutics: using 'diaries, documents, interviews, political philosophies, the subject's actions and artistic productions, and any relevant films or audio material', as well as visits to important sites (1997: 22). Psychoanalytic methods provide important qualitative methods in accessing the more tacit and complex, yet arguably crucial, aspects of character and personality: the sources of vision and values, power, and authority that constitute the administrative and leadership roles.

References

Bettelheim, B. (1982) *Freud and Man's Soul*, New York: Vintage.

Bion, W. (1961) *Experiences in Groups*, New York: Basic Books.

Burns, J.M. (1978) *Leadership*, New York: Harper & Row.

Cartwright, D. (2004) 'The psychoanalytic research interview: Preliminary suggestions', *Journal of the American Psychoanalytic Association*, 52: 209–42.

Dauphin, B. (2000) 'Tantalizing times: An examination of discontent and disconnects in contemporary American society', *Journal of Applied Psychoanalytic Studies*, 2, 3: 219–45.

Diamond, M. (1993) *The Unconscious Life of Organizations: Interpreting Organizational Reality*, Westport: Quorum.

Elliott, A. (1992) *Social Theory and Psychoanalysis in Transition*, Oxford: Blackwell.

Elms, A. and Song, A. (2005) 'Alive and kicking: The problematics of political psychobiography', in W.T. Schultz (ed.) *Handbook of Psychobiography*, Oxford: Oxford University Press.

Erickson, E. (1962) *Young Man Luther: A Study in Psychoanalysis and History*, New York: W.W. Norton.

Essman, A.H. (1998) 'What is "applied" in "applied" psychoanalysis?' *International Journal of Psychoanalysis*, 79: 741–52.

Falk, A. (2004) *Fratricide in the Holy Land: A Psychoanalytic View of the Arab–Israeli Conflict*, Madison: University of Wisconsin Press.

—— (2008) *Antisemitism: A History and Psychoanalysis of Hatred*, Westport: Praeger.

Frankl, V. (1963) *Man's Search for Meaning: An Introduction to Logotherapy*, Boston: Beacon Press.

Freud, S. (1910) 'Leonardo da Vinci and a memory of his childhood', *Standard Edition*, vol. 11, London: Hogarth Press.

—— (1921) 'Group psychology and the analysis of the ego', *Standard Edition*, vol. 18, London: Hogarth Press.

—— (1926) 'Inhibitions, symptoms and anxiety', *Standard Edition*, vol. 20, London: Hogarth Press.

—— (1930) *Civilization and Its Discontents*, London: Hogarth Press.

—— (1939) 'Moses and monotheism', *Standard Edition*, vol. 23, London: Hogarth Press.

—— (1954) *The Origins of Psychoanalysis: Letters to Wilhelm Fleiss, Drafts and Notes: 1887–1902*, New York: Basic Books.

Fromm, E. (1941) *Escape from Freedom*, New York: Holt, Rinehart & Winston.

—— (1979) *Greatness and Limitations of Freud's Thought*, New York: Harper & Row.

Gabriel, Y. (1999) *Organizations in Depth*, London: Sage.

Glad, B. (2005) 'Psychobiography in context: Predicting the behavior of tyrants', in W.T. Schultz (ed.) *Handbook of Psychobiography*, Oxford: Oxford University Press.

Gould, L., Stapely, L.F., and Stein, M. (eds) (2001) *The Systems Psychodynamics of Organizations*, New York: Karnac.

Hughes, H.S. (1964) *History as Art and as Science: Twin Vistas on the Past*, New York: Harper & Row.

Isaacson, K. (2005) 'Divide and multiply: Comparative theory and methodology in multiple case psychobiography', in W.T. Schultz (ed.) *Handbook of Psychobiography*, Oxford: Oxford University Press.

Kernberg, O. (1998) *Ideology, Conflict, and Leadership in Groups and Organizations*, New Haven: Yale University Press.

Kets de Vries, M. (1980) *Organizational Paradoxes: Clinical Approaches to Management*, London: Tavistock.

—— (1989) 'Can you survive an entrepreneur?' in J. Kao (ed.) *Entrepreneurship, Creativity and Organization*, Englewood Cliffs: Prentice-Hall.

—— (1998) 'Beyond the quick fix: The psychodynamics of organizational transformation and change', *European Management Journal*, 16, 5: 611–22.

Kets de Vries, M. and Miller, D. (1984) *The Neurotic Organization: Diagnosing and Changing Counterproductive Styles of Management*, San Francisco: Jossey-Bass.

Khaleelee, O. and Woolf, R. (1996) 'Personality, life experience and leadership capability', *Leadership & Organization Development Journal*, 17, 6: 5–11.

Kirsner, D. (2000) *Unfree Associations*, London: Process Press.

Marvick, E.H. (1983) *The Young Richelieu: A Psychoanalytic Approach to Leadership*, Chicago: University of Chicago Press.

Miller, E. (1989) 'The Leicester model: Experiential study of group and organizational processes', Occasional Paper No. 10, London: Tavistock Institute of Human Relations.

Mitscherlich, A. (1993) *Society without the Father: A Contribution to Social Psychology*, New York: HarperCollins.

Obholzer, A. (1996) 'Psychoanalytic contributions to authority and leadership issues', *Leadership & Organization Development Journal*, 17, 6: 53–6.

Offer, D. and Strozier, C. (1985) 'Reflections on leadership', in C. Strozier and D. Offer (eds) *The Leader: Psychohistorical Essays*, New York: Plenum Press.

Rosenthal, L. (2005) 'Resistance in group therapy: The interrelationship of individual and group resistance', *Modern Psychoanalysis*, 30B: 7–25.

Sperling, O. (1950) 'Psychoanalytic aspects of bureaucracy', *Psychoanalytic Quarterly*, 19, 88–100.

Twemlow, S. and Sacco, F. (1999) 'A multi-level conceptual framework for understanding the violent community', in H. Hall and L. Whitaker (eds) *Collective Violence: Effective Strategies for Assessing and Intervening in Fatal Group and Institutional Aggression*, New York: CRC Press.

Twemlow, S., Fomagy, P., Sacco, F.C., Gies, M.L., Evans, R., and Eubank, R. (2000) 'Creating a peaceful school learning environment: A controlled study of an elementary school intervention to reduce violence', *Medical Science Monitor*, 11, 7: 317–25.

Volkan, V.D. (2008) 'On Kemal Atatürk's psychoanalytic biography', in K. Babir and B. Tezcan (eds) *Identity and Identity Formation in the Ottoman Middle East and the Balkans*, Madison: University of Wisconsin Press.

Volkan, V.D. and Itzkowitz, N. (1984) *The Immortal Ataturk: A Psychobiography*, Chicago: University of Chicago Press.

Volkan, V.D., Itzkowitz, N., and Dod, A. (1997) *Richard Nixon: A Psychobiography*, New York: Columbia University Press.

Zaleznik, A. (1990) *Executive's Guide to Motivating People: How Freudian Theory Can Turn Good Executives into Better Leaders*, Chicago: Bonus Books.

—— (2006) *Learning Leadership: Cases and Commentaries on Abuse of Power in Organizations*, Chicago: Bonus Books.

5 Towards a critical theory of emotions in educational leadership and administration

Building on concepts from Jürgen Habermas

Peter Milley

Educational organisations and learning processes are 'powerhouses of emotion' (Harris 2007: 3). They are sites of pleasure, excitement, joy, fulfilment, and minefields of disappointment, envy, fear, anguish, depression, humiliation, grief, and guilt (Ackerman and Maslin-Ostrowski 2004). Thus it should not be surprising that there are important emotional aspects to the work of those who lead and administer schools, colleges, universities, and other educational concerns. But what is surprising is that it took educational researchers until the mid-1990s to recognise this. Since then, a growing body of research has emerged; it is now acceptable to study, think about, teach, and develop this emotional dimension (Beatty and Brew 2004). There are, however, differing opinions as to why emotions are on the agenda and whose interests are best served by this new approach. Questions about power and politics are emerging around the significance of emotions in educational leadership (Boler 1999).

There is a growing critique regarding the instrumental perspective and practices that appear to regulate emotional leadership in education. McWilliam and Hatcher (2007) describe how harnessing feelings as a means to increase motivation and productivity underwrites much of the current emphasis on emotions in educational leadership. Beatty observes how emotional intelligence in research and practice integrates with the prevailing view of leadership as an influence process to become another tool in the 'arsenal of productivity devices' (2000: 354; Goleman 2002). Elsewhere, Hartley observes that the adoption of emotions in educational leadership is a 'rationalist make-over of the emotions for performative purposes' and 'an emerging technology of control' (2004: 584). And Blackmore (1999) reveals distinctively gendered aspects to the contemporary productivity and control agenda. As in other service organisations (see Hochschild 1983), women educational leaders increasingly find their rich emotional capabilities exploited to their personal detriment.

In the literature on educational leadership, there is also a focus on how emotions can contribute to a deeper understanding of selves, others, and cultures, leading to greater social cohesion, care, compassion, self-expression, and emancipation (Beatty 2000; Zorn and Boler 2007). These perspectives look at how emotions are implicated in, and can help to attain, the social goals of most educational systems, and thereby improve the quality of education (Hargreaves 1998).

On balance, the literature is increasingly critical and negative in its concepts and findings. This leads to a question regarding the kind of conceptual resources that are required to help educational researchers and practitioners continue their critique while recuperating the important social, cultural, self-expressive, and emancipatory potential of emotions in learning, leadership, and educational organisations. Drawing on Jürgen Habermas' critical social theory, this chapter develops theoretical resources that aim to address this question.

Perspectives on emotions

Before these conceptual ideas are introduced, it is important to provide a perspective on some key ideas about emotions, including their relationship to politics and power in educational organisations.

Humans are physiologically wired for some kinds of emotional responses (Crossley 1998), but it is also now widely believed emotions are intimately connected to psychological, social, and cultural contexts. There is much to emotions that is 'learned, "social", interpretive, culturally specific' (Fineman 1993: 10). Emotions are 'high intensity feelings that are triggered by specific stimuli, either internal or external to the individual, that demand attention, and interrupt cognitive processes and behaviours' (George 2000: 1029), consisting of 'an awareness of four elements that we usually experience at the same time: (a) appraisals of a situation; (b) changes in bodily sensations; (c) the free or inhibited display of expressive gestures; and (d) a cultural label applied to specific constellations of the first three elements' (Hochschild 1990: 118–19). In different cultures we will find different emotional meanings, responses, and displays (Markus and Kitayama 1994). Emotions are not only individual, private, and autonomous psychological traits and states, but are collaboratively and publicly formed (Denzin 1984). We have expectations about reasonable and appropriate emotional responses in situations, and we make judgements based on these. We can contest emotions on the same validity claims as other social actions – that is, whether they are efficacious, true, correct, sincere, and authentic (Crossley 1998; Habermas 1989).

Feeling and thinking are two sides of the same coin (Ratner 1989): we can name emotions (Frijda *et al.* 1994), learn emotional scripts (Fischer *et al.* 1990), consciously reflect on, describe, and probe the source of our emotions, and learn to better control, manage, and alter our emotions using cognitive means (Beck 1976). Feelings influence our judgement, reasoning processes, memory, and creativity (Ashkanasy *et al.* 2002).

Emotions form part of our personalities, sense of self, and impressions that others have of us (Markus and Kitayama 1994). Our personal repertoires of emotion, how we manage our emotions, and our levels of emotional maturity and competence are fundamental to our self-efficacy (Saarni 1999). Appropriate emotional responses can help us to get what we want in our exchanges with others. Equally important, inappropriate emotional responses create interpersonal stumbling blocks, thwarting our self-efficacy, reducing our self-esteem, and eroding our capacity to confront challenges and recover from adversities (Saarni 1999). Emotions are also intimately bound up with our moral character. When we are emotionally competent, we live and act in accord with our moral dispositions; when we are emotionally immature, we may find it difficult to maintain our personal integrity (Saarni 1999).

Emotions help to bind us together with others. When we talk about and share our feelings, we potentially reach deep, intersubjective understandings and commitments with others (Denzin 1984). Yet emotions can also be the source of great misunderstanding and conflict: we can wrongly interpret or falsely attribute meanings and motivations to others' displays of emotion (Denzin 1984), use emotions to deceive and manipulate others, and be deceived about our own emotions (Baron 1988). At the same time, they are a 'social glue' (Fineman 1993: 15) stabilising deeply held beliefs. But the (re)creation of social order occurs, in part, through political action. Emotional energy can mobilise conflict, destabilise beliefs, and alter social order (Collins 1990).

Emotional dramaturgy is an important component in both the maintenance and transformation of social order. We perform on a social 'stage' where we present ourselves to others in terms of our expected social roles. In this process we often conceal some or all of our feelings and adopt socially acceptable masks (Goffman 1959). We engage in impression management, on the one hand, to protect our interests and deal with the politics of negotiating social order and, on the other, to 'fit in' with others and coordinate our actions (Fineman 1993).

Finally, because ideas about emotions are both culturally and historically specific, there is often an ideological character to them that is connected to specific power relations. Ideologies 'shape norms or scripts on the dos and don'ts of particular feelings' (Fineman 1993: 15). Prevailing gendered ideas about emotion, such as women being more emotional than men and men being more rational than women, serve as an important example (Hearn 1993).

Building on critical concepts from Habermas

The grist for the theoretical mill here comes from the highly regarded work of Jürgen Habermas. Similar to most critical theories, the normative concerns of freedom, equality, and social justice are at the heart of his work (Cannon 2001). His interest has been in defining the conditions under which people are able to identify and criticise ideologies, authentically express their interests, and resolve conflicts non-violently. This outlook stems from his concern that people in advanced industrial societies continually run the risk of losing their capacity for critical reflection. As a result, they readily succumb to various forms of domination. To avoid these problems, we need to work to ensure our societies have a robust public sphere, enabled by key institutions in civil society (including public education), in which authentic interactions, genuine dialogue, and collective learning can take place about needs, interests, issues, and goals.

Habermas' work may seem to be a curious place from which to draw conceptual resources regarding emotions which have not figured substantially in his work, however, emotional considerations are commensurable with his theoretical perspective (Crossly 1998). Three key sets of concepts from across Habermas' oeuvre are explored and adapted here: a typology of human interests and corresponding forms of rationality; Habermas' perspective on communicative and strategic action; and his model of the lifeworld and system.

Human interests, reason and emotions

Early in his career, Habermas (1971) developed a typology of fundamental human interests and corresponding forms of reason that had emerged in western societies as they modernised and became 'enlightened'. According to this typology, we have fundamental interests in understanding, explaining, and controlling our environments. Scientific reason, grounded in its claims to truth and effectiveness, supports these interests. We also have an interest in understanding each other and coordinating our collective lives in fair and just ways. Moral reason, grounded in its claims to rightness or correctness, supports these goals. And we have an interest in pursuing our individual freedom and happiness. Aesthetic reason, grounded in its claims to truthfulness and authenticity, supports these intents. Table 5.1 presents an interpretation of the typology, adapted to reflect emotional considerations (for discussion on power and politics see Milley 2005; 2008). In its new form, this typology provides insights for integrating reason and emotion in critically reflective ways in the context of educational leadership.

Strategic–instrumental emotional reason supports the interests we have in predicting and, ultimately, controlling our natural, social (including educational and emotional) contexts through emotional means. This form of reason can be deemed valid if it helps meet the objectives to which it is put to use, and in particular if the emotions and emotional work involved in using it prove to be reliable and effective in achieving goals. This kind of emotional reason (and reasoning about emotions) is very common in educational leadership. It constitutes instrumental and technological approaches to emotions, outlined earlier.

Scientific–cognitive emotional reason supports the interests we have in accurately describing and explaining emotions in order to better understand them, their sources and effects. Here, emotional reason is deemed valid based on the extent to which it can produce reliable knowledge about emotions,

Table 5.1 Emotional interests, corresponding forms of emotional reason, and valid emotional claims

Emotional interests	*Forms of emotional reason/knowledge*	*Valid emotional claims*
Prediction, control, efficacy, success	Strategic–instrumental	Reliability and effectiveness of emotions
Description, explanation	Scientific–cognitive	Verity of emotions (experience, display, description, source)
Legitimate interpersonal relationships, action coordination, fairness, justice	Moral–practical	Suitability, correctness, rightness of emotions
Self-expression, emancipation	Aesthetic–expressive	Sincerity, authenticity, truthfulness of emotions

including the verity of emotions themselves. This is a tricky business because emotions are not like other, more objectively assessable phenomena. But that should not stop us from trying. Doing so continually bolsters our 'our confidence in the general validity of our emotions' (Solomon 1993: 56). It also builds our capacities for living authentic lives with personal integrity. It helps us to establish genuine emotional attachments with others and to discern emotional distortions in our inner and social worlds. In the context of educational organisations, this kind of emotional reason supports educational leaders and members of educational communities in feeling, expressing, and recognising authentic emotions and forming genuine emotional connections with others, with their learning and work. It is also useful in helping them to identify inauthentic or deceptive emotions in their working relationships and organisations, including the likely sources and effects of these.

Moral–practical emotional reason supports the interests we have in establishing legitimate interpersonal relations in order to coordinate our actions with others in mutually agreeable, fair ways. This kind of emotional reason can be deemed valid based on how suitable, correct, or just our emotional knowledge and actual emotions are in specific social contexts. In the context of educational administration, moral–practical emotional interests and knowledge can be viewed, first and foremost, as a key part of the foundation upon which leaders (could) establish legitimate relationships with members of their educational institutions and communities. It also (could) help inform moral reasoning, ethical judgements, and policy making and implementation, although the research findings discussed earlier suggest this is not generally the case (e.g. Jenkins and Conley 2007).

Aesthetic–expressive emotional knowledge informs the interests we have in conveying our (emotional) needs, interests, and (emotional) identities. It also provides a means for us to free ourselves from illegitimate forms of domination and repression, whether emotional, psychological, social, cultural, economic or political. Aesthetic–expressive emotional knowledge can be deemed valid based on how authentically we understand our emotions, how truthfully we express our emotions, and how sincerely we attempt to understand the emotions of others. This kind of emotional reason is the source of self-awareness, virtue, and charisma that forms an important foundation of educational leadership (Samier 2006). It is also a potent source of personal and political power. Educational leaders can draw strength and resilience from the insights it provides (Beatty 2000). It can help them build coalitions and solidarity with others.

With his original typology, Habermas (1971) aimed to release the ideological stranglehold that 'positivism' had at the time on the human sciences. He believed that the unreflective application within the human sciences of the interests, epistemologies, and methods from the physical sciences was a significant intellectual and moral failing. It facilitated the use of the human sciences in psychological and social domination. His solution was to show how the human sciences address a broader range of interests than the physical sciences, including moral, aesthetic, scientific, and instrumental interests, and also rely on additional forms of reason and a wider array of validity claims. Genuine, intellectually honest debates and socially progressive knowledge production in the human sciences needed to accommodate all four forms of reason.

Later, Habermas (1984; 1989) observed that advanced industrial societies exhibited a very strong instrumental impulse that co-opts and distorts scientific, moral, or aesthetic reason. He worried that societies with such an ideological affection for instrumental rationality would more readily become totalitarian, as people in them lost the aptitude and conditions for self-expression, moral judgement, and truth-seeking.

Habermas' observations have relevance for the current status of emotions in educational leadership; they suggest we should be more vigilant about how emotions should be understood and used in educational organisations. There is evidence that a 'positivist' bias exists in the understanding and use of emotions in educational administration via the reliance of practitioners and professional developers on the emotional tools arising from the organisational behaviour and business management fields (McWilliam and Hatcher 2007). This bias can be seen in the application and use of psychometric instruments to measure emotional capabilities in organisational leaders with a view to making sure they have the right emotional profile to control themselves and their staff to support the meta-values of effectiveness and efficiency. This literature on emotions in educational administration suggests how these instrumental values masquerading as substantive principles in policy and practice have narrowed the scope of emotional reason in the field. This may result in socially and emotionally regressive educational scholarship, practices, and organisations.

Habermas observes that, 'We call a person rational who interprets the nature of his desires and feelings in light of the culturally established standards of value, but especially if he can adopt a reflective attitude to the very value standards through which desires and feelings are interpreted' (1984: 20). The lesson here for researchers and practitioners is they need to be vigilant about the interpretive frameworks they use to represent emotions to themselves and others, including where these frameworks come from, whether and how they are valid, and who benefits from them. The typology offered here provides one means for doing this work. It encourages a decentred perspective that considers both the instrumental utility and social significance of emotions.

Communicative and strategic dimensions of emotional praxis

According to Habermas (1984), two basic modes of communication and human interaction inform all social action, defined as any human activity to which people ascribe meaning, a definition derived from Weber (1968). Through communicative action, people derive and express their individual and collective goals and coordinate their actions in a consensual manner. Through strategic action people work to achieve individual and collective goals. The primary role of communicative action is to foster reciprocity and mutual understanding. The main purpose of strategic action is to pursue and attain goals. These two types of social action are dialogically related: an appropriate balance of each is required for people to maintain their lives, families, communities, organisations, and societies. It is important to note that for Habermas (1984; 1989) human communication exists, in the first instance, to support communicative action, aimed at creating reciprocity and understanding and representing the ideal case of 'normal' human communication. Strategic communication is derived from this fundamental mode.

While Habermas' concepts of communicative and strategic action offer insights about politics and power, here the focus is on adapting his ideas in a way that accounts for emotions. Figure 5.1 does this, beginning from the assumption that emotions are an intrinsic aspect of all social action.

The first thing to note is that somatic processes constitute, and are constituted by, emotions and cognitions (Crossley 1998). These somatic processes are pre-reflective (e.g. the sinking feeling in our stomachs before we realise we are fearful) and ongoing (e.g. sweaty palms, elevated heart rate, and dry mouth throughout a stressful situation).

Habitual authentic emotional expressions are the ones we genuinely feel (or suppress) and display (or conceal) without thinking about them, customary in the cultural, social, and organisational context. They provide part of the dramaturgical resources and social glue that allows us to pursue our collective goals and coordinate our actions. We can call these emotions into question on the basis of validity claims, subjecting them to intra- or interpersonal scrutiny through 'discursive emotional reflection'. For example, in a

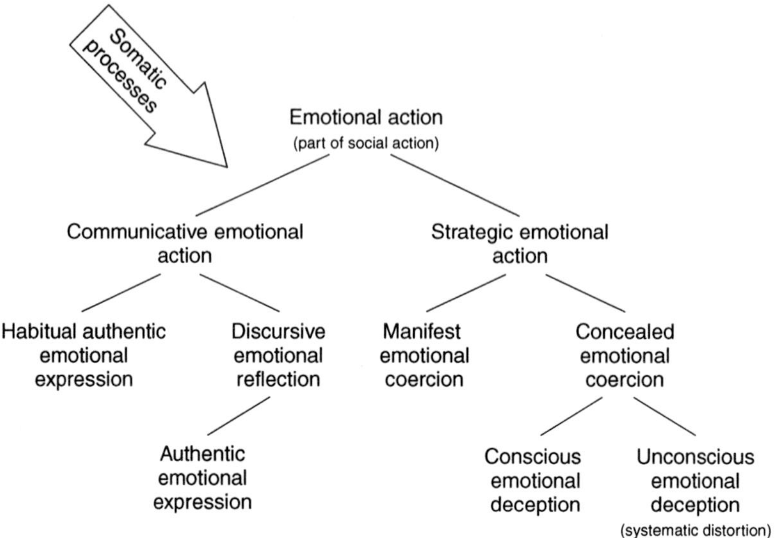

Figure 5.1 Communicative and strategic emotional action.

town hall meeting with educational officials, some parents might begin the event with positive feelings, impressed that the officials want to engage with them and optimistic about the potential outcome. As the event unfolds, they may experience increasingly negative feelings if the officials do not seem as open to discussion as they had hoped. The parents might begin to feel disappointment, frustration, and anger. Their faces might get flushed, their heartbeats might increase, their muscles might tense up. At first, they may engage in an internal dialogue that asks questions such as: What am I feeling? Why (scientific–cognitive validity claims)? Are these feelings justified (a moral–practical validity claim)? What am I going to do about them (an aesthetic–expressive validity claim)? Will these feelings help me get what I want out of this meeting (an instrumental validity claim)? Then a parent might question the officials in ways that raise emotional validity claims, perhaps beginning with a statement such as 'I'm feeling frustrated because you're not listening and don't seem to care'. This statement would raise both moral–practical and aesthetic–expressive validity claims, challenging the officials regarding the appropriateness and sincerity of their actions, including their emotional displays.

At this point the officials have a choice. They can try to engage communicatively with the parents in addressing their concerns, which are in part emotional, or they can strike a strategic attitude. Doing the former would keep the interaction within the realm of 'discursive emotional reflection' and might eventually push the relationship into a situation of 'authentic emotional expression', where both parties feel they have a strong intersubjective emotional understanding (Zorn and Boler 2007). For this to happen, certain conditions resembling what Habermas (1989) calls situations of 'ideal speech' would likely need to be in place. Here, the officials might need to embrace discomfort and conflict (Boler 1999). They would need to overcome mainstream cultural pressures to maintain their power and authority in a way that silences emotions such as anger and constitutes a regime of 'emotional absolutism' (Beatty and Brew 2004: 334). To do this they would need appropriate linguistic, interpersonal, and cognitive capacities to express and understand emotions, including an embodied awareness of them (Beatty and Brew 2004). They would need to demonstrate a genuine openness to feel and understand what fundamental emotions (e.g. fear, shame) are below the surface of the parents' secondary emotions (e.g. frustration, anger) (Beatty and Brew 2004).

When educational leaders ignore fundamental emotions in themselves and others they can create 'dysfunction in individuals and organizations' (Beatty and Brew 2004: 335). The denial of emotionality can limit the potential for professional renewal in educational organisations, and can also increase stress and anxiety, reduce creativity, and create barriers to achieving educational goals (Beatty 2000), whereas, the communication of feelings in the context of organisational experience can change the activities and relationships that 'cause errors, distortions, demoralization and ineffectiveness at work' (Diamond 1993: 118).

If the educational officials in our hypothetical case respond with 'strategic emotional action', there are at least two avenues they might end up pursuing. One of these could be 'manifest emotional coercion'. There is a continuum of possibilities here. They might make an emotional appeal (Crossley 1998) to the parents to see the merits of the initiative. They might try to show the parents how their feelings of frustration are unfounded by pointing out that no one else in other town halls expressed or harboured such emotions. They might chide the parents to start behaving appropriately or call an end to the meeting. Such a reaction would not be uncommon amongst educational administrators.

A second kind of strategic emotional action in which the educational officials might engage is 'concealed emotional coercion'. There are two related pathways here: 'conscious emotional deception' or 'unconscious emotional deception'. Typically, people deceive one another, and themselves, to protect their feelings and the emotional attachments they have with significant others and meaningful phenomena such as their work, profession, and goals (Saarni and Lewis 1993). The educational officials in our example might thus sense the need to protect each other and their professional identities, which are deeply invested in the proposed initiative. They might resort to emotional deception to protect these emotional attachments.

Conscious emotional deception usually entails deliberately pretending we have a certain emotion when we do not or when we are feeling something else entirely (Solomon 1993). The educational officials in our example might thus pretend to be 'on side' with the parents by acknowledging and mirroring the parents' feelings. There is a question here as to whether the emotional closeness the officials might be able to build with the parents would constitute a communicative or strategic interaction. Emotional interactions may appear similar on the surface in terms of whether they are communicative or strategic but there can be a radical difference underneath. This difference stems from the nature of the relationships between the emotions we may be experiencing, the emotional expressions we choose to make, and our underlying motivations (Solomon 1993). It boils down to whether we are attempting to build a genuine relationship of trust and authentic emotional understanding, or whether we are trying to protect ourselves and get our way, in part, through emotional means.

To make things more complicated, there is a significant amount of self-deception in emotional experience. Emotional pretences can turn into emotional realities (Solomon 1993). When we put on (or hide) emotions, we can come to believe we actually feel (or do not feel) them. This helps us to make convincing shows of emotion. It also often forms a cornerstone of how emotional labour is accomplished in organisations (Ashkanasy *et al.* 2002: 322). Through pretence, the educational officials in our example might thus believe they actually feel the frustration of the parents, and they might come to truly believe they have established greater emotional proximity to the parents.

While emotions are a conduit from deception to self-deception, some form of conscious rationalisation is usually a sign that this process is underway (Solomon 1993). In our example, in preparing for their town hall, the educational officials may have discussed a communication plan, including how they might diffuse parents' concerns by displaying empathy and care. Despite knowing this would be a 'rigged' performance, they may have reasoned it was worth doing as it would help them achieve their desired outcomes. And if they were successful, they might even come to perceive themselves to be genuinely empathic and caring administrators.

Too much strategically-oriented deception in social life can dramatically and deleteriously affect individual and social psychology (Saarni and Lewis 1993). Particularly problematic are cases where we are not just deceived *about* emotions, but are deceived *within* them (Solomon 1993). Our ideas about emotions can go wrong in a number of ways: they can be based on mistaken information, faulty inferences, insufficient evidence, spurious claims, and unjustified evaluations (Solomon 1993). We can deceive ourselves about what we believe, so our beliefs and judgements about our emotions can also be deceptive. In these cases, we may be self-deceived but our emotions are not entirely 'phony'. Truly self-deceptive emotions are the ones that become 'detached' from the social context in which they were first misperceived or distorted and become a more-or-less permanent feature of our individual or social psychology. McWilliam and Hatcher's (2007) analysis of the current ideology of what constitutes emotional leadership suggests this has happened in contemporary practice.

Finally, self-deceptive emotions, like deception in general, can have a rippling effect (Solomon 1993). When we lie, we often have to tell more lies in order to protect our original lie. A similar dynamic exists for self-deceptive emotions, which need to continually expand their boundaries in order to be effective. As a result, self-deceptive emotions can corrupt our belief-forming processes (Baron 1988). They can lead us to rationalise away our immoral actions, reinforce our bad habits, allow us to blame others, and cement fraudulent emotions in our ways of life that are fraudulent as well (Solomon 1993).

Lifeworld and system: emotional domains of educational leadership

As a core part of his theory, Habermas (1979; 1997) describes how progressive social evolution in advanced industrial societies occurs through a dialogical learning process involving two developmental trajectories. On one developmental path, we can learn to coordinate our lives in increasingly reasonable and non-violent ways, despite different values, interpretations of need, interests, and goals. On the other, we can establish and learn to participate productively in economic and administrative systems and institutions that provide the material infrastructure that sustains diverse, large-scale populations. Habermas (1984; 1989) refers to the former developmental path as 'cultural rationalization' and the latter as 'social modernization'.

Processes of cultural rationalisation rely on our capacity to think and interact communicatively. We create cohesive societies with psychologically healthy populations, and vibrant, dynamic cultural institutions. Processes of social modernisation that rely on successful forms of strategic action, create well-off societies characterised by efficient organisations and effective systems of administration. Both are required to maintain and reproduce advanced industrial societies, but they need to be dialogically connected in order for us and our societies to develop in socially progressive ways (Habermas 1984; 1989).

Habermas' (1989) influential model of advanced industrial societies consisting of a lifeworld and system foregrounds the importance of the dialogical relationship between cultural rationalisation and social modernisation. In the lifeworld, we coordinate our private and public activities in reciprocal ways with others through communicative action. In the system, we engage in actions that implement decisions to which we consent in the lifeworld. A healthy lifeworld is central to the establishment and maintenance of a functional system, while a functional system offers some of the key infrastructures that support a healthy lifeworld. The main functions of the lifeworld include socialisation and identity formation, enculturation and cultural reproduction, and social integration. Education plays a fundamental role in each of these areas (Habermas 1987). Habermas observes that there is a tendency in advanced industrial societies for processes of social modernisation in the system to 'colonise' (1989: 186) and distort communicative action in the lifeworld. In such moments, social cohesion may begin to unravel, shared norms and cultural values may fragment, cultural institutions may suffer a crisis of legitimacy, and individuals may suffer psychosocial problems.

This model and related concepts have been discussed elsewhere, both generally (e.g. Braaten 1991; Outhewaite 1994) and in education and its administration (e.g. Bates 1989; Milley 2005; 2008; Welton 1995). The focus here is on adapting this model for emotional considerations in educational administration. Figure 5.2 provides a provisional interpretation towards this end.

The lifeworld can be seen as the institutions (including educational organisations), relationships (including those involving leadership and learning), and communicative practices (including leadership and curricular practices), through which individual and collective emotional development takes place. In educational organisations, healthy emotional development contributes to emotionally mature leaders, educators, and learners who are 'more differentiated, better adapted, effective and confident' (Saarni 1999: 4). According to Saarni (1999), in western nations, such people have developed a number of emotional competencies. These are the types of skills that allow leaders, educators, and learners to build, maintain, renew, and protect their own unique emotional habitus. The development and exercise of emotional competence also contributes to the (re)production of a collect-

Lifeworld Domain of emotional development through communicative action	**Steering mechanisms** (P) = power (M) = money	**System** Domain of emotional management through strategic action
Private sphere Emotional development for identity formation and (re)production of personal emotional habitus	← (P) Definition of employable, professional emotions (P) Emotional labour → ← (M) Wages, pecuniary benefits (P) Financial means → ← (P) Emotional management technologies	**Economic system** Emotional management for productivity, efficiency, creation, and exploitation of emotional capital
Public sphere Emotional development for (re)production of collective emotional habitus, social integration, and cohesion	(P) Emotional competence, maturity → ← (P) Policy decisions (P) Critique and emotional activism → ← (M) Institutional resources ← (P) Administrative acts (P) Feelings of loyalty, commitment →	**Administrative system** Emotional management for policy implementation, maintaining social order and institutions

Figure 5.2 Emotional elements of the lifeworld and system.

ive emotional habitus. Healthy emotional development allows people genuinely to get along with each other and to have real self-efficacy in their relationships. It also contributes to robust, dynamic, diverse, and cohesive cultures in their organisations, communities, and societies.

To be sure, there are emotional politics in private and public spheres of the lifeworld. These occur around emotional self-expression, including the expression of emotional needs and interests, and the emotional climates of families, organisations, and other collective social entities. Emotional politics can contribute to healthy processes of emotional development if they are practised communicatively and under conditions that resemble Habermas' (1989; 1990) concept of 'ideal speech' outlined earlier.

Emotional development in the lifeworld can go wrong in a number of ways. People may suffer psychological problems that stem from any number of sources, from neuro-biology to trauma. Saarni (1999) observes that our developmental histories are especially significant in shaping the emotional components of self-concepts and moral characters. Many life experiences can dramatically alter our emotional make-up, including those involving psychological abuse. Emotional politics can take a very wrong turn when they head in the direction of abuse. A wide range of negative consequences may ensue, from immature forms of acting out (Hochschild 1983) to psychopathologies (Jenkins 1994). These implications should serve as red flags to educational leaders and policy makers who approach their work without due regard to people's feelings (Hargreaves 2004). Importantly, 'abusive' leadership behaviour can be both active and passive (Samier in press) and emotional neglect is considered to be a form of abuse in the context of emotional development (Glaser *et al.* 2001). The questions here are not just humanistic and moral. Instrumentally speaking, leaders and policy makers may not get the results they intend without factoring in the emotional dimension of leadership, learning, and organisations (Hargreaves 2004).

Emotional development processes can also go wrong as a result of undue strategic and instrumental influences emanating from the system. To understand the ways in which this can happen, we first need to outline the role of emotions from the perspective of the economic and administrative systems. Action in the system concerns itself with the administratively effective and economically efficient execution of the educational goals established in the lifeworld. Here, emotions are subject to an economic calculus that aims to exploit them for productivity gains, and an administrative emphasis on managing emotions to support policy implementation and maintain institutional order. If actors in educational organisations and communities have consented in some communicatively reasonable fashion to the educational goals, and if the emotional management practices used in the system are commensurate with these goals and with the expectations set out in the process by which the goals were derived, the result should be an emotionally healthy balance from the perspective of social action in the lifeworld and the system.

The relationships between emotional development in lifeworld and emotional management in the system can be seen to be mediated through a series of emotional 'steering mechanisms'. These are essentially different forms of power, including the power of money, as indicated in Figure 5.2. There is not room here to explain all of these mechanisms. Two important ones for the current discussion are the 'emotional management technologies' that impinge as a form of power from the system into the lifeworld and the 'emotional competence and maturity' that serve as a form of power towards the system from the lifeworld.

Some of the emotional management technologies, such as instruments that measure the emotional capabilities and performance of educational leaders, began from robust knowledge about emotional competence and maturity gained in the lifeworld but ended in a narrow interpretation of the organisational, cultural, and social utility of emotions (Hartley 2004). This demonstrates how the power of instrumental reason in the system can colonise and distort concepts and practices born in the lifeworld. This dynamic can have deleterious consequences in the context of educational administration. For example, under pressure from the system, leaders or educators might burn-out from being required to do too much emotional labour (Kruml and Geddes 2000) and from trying to cope with the emotional dissonance that stems from the nature and volume of their emotional work (Grandey 2000). Scripted to feel and behave in certain ways (McWilliam and Hatcher 2007), educational leaders may find they have problems with being authentic and living within personal integrity, undermining fundamental expectations people have of them, and eroding their legitimacy. Or, subject to strategic concerns to 'produce' particular organisational cultures, in part through emotional management technologies, leaders may find they actually generate emotional resistance, disillusionment, and distrustful cultures.

A good deal of the current critical literature on emotions in educational leadership foregrounds how emotions have largely come to be seen and used as a technology of productivity and control in educational organisations (e.g. Beatty 2000; McWilliam and Hatcher 2007). If this is the case, the model presented here reveals how more research and practical action is required to promote robust emotional capabilities in the lifeworld of educational organisations, including capabilities for emotional activism against the power of emotional technologies. This is one example of how the model offers a framework for critically investigating and thinking about where and how emotional politics and power play a role in educational administration. Readers are encouraged to adapt and use it on other examples in their research and practice.

Concluding thoughts

Educational administration and leadership are now understood to have emotional dimensions. Among their other meanings, emotions are seen to have political importance in and around educational organisations. Researchers are increasingly concerned that in policy and practice emotions are becoming a technology of control that helps to centralise and augment administrative power and produce productivity gains. Researchers are also increasingly able to demonstrate there are deleterious unintended consequences for educational leaders, educators, learners, and organisations stemming from the contemporary agenda for emotions.

The three conceptual models from Habermas' oeuvre explored and adapted here hopefully can support researchers, practitioners, and policy makers in further thinking through the contemporary situation. A key feature of each of these models is their dialogical construction. This encourages us to look at emotions from different angles. It opens up possibilities to see how emotions (ought to) serve both instrumental and sociocultural purposes, how they (ought to) help us to achieve goals through others and how they (ought to) help us to have deep attachments with others as an important social purpose in itself, and how they (ought to) help us to create economic value and exercise administrative power while also protecting and developing healthy personalities and cultures.

Habermas' concepts also serve as an important reminder that, while emotions play a role in educational organisations and their administration, educational organisations play an important role in the emotional development and maturation of our individual and collective lives. Habermas (1987) made it clear that education is (or ought to be) first and foremost a contributor to sociocultural development, in which we can locate healthy emotional development. On this view, a core goal of education is to build and sustain the emotional capacity in individuals and society more generally. This capacity includes emotional critique, which contributes to a robust, highly reflexive public sphere, strong emotional bonds between people in communities, and is a key source of power in civil society for steering economic interests and administrative actions.

References

Ackerman, R.H. and Maslin-Ostrowski, P. (2004) 'The wounded leader and emotional learning in the schoolhouse', *School Leadership and Management*, 24, 3: 311–28.

Ashkanasy, N., Härtel, C., and Daus, C. (2002) 'Diversity and emotion: The new frontiers in organizational behaviour research', *Journal of Management*, 28, 3: 307–38.

Baron, M. (1988) 'What is wrong with self-deception?' in B. McLaughlin and A. Rorty (eds) *Perspectives on Self-deception*, Los Angeles: University of California Press.

Bates, R. (1989) 'Leadership and the rationalization of society', in J. Smyth (ed.) *Critical Perspectives on Educational Leadership*, London: Falmer.

Beatty, B. (2000) 'The emotions of educational leadership: Breaking the silence', *International Journal of Leadership in Education*, 3, 4: 331–57.

Beatty, B. and Brew, C. (2004) 'Trusting relationships and emotional epistemologies: A foundational leadership issue', *School Leadership and Management*, 24, 3: 329–56.

Beck, A.T. (1976) *Cognitive Therapy and Emotional Disorders*, New York: International Universities Press.

Blackmore, J. (1999) *Troubling Women: Feminism, Leadership, and Educational Change*, Buckingham: Open University Press.

Boler, M. (1999) *Feeling Power: Emotions and Education*, New York: Routledge.

Braaten, J. (1991) *Habermas's Critical Theory of Society*, Albany: SUNY Press.

Cannon, B. (2001) *Rethinking the Normative Content of Critical Theory: Marx, Habermas and Beyond*, New York: Palgrave.

Collins, R. (1990) 'Stratification, emotional energy, and the transient emotions', in T. Kemper (ed.) *Research Agendas in the Sociology of Emotions*, Albany: SUNY Press.

Crossley, N. (1998) 'Emotion and communicative action: Habermas, linguistic philosophy and existentialism', in G. Bendelow and S. Williams (eds) *Emotions in Social Life*, London: Routledge.

Denzin, N. (1984) *On Understanding Emotion*, San Francisco: Jossey-Bass.

Diamond, M. (1993) *The Unconscious Life of Organisations*, Westport: Quorum Books.

Fineman, S. (1993) 'Organisations as emotional arenas', in S. Fineman (ed.) *Emotion in Organisations*, London: Sage.

Fischer, K., Shaver, P., and Carnochan, P. (1990) 'How emotions develop and how they organize development', *Cognition and Emotion*, 4, 2: 81–127.

Frijda, N. *et al.* (1994) 'Emotions and emotion words', in J. Russell *et al.* (eds) *Everyday Conceptions of Emotion: An Introduction to the Psychology, Anthropology and Linguistics of Emotion*, Norwell: Kluwer Academic.

George, J.M. (2000) 'Emotions and leadership: The role of emotional intelligence', *Human Relations*, 53, 8: 1027–55.

Glaser, D., Prior, V., and Lynch, M. (2001) *Emotional Abuse and Emotional Neglect: Antecedents, Operational Definitions, and Consequences*, York: British Association for the Study and Prevention of Child Abuse and Neglect.

Goffman, E. (1959) *The Presentation of Self in Everyday Life*, New York: Doubleday.

Goleman, D. (2002) *The New Leaders: Transforming the Art of Leadership into the Science of Results*, London: Little, Brown.

Grandey, A. (2000) 'Emotion regulation in the workplace: A new way to conceptualise emotional labour', *Journal of Occupational Health Psychology*, 5: 95–110.

Habermas, J. (1971) *Knowledge and Human Interests*, trans. J. Shapiro, Boston: Beacon Press.

—— (1979) *Communication and the Evolution of Society*, trans. T. McCarthy, Boston: Beacon Press.

—— (1984) *The Theory of Communicative Action: Reason and the Rationalization of Society*, trans. T. McCarthy, Boston: Beacon Press.

—— (1987) 'The idea of the university – Learning processes', *New German Critique*, 41: 3–22.

—— (1989) *The Theory of Communicative Action: The Lifeworld and the System*, trans. T. McCarthy, Boston: Beacon Press.

—— (1990) *Moral Consciousness and Communicative Action*, trans. C. Lenhardt and S. Weber Nicholsen, Cambridge: MIT Press.

—— (1997) 'Modernity: An unfinished project', in M. Passerin d'Entrèves and S. Benhabib (eds), *Habermas and the Unfinished Project of Modernity: Critical Essays on The Philosophical Discourse of Modernity*, Cambridge: MIT Press.

Hargreaves, A. (1998) 'The emotional politics of teaching and teacher development: With implications for educational leadership', *International Journal of Leadership in Education*, 1, 4: 315–36.

—— (2004) 'Inclusive and exclusive educational change: Emotional responses of teachers and implications for leadership', *School Leadership and Management*, 24, 2: 287–309.

Harris, B. (2007) *Supporting the Emotional Work of School Leaders*, London: Sage.

Hartley, D. (2004) 'Management, leadership and the emotional order of the school', *Journal of Educational Policy*, 19, 5: 583–94.

Hearn, J. (1993) 'Emotive subjects: Organizational men, organizational masculinities and the (de)construction of "emotions"', in S. Fineman (ed.) *Emotions in Organizations*, London: Sage.

Hochschild, A.R. (1983) *The Managed Heart: The Commercialization of Human Feeling*, Berkeley: University of California Press.

—— (1990) 'Ideology and emotion management: A perspective and path for future research', in T.D. Kemper (ed.) *Research Agendas in the Sociology of Emotions*, Albany: SUNY Press.

Jenkins, J.H. (1994) 'Culture, emotion and psychopathology', in S. Kitayama and H. Markus (eds) *Emotion and Culture: Empirical Studies of Mutual Influence*, Washington, DC: American Psychological Association.

Jenkins, S. and Conley, H. (2007) 'Living with the contradictions of modernization? Emotional management in the teaching profession', *Public Administration*, 85, 4: 979–1001.

Kruml, S. and Geddes, D. (2000) 'Catching fire without burning out: Is there an ideal way to perform emotional labour?' in N. Ashkanasy, C. Härtel, and W. Zerbe (eds) *Emotions in the Workplace: Theory, Research and Practice*, Westport: Quorum Books.

Markus, R. and Kitayama, S. (1994) 'The cultural construction of self and emotion: implications for social behaviour', in S. Kitayama and H. Markus (eds) *Emotion and Culture: Empirical Studies of Mutual Influence*, Washington, DC: American Psychological Association.

McWilliam, E. and Hatcher, C. (2007) 'Killing me softly: The making up of the educational leader', *International Journal of Leadership in Education*, 10(3): 233–46.

Milley, P. (2005) 'Social and educational implications of university co-operative education: A Habermasian perspective', unpublished thesis, University of Victoria.

—— (2008) 'On Jürgen Habermas' critical theory and the political dimensions of educational administration', in E.A. Samier (ed.) *Political Approaches to Educational Administration and Leadership*, New York: Routledge.

Outhwaite, W. (1994) *Habermas: A Critical Introduction*, Stanford: Stanford University Press.

Ratner, C. (1989) 'A social constructionist critique of the naturalistic theory of emotion', *Journal of Mind and Behavior*, 10: 211–30.

Saarni, C. (1999) *The Development of Emotional Competence*, New York: Guilford Press.

—— (2000) 'Emotional competence', in R. Bar-On and J.D. Parker (eds) *The Handbook of Emotional Intelligence: Theory, Development, Assessment and Application at Home, School and in the Workplace*, San Francisco: Jossey-Bass.

Saarni, C. and Lewis, M. (1993) 'Deceit and illusion in human affairs', in M. Lewis and C. Saarni (eds) *Lying and Deception in Everyday Life*, New York: Guilford Press.

Samier, E.A. (2006) 'The aesthetics of charisma: Architectural, theatrical, and literary dimensions', in E.A. Samier and R. Bates (eds) *Aesthetic Dimensions of Educational Administration and Leadership*, New York: Routledge.

—— (2008) 'The problem of passive evil in educational administration: Moral implications of doing nothing', *International Studies in Educational Leadership*, 36, 1: 2–21.

Solomon, R.C. (1993) 'What a tangled web: Deception and self-deception in philosophy', in M. Lewis and C. Saarni (eds) *Lying and Deception in Everyday Life*, New York: Guilford Press.

Weber, M. (1968) *Economy and Society: An Outline of Interpretive Sociology*, trans. R. Gunter and C. Wittich, New York: Bedminster Press.

Welton, M. (1995) 'In defense of the lifeworld: A Habermasian approach to adult learning', in M. Welton (ed.) *In Defense of the Lifeworld: Critical Perspectives on Adult Learning*, Albany: SUNY Press.

Zorn, D. and Boler, M. (2007) 'Rethinking emotions and educational leadership', *International Journal of Leadership in Education*, 10(2): 137–51.

Part II

Types of emotional analysis

6 Desks and office spaces

Personal, emotional, and organisational sites for leading

Sheri Klein

Current approaches to leadership, such as primal leadership, suggest that the awareness and regulation of leaders' emotions and feelings plays a pivotal role in employee motivation, retention, and performance and the success of leaders (Goleman *et al.* 2002). Other approaches, such as transformational and artful leadership (Klein and Diket 2006), suggest that education requires leaders who have a sensitivity and awareness toward *nuances* of thinking, relating, and physical spaces. With growing accounts of bullying and mobbing in the workplace worldwide (Davenport *et al.* 1999; Namie and Namie 2000; Westhues 2004), that include K-16 contexts, it is becoming increasingly important for leaders and participants to pay attention to the aesthetic and emotional components of workspaces. In this sense, leaders may be envisioned as 'architects in the construction of spaces that can promote more humane, thoughtful, and aesthetic leading' (Klein and Diket 2006: 99).

The physical special considerations within educational organisations that include office location, layout, and décor, impacts 'social interactions, arousal levels, affective reactions, [and] morale' (Rafeli and Worline 1999: para. 13). Leaders influence not only where, how, and when organisational participants interact, but also how their spaces look and feel. Organisational participants today are paying more attention to the aesthetics of work spaces as they tend to spend more time at work. As 'physical objects are concrete manifestations of the psychological dynamics of organizational life' (Rafeli and Worline 1999: para. 17), and leadership, it is important to understand what constitutes office artefacts, or the 'symbols of organizational life' (Rafeli and Worline 1999) and how they contribute to the emotional life of organisational participants.

Halford calls for attention to the sociology of work for 'space itself remains largely under-theorized', and that 'most attention to the physical setting of organizations has focused on ergonomics' (2008: 4). There has been considerable research within organisational studies and environmental and applied psychology (Canter 1997) concerning the physical layout of organisational spaces, and the sensory and aesthetic artefacts of office spaces (Gagliardi 1990; Ornstein 1986). What emerges as a critical issue from this research is the notion of the artefact as symbol. Rafeli and Worline write, that symbols within organisational culture 'reflect underlying aspects of culture, generating emotional responses from organizational members and representing organizational values and assumptions' (1999: para. 57). Furthermore, Rafeli and Worline add that 'the study of symbols can provide a deep, rich, and worthwhile understanding of organisational cultures' (1999: para. 59). A second and equally important issue that emerges is that of the physical space of workspaces as *dynamic*; that 'organisational spaces are made and re-made' (Halford 2008: 14) by participants through the act of working, thinking, feeling, and leading. Although the 'architecture, layout, and décor contribute to a kind of ideological superstructure' (Halford 2008: 7), organisational spaces are suspect to changes based on participant interactions, conversations, daily activities, and changes to status (Baldry 1999). Citing Canter (1997), Rafeli and Worline write 'researchers from the architecture tradition have called the interaction of activity and setting "place"' (1999: para. 16). This may help to explain how office spaces, and in particular desks, furniture, and other aesthetic objects, create personal and organisational identities as well as fulfil emotional needs of organisational participants – to have a sense of place and belonging while at work.

In this chapter, I will discuss the role and purpose of *desks* as symbols within the place of K-16 educational organisations, and how the desk serves as a site for the emotions, thoughts, and actions of organisational participants. The desk within historical and contemporary office spaces is a standard and prominent piece of furniture. Given its complexity as a personal, social, and cultural artefact and symbol, I turn to semiotic theory as it 'investigates how resources [desks] are used in specific historical, cultural, and institutional contexts' (Van Leeuwen 2004: 3). As desks are also symbols of aesthetic and personal taste, aesthetic theory may help to explain how the embellishment of desks and surrounding areas may serve a basic human need to make our immediate environments special (Dissanyake 1998: 61) in ways that fulfil basic emotional needs to feel safe, well, and unique. Finally, as 'we see the emergence of new working spaces: shared offices, remote working, and varieties of cyberspace' (Halford 2008: 14), I will address how the contemporary virtual desktop serves as a site for leading, and a symbol of personal and organisational identity.

Historical overview of desks in educational settings

Desk: 'a table, frame, or case with a sloping or horizontal surface for writing and reading and often with drawers or compartments; a place from which a person performs his/her duties' (*Webster's New Collegiate Dictionary* 1980: 305). Desks are associated, particularly, in academic environments with study, scholarship, writing, reading, and preparation for teaching, and leading. K-16 education in the US is synonymous with hierarchical organisational structures. Harter *et al.* write:

> ... each higher level on the chart presupposes another level of supervision and control ... it is classic hierarchy ... analytical hierarchicalism ... it 'stands for the position that there is a conceptual difference between the leader and the follower and this difference entails inequality of some sort'.
> (2006: 277)

In hierarchically designed organisations, such as schools and universities, individuals at the top of the organisational chart (administrators or heads of units, programmes, or schools) who have control over how human and financial resources are distributed typically have larger offices and bigger and better quality desks and other furniture compared with other members of the organisation. This practice can be illustrated in education, corporate, and government sectors; large desks within spacious offices communicate power (Ornstein 1986).

Historically, the desks of teachers and office workers have been functional, smaller, and less adorned. In the nineteenth century, desks of American school teachers symbolised functionality and authority. Wooden handcrafted desks, often oak, with drawers on each side of a long narrow central drawer provided some degree of security for teachers, but little privacy. Around 1915, Steelcase designed the Modern Efficiency Desk, a metal-top desk with drawers on each side and one central drawer which transformed school office furniture. The desk, seen as purely utilitarian, was adorned with only the most rudimentary accessories to enable the user to perform tasks. The Modern Efficiency Desk was designed for efficiency, replacing the roll-top desk which 'encouraged disorder and a lack of neatness' (Galloway 1919: 90).

The function, types, and placement of worker and teacher desks versus management, administrator, and executive desks in business and educational contexts sharply differed. In *Office Management Principles and Practice*, Galloway writes, 'The executive desk should be a center of consultation and conference ... where orders and instructions are issued ... while a clerk's duties are to carry out orders and get work done' (1919: 90). He further added that executive desks be 'free of encumbrances ... with a size of 36 × 60 inches' (1919: 90). The design of the executive desk was the standard double pedestal flat-top desk with six drawers in contrast to the three shallow drawers of the Modern Efficiency Desk typically given to workers, staff, and teachers. Variations on the Modern Efficiency Desk still permeate the aesthetic of K-16 education work spaces, and variations of the executive desk still permeate the aesthetic of K-16 administrator work spaces. New executive desks are constructed out of metal, glass, and exotic woods; stylistically they may be antique or contemporary, U-shaped or L-shaped. Depending on the style and materials, executive desks may convey strength, charm, luxury, hi-technology, and trust.

Historically, productivity and efficiency were aims of 'mechanistic and hierarchical systems of organisations' (Samier *et al.* 2006: 3), and educational leadership and administration focused on the management of people and tasks. School design in the US beginning in the twentieth century was marked by the individual and segregated classroom space. While progressive educators of the 1930s challenged traditional school classroom designs, segregated classrooms within school design remained a constant feature.

School and classroom design of the 1960s and 1970s did see some changes with respect to the incorporation of movable desks for students and teachers, the use of plastics and laminates in school furniture, carpeted classrooms, and installation of more energy-efficient window systems. The introduction to the open-floor plan for office design in the 1960s and 1970s, that is, a large open space where desks were placed side-by-side, or with partitions, resulted in non-segregated workspaces for school non-instructional staff (secretaries and office workers). However, classroom and administrator office spaces remained segregated. Historically, teachers and administrators with more education have been afforded more privacy within the workplace. Those with higher rank and status in the organisation have been afforded larger offices, better furniture, greater privacy, larger office windows, and nicer views of the outside world. University administrators (Chairs, Deans, Vice-Presidents, and Presidents) often have larger offices that are located behind, or are buffered by, administrative support staff spaces.

What has changed over the years is the degree to which the personalisation, privatisation, and the articulation of the desk space within educational contexts has occurred, and how the desk now serves as a multi-purpose space for all organisational participants. Desks in educational contexts are spaces where participants and leaders multi-task: communicate (phone, email), collaborate (discuss, share, meet), envision (write, plan), reflect, create, and feel (experience frustration, anger, joy, peace, etc.). They are spaces where the aesthetic merges with the bureaucratic, personal, political, social, and philosophical. The desk is where participants can express, subvert, and regulate emotion, engage in creative and intellectual work, and may find pleasure through looking at and contemplating images or objects that have personal meaning. Desks in this sense are highly complex and dynamic spaces.

Desks as 'semiotic resources'

Van Leeuwen's (2004) semiotic theory can assist us to understand desks as highly complex spaces and signs, and what is communicated through office and desk design, placement of desks, and what is on, and around desks. The phrase, 'semiotic resource' is used to describe 'actions or artefacts we use to communicate [with]' (Van Leeuwen 2004: 3). The semiotic analysis of office spaces must also consider the way that artefacts (in this case, desks) are framed, that is, what is occurring in the physical space around the resource, or artefact. What occurs around the desk is important to semiotic analyses: how desks are positioned, whether or not there are chairs adjacent to allow for visitors, and what kinds of objects and images are on and around the desk, or on the walls. What is placed on or around the desk communicates something about a participant, or a leader's gender and status within the organisation. As such, the desk must be viewed in the context of the office as a dynamic social space.

Van Leeuwen explains that semiotic resources may be framed by either separation or segregation (2004: 13). The application of these concepts to the analysis of school and office buildings, and the desk as one artefact of an office space, may help explain how desks may be used to segregate and separate participants. The desk physically separates and provides distance from the occupant and visitors through the desktop and surrounding chairs. In addition, they may also be physically segregated from other desks in surrounding areas and offices through walls, partitions, and doors.

Van Leeuwen writes, 'Prior to 1950, rank determined how many people occupied an office and how much space one needed' (2004: 20). Typically, educational leaders and administrators are segregated and separated from support staff and visitors through privatised spaces with secure walls and doors. In addition, staff may be separated and segregated from other staff based on work-related tasks, or relationship to the leader.

Open office plans resulted in the desegregation of desks, however, the use of modular desks often resulted in arrangements of workers facing inward toward computers, rather than outward toward the public. In spite of open office plans that now permeate many K-16 support staff spaces, leaders and administrators still have private office spaces that are separated and segregated, and that afford them 'greater privacy, security, a sense of identity, and the ability to get on with concentrated work' (Van Leeuwen 2004: 21).

The contents of one's desk provide opportunities for utilising interpretive research methodologies, such as semiotics. The organisation of desktops, in terms of clean versus messy, piles versus files, suggests how participants think, and what they think about. Green writes:

> In the semiotics of mess, desks may be the richest texts. Messy-desk research borrows from cognitive ergonomics, a field of study dealing with how a work environment supports productivity. Consider that desks, our work landscapes are stand ins for our brains, and so the piles we array on them are 'cognitive artifacts', or date cues of our thoughts as we work.
>
> (2006)

Using interpretive research to understand desks

Recently, I came across a piece in *Vanity Fair* (2007) – a photo-essay in the section called 'FanFair' that featured high-profile celebrity desks. 'My Desk', highlighted the desk of Liz Smith, syndicated columnist, journalist, leader within the entertainment industry, and writer for *Vanity Fair.* Two main features of this one-page essay included a photograph of her desk with captions that highlight specific objects in the space. This photo-journalistic format offers educators a methodology for documentation of visual signs and a semiotic and interpretive analysis of the desk and office space within educational organisational life, with the photograph becoming part of the analysis. This format may offer a glimpse into the emotional and psychological needs of the office occupant(s) as well as insights into the desk and office space as a social, thinking space, organisational, and aesthetic space.

Semiotic methodology has been applied to the analysis of photographs in visual culture and media (e.g. Bignell 2002; Danesi 2002). Norwood (2005) suggests that the photograph should be part of a semiotic analysis in terms of lighting, focus, and depth of field. Some other criteria to consider in the analysis of a photo of an organisational space may be the vantage point of a photographer – whether the photographer was the researcher, an organisational participant, and whether the photograph was staged.

Concerning the semiotic analysis of the desk, other considerations may include the desk location and materials, contents on and near the desk (objects, books, papers), arrangements on the desk, the degree of organisation and personalisation of the desk and office, surrounding objects (chairs, baskets, etc.), and the frequency to which objects and images appear. Reporting observations may occur through narrative, photographs, and/or videotaping.

While semiotic analysis can provide rich interpretations, Rafeli and Worline note that there are 'difficulties in analyzing symbols in organisational cultures ... that meanings given to symbols by a researcher may not necessarily be meanings inferred by members' (1999: para. 8). Other qualitative and interpretive research methods, such as interviews with organisational participations, researcher observations of the desk and workspace, and participants' narratives about their desks and offices, may help to explain the 'lived spaces and temporality, and human relations' (Van Manen 1990: 101). To better understand the desk as a complex and dynamic space (social, cognitive, aesthetic, personal, contemplative, emotional, and virtual) we can also turn to material culture studies and critical hermeneutics. Material culture studies offer several models for the analysis of material culture that includes objects within built environments and spaces, such as desks and office spaces (Hodder 2000). Considerations for material culture analysis include criteria such as construction, materials, design, and the history of object(s) with an in-depth analysis of the desk. Both semiotic and material culture research methods may assist researchers in fieldwork within organisational settings such as office spaces to explore the terrain of the office as a cultural text, and a site for self-representation and work-related drama.

Desks as social spaces

If leadership may be likened to art and drama with leaders engaging in 'roles and scripts, plots and play ... charismatic intervention, dramas of domination ... human comedy and tragedy' (Starratt 1993: 134), then the desk and office may serve as theatre where participants/actors interact with one another and organisational props: objects, papers, piles, etc. In this sense, the desk becomes part of a broader collective and social space where the personal, political, and dramatic converge. Participants/workers may also use the desk and space to 'resist the space, and in doing so, come to remake uses and meanings of space' (Halford 2008: 6). We can turn to 'dramaturgy', or the study of human performative interaction (Rafeli and Worline 1999: para. 34) to understand the inter-relationships between aesthetic artefacts, discourse, and human interaction within organisational life.

To also better understand the drama of office spaces, and desks as social spaces, one might analyse actual office spaces, as well as use the BBC series *The Office* or the US film *Office Space* as aesthetic sources of critique.

Desks as cognitive space

Piles and files serve as a semiotic resource of labour (work completed or unfinished) – and thinking in the broadest sense. Books that are open, closed, or stacked on or around desks are signs/symbols of participant thinking. Note pads, reminders, and calendars reflect thinking and planning. The desk as a space for cognition cannot be underestimated; it is a place for decision-making, reflection, and problem-solving. Thinking about one's practice, that is, engaging in reflective practice, imagining, and envisioning are important for leaders. The leader's desk then becomes a space for creative and imaginative thinking, and the generation of new ideas and visions. Given the contemporary role of scholar–practitioner, the desk may also serve to foster the production of scholarship. Inquiry into the times of day or night that best support thinking (morning, afternoon, evening), the traffic flow around desks (busy versus quiet), and the physical environment of the office (climate/temperature, sunny/dark, aesthetics), may illuminate how desks may function as thinking-spaces. While philosophic approaches to educational leadership may vary, the emphasis in current educational leadership practice upon reflection, emotional intelligence, and creating toxic-free work environments appear to be dominant themes. As such, organisational participants are creating desks and surrounding spaces that are also aesthetically and personally pleasing.

Desks as aesthetic and personal spaces

American workers on average spend three hours a day at their desks. Attempts are made by office workers, teachers, and administrators to humanise workspaces that are sterile and impersonal. The degree to which this occurs depends on the kind of desk and office space one has, the inclination of the desk occupant, their tastes, their budget, and how much time they spend at their desks. How important is the personalisation of the desk space? Harris writes that 'Collingwood contends that various forms of organizational life have a numbing effect on people's emotions' (2006: 52). A recent study shows that personalisation of the workspace matters

> in a time where corporate identity and the power of 'the Brand' plays such a key part in the corporate world ... Research shows that 67 percent of workers keep personal items on or around their desks, and 36 percent of workers keep personal items – a mug, bowl, or food, for example – in their office kitchen.
>
> (United Kingdom Tea Council n.d., para. 9)

Advances in technology, with the mass production of objects and digital photography combined with access to the Internet, have made it possible to easily produce images for and about the desk and office. As the desk becomes a second home to many during the day, attempts to make this space pleasant, homey, and inviting are undertaken in varying degrees. Some of the ways that educators and educational leaders are embracing aesthetics with respect to their desks include the integration of aesthetic objects and images: photographs, children's drawings, fresh or dried flowers and plants, paperweights and small art objects, lamps, books, and documents that provide evidence of academic preparation and achievement.

Gablik (1991), like other educators, philosophers, health care workers, and artists of our time, understands that we have become lost, to ourselves, our own spirits, and to one another. The degree to which desk spaces are individualised is always a matter of personal choice and taste and may be impacted by gender, school/work policy, job responsibilities, and the location of the desk, and how public or private it is. If Lippard's definition of place is the 'space where culture is lived' (1997: 10), then desks are spaces where work culture is lived.

The photograph is one of the most popular desk artefacts. This can be illustrated with the photos of family and friends that permeate the space. The photographer Emmit Gowin reflects on the power of images: 'A picture is like a prayer ... it is offered as a place where the heart can stand, or better still, rest. It is a call for reflection, meditation, and to be more intimate with the world' (2003: 57). Photographs of family, pets, loved ones, and of memorable and happy occasions provide images for reflection and a moment's retreat within the busy, and often stressful workday; they communicate participants' values and passions. In addition, photographs of landscapes or posters of art may also provide pleasantly stimulating images to allow participants to stand still and rest.

Flowers and plants (real, dried, or fake) provide an element of nature and colour within educational environments that are often bland (beige, white, grey), and devoid of colour and texture. Flowers and plants also provide an element of texture and simulate nature within offices where no views of the outside may exist. Books on desks, or diplomas and awards on walls and in cases surrounding one's desk are symbols of authority, trust, knowledge, scholarship, competence, and recognition. Additionally, children's drawings or art work can be found in and around desk spaces as well as decorative calendars and desk accessories, and kitsch and consumer objects, such as humorous coffee mugs.

The humanisation of the workplace within school contexts is exemplified in recent examples of K-12 school design that embrace colours and textures of the local landscape. Schools are now recognised as 'community spaces ... aesthetic spaces embedded with social, political and cultural values' (Klein 1995: 30–1). The increasingly high stress levels in work environments suggests that desks may help to foster moments of much-needed contemplation, reflection, and the regulation of emotions within the workday. The infusion of aesthetic features may indeed assist organisational participants to regulate emotions and foster contemplation.

Desks as contemplative spaces

What would be a better way to contemplate and reflect than to sit down with a cup of tea? Electric tea pots and microwaves have become office fixtures and 'Psychologists have discovered that making tea is such an influential part of office life' (United Kingdom Tea Council n.d., para. 4). Taking a tea or coffee break at the desk is one way to regulate the emotions and slow down. Regulating emotions is critical to being emotionally intelligent (Goleman *et al.* 2002) and plays an important role in teaching, leading, and working. Desks can be sites for self-regulation of emotions (anxiety, anger, fear) through meditation, guided visualisation, stating positive affirmations, and having aesthetically pleasing images and objects in one's immediate surroundings.

The incorporation of small desktop water fountains, pleasing images, inspirational quotes, shells, and candles can support the desk as a contemplative and imaginative space. Linn explains that 'clustering special items around a computer monitor or on a desk can be an unintentional way of establishing an altar' (1999: 12). Eisner reminds us that 'Judgments about qualitative relationships depend on somatic knowing' (2002: 231). Creating desk and office spaces that allow for sensory and aesthetic experiences, reflection, and contemplation can assist leaders and organisational participants to connect with their emotions and feelings and engage in somatic and intuitive knowing.

Desks as virtual spaces, virtual spaces as desks

K-16 organisational participants use computers for the purposes of communication (e.g. email, wordprocessing, wikis, blogs) and the production of scholarship and dissemination. Some educational leaders may teach online courses, contribute to blogs and online discussion groups, and/or may be enrolled in online distance education degree programmes. To this extent, educational leaders are spending a great deal of time in virtual space.

The extensive use of the laptop/desktop to conduct business is likely to continue. The virtual desk, like the physical desk, presents opportunities for personalisation and connecting. The virtual desktop offers leaders ways for connecting that are not often possible with conventional desks; they can have an international presence through the World Wide Web and seek out collaborations, dialogue, and connections with others globally. Attention to the aesthetics of the presentation of self and organisation in virtual arenas, such as through website design, production of digital documents and presentations, and desktop screensavers, should matter to leaders who understand the power of images to convey personal and organisational values and beliefs.

Conclusion

Historically, approaches to leadership within K-16 educational contexts have had an aim of efficiency and productivity, and 'universities and schools were built according to a factory model, [and] not designed to address the psychological needs of inhabitants' (Klein and Diket 2006: 99). Looking toward humanistic models of leadership, and organisational, spatial, and aesthetic theory, may help us to understand and explain the psychological impact of interior planning and the power of aesthetic components (images and objects) within workspaces and their role in sustaining the emotional, social, cognitive, and aesthetic needs of organisational participants. The desk is a physical object in the educational workspace that is a symbolic, functional, dynamic, aesthetic, emotional, and contemplative space for intellectual work as well as the processing of emotions. Having one's own reasonably secure space that can be personalised to some degree is psychologically very important to most people (Eley and Marmot 1995). As such, K-16 participants personalise their spaces to the degree that is in keeping with their respective organisational culture, job responsibilities, and personal taste.

However, one must be cautious in making assumptions about the skills, knowledge, abilities, race, culture, religion, etc., of effective leadership, or the emotional state of a participant based on the aesthetics of a desk (neat versus cluttered, image-laden or image free, etc.). At the present time, there is no data to indicate that educational leaders who have tidier or more aesthetically pleasing desks or office spaces, are more competent, ethical, inspiring, compassionate, or humanistic. Nonetheless, one may infer that those leaders who do embrace the desk as an aesthetic, emotional, and contemplative space may be more attuned to the *nuances* of their own and others' feelings, thoughts, ideas, and spaces within their organisations. In doing so, these leaders may be more inclined to 'overcome invisibility in administrative life' (English 2006: 133) and be to be vitally present within their organisation.

Halford suggests that we have to look holistically at organisational spaces in order to understand office spaces as a social construct. In doing so, we might consider factors, such as, 'managerial paradigms and industrial heritage, furniture, friendship, new technologies and memories [and emotions]' (2008: 16) to better understand office spaces. Educational researchers and practitioners, including leaders, should be encouraged to investigate their own desks and office spaces as sites for social, emotional, intellectual, creative, political, and aesthetic dimensions of practice. In doing so, they may find greater self-understanding and connections to self, others, and their organisations.

References

Baldry, C. (1999) 'Space – the final frontier', *Sociology*, 33: 535–53.

Bignell, J. (2002) *Media Semiotics: An Introduction*, New York: Manchester University Press.

Canter, D. (1997) 'The facets of place', in G.T. Moore and R.W. Morans (eds) *Advances in Environment, Behavior, and Design 4*, New York: Plenum Press.

Danesi, M. (2002) *Understanding Media Semiotics*, New York: Oxford University Press.

Davenport, N., Schwartz, R., and Elliot, G. (1999) *Mobbing: Emotional Abuse in the Workplace*, Ames: Civil Publishing.

Dissanayake, E. (1998) *What is Art for?* Seattle: University of Washington Press.

Eisner, E. (2002) *Art and Creation of Mind*, New York: Teachers College Press.

Eley, J. and Marmot, A. (1995) *Understanding Offices: What Every Manager Needs to Know About Office Buildings*, Bingley: Emerald.

English, F. (2006) 'Understanding leadership in education: Life writing and its possibilities', *Journal of Educational Leadership*, 38, 2: 126–40.

Gablik, S. (1991) *The Re-enchantment of Art*, London: Thames & Hudson.

Gagliardi, P. (ed.) (1990) *Symbols and Artifacts: Views of the Corporate Landscape*, New York: Aldine de Gruyter.

Galloway, L. (1919) *Office Management: Principles and Practice*, New York: Ronald Press.

Goleman, D., Boyatzis, R., and McKee, A. (2002) *Primal Leadership: Realising the Power of Emotional Intelligence*, Cambridge: Harvard Business School.

Gowin, E. (2003) 'Where the heart stands', *Parabola*, 58: 57.

Green, P. (2006) 'Saying yes to mess', *New York Times*, 21 December, 12. Online at www.nytimes.com/2006/12/21/garden/21mess.html (accessed 25 April 2008).

Halford, S. (2008) 'Sociologies of space, work and organisation', *Sociology Compass*, 2, 3: 925–43. Online at www.blackwell-synergy.com/doi/pdf/10.1111/j.1751–9020.2008.00104.x (accessed 23 April 2008).

Harris, C. (2006) 'Collingwood on imagination and expression: Advancing an aesthetically critical study of educational administration', in E.A. Samier and R. Bates (eds) *Aesthetic Dimensions of Educational Administration and Leadership*, London: Routledge.

Harter, N., Ziolkowski, F.J., and Wyatt, S. (2006) 'Leadership and inequality', *Leadership*, 2, 3: 275–94.

Hodder, I. (2000) 'The interpretation of documents and material culture', in N. Denzin and L. Lincoln (eds) *Handbook of Qualitative Research*, Thousand Oaks: Sage.

Klein, S. (1995) 'Reshaping a place called school', *Cat's Cradle*, 1, 1: 25–36.

Klein, S. and Diket, R. (2006) 'Aesthetic leadership: Leaders as architects', in E.A. Samier and R. Bates (eds) *Aesthetic Dimensions of Educational Administration and Leadership*, London: Routledge.

Linn, D. (1999) *Altars: Bringing Sacred Shrines into Everyday Life*, New York: Ballantine.

Lippard, L. (1997) *The Lure of the Local: Senses of Place in a Multicentered Society*, New York: The New Press.

Namie, G. and Namie, R. (2000) *The Bully at Work*, Naperville: Sourcebooks.

Norwood, J.L. (2005) 'A semiotic analysis of bio-technology and food safety photographs', unpublished thesis, University of Texas at Austin.

Ornstein, S. (1986) 'Organisational symbols: A study of their meanings and influences on perceived psychological climate', *Organisational Behavior and Human Decision Process*, 38: 207–29.

Rafeli, A. and Worline, M. (1999) 'Symbols in organizational culture'. Online at http://iew3.technion.ac.il/Home/Users/anatr/symbol.html (accessed 9 May 2008).

Samier, E.A. and Stanley, A. (2006) 'The art and legacy of the Romantic tradition: Implications for power, self-determination and education', in E.A. Samier and R.J. Bates (eds) *Aesthetic Dimensions of Educational Administration and Leadership*, London: Routledge.

Samier, E.A., Bates, R.J., and Stanley, A. (2006) 'Foundations and history of the social aesthetic', in E.A. Samier and R.J. Bates (eds) *Aesthetic Dimensions of Educational Administration and Leadership*, London: Routledge.

Starratt, R. (1993) *The Drama of Leadership*, Bristol: Falmer Press.

United Kingdom Tea Council. (n.d.) 'Tea and work: Employabilitea – life in the 21st century workforce'. Online at www.tea.co.uk (accessed 26 April 2008).

Van Leeuwen, T. (2004) *Introducing Social Semiotics*, London: Routledge.

Van Manen, M. (1990) *Researching Lived Experience: Human Science for an Action Sensitive Pedagogy*, Albany: SUNY Press.

Vanity Fair, 'My Desk' (March 2007): 206.

Webster's New Collegiate Dictionary (1980) Springfeld: G. & C. Merriam Company.

Westhues, K. (2004) *Workplace Mobbing in Academe: Reports from 20 Universities*, Lewiston: Mellen Press.

7 The politics of emotions

Affective economies, ambivalence, and transformation

Michalinos Zembylas

Within education, there have been calls for 'rethinking educational change with heart and mind' (Hargreaves 1997), for 'passionate leadership' (Davies and Brighouse 2008), and for 'balancing logic and artistry in leadership' (Deal and Peterson 1994). Moreover, empirical work has indicated that emotions are powerful forces in school leaders' lives warranting attention (Beatty 2000; 2002; 2005; Beatty and Brew 2004; Blackmore 1996; 2004; Revell 1996; Sachs and Blackmore 1998). The emotionality of school leadership is an area that has not been explored in depth to date (Beatty 2005). However, there is much evidence in the research literature that the affective world of school leaders is both complex and intense. School leaders are confronted on a daily basis with a variety of emotions – such as anger, bewilderment, anxiety, caring, and excitement – that are inextricably linked to personal, professional, relational, political, and cultural issues.

The school leaders' constant struggles to cope with (or 'manage') emotions embedded in the multiple issues associated with educational leadership have significant implications for their decision-making, well-being, and overall leadership style. For instance, there is research that shows how school leaders (especially women) are constantly engaged in emotion management processes, often with serious implications not only for their emotional health but also for their professional effectiveness (Blackmore 1996; 2004; Sachs and Blackmore 1998); at the same time, however, research also documents how mechanisms of emotion management help school leaders promote their own agenda, survive the high emotional demands of school leadership, and bring meaningful changes to their school (Beatty and Brew 2004). School leaders' handling of the emotions in their own reflective practices and in their relationships with parents, students, and faculty, shape and reflect the climate and culture of their schools (Beatty 2000).

In educational administration and leadership theory and research, the emotions have been treated, if are they mentioned at all, as little more than psychological and cognitive forces that distract rational processes (Beatty 2005). However, recent work in the social sciences (including cultural studies, feminist studies, sociology, political science, and communications) increasingly recognises emotions as part of everyday social, cultural, and political life. Emotions in leadership, for example, are not only a private matter for individuals but also a *political* space in which administrators, teachers, students, and parents interact, with implications for larger political and cultural struggles for change (Albrecht-Crane and Slack 2003; Zembylas 2005). The notion of 'politics' here refers to 'a process of determining who must repress as illegitimate, who must foreground as valuable, the feelings and desires that come up for them in given contexts and relationships' (Reddy 1997: 335). That is, power is located in who gets to express and who must repress various emotions. The *politics of emotions*, then, is the analysis that challenges the cultural and historical emotion norms with respect to what emotions are, how they are expressed, who gets to express them and under what circumstances. It is in this sense that it may be argued that a political analysis of the emotions of school leaders highlights the connections among power relations, resistance, and transformation.

But how are emotions implicated in power relations, resistance, and transformation in education? How do emotions circulate in educational spaces and form particular 'affective economies', and what are the (political) implications of these economies, especially in the context of contemporary calls for emotional intelligence in management and organisation? The goal of this chapter is to offer a theoretical framework that: (a) acknowledges how emotions connect macro-politics to the micro-politics of school leadership and culture; (b) pays attention to tensions and ambivalences associated with attempts to express, regulate, or ignore emotions within school leadership and culture; and (c) considers the role of emotions in creating openings for transformation of school leadership and culture. By paying attention to the politics of emotions in school leadership, the aim is to engage school leaders in meaningful dialogue that moves beyond the usual concern with cognition, rationalism, and management. By staking out this theoretical territory, this chapter goes beyond burgeoning research in this area that mainly treats emotions as merely an object of management. Most significantly, it is argued that emotions play an important political role in enabling resistance and transformation, something that is currently missing from many contemporary accounts of emotions in school leadership.

First, I briefly clarify the different theoretical approaches of emotion and then analyse the power of emotions as transformative forces. In the next part of the chapter, I discuss the notion of *affective economies* and its implications for theorising transformation. Affective economies refer to relations, practices, and discourses about emotions, how they are constructed, and how they constantly change. In other words, it is emphasised that emotions do not reside in individuals but are circulated, and one of the effects of this circulation is that some bodies, objects, or events are endowed with particular emotional meanings and values. It is in this context that the presence of *emotional ambivalence* acquires political significance in forming a subversive analysis. The chapter ends with a discussion on the implications of this theorisation for educational leadership in light of contemporary calls for performing *emotional intelligence* in management and organisation.

Different theoretical approaches of emotion

Different definitions of emotions have produced conceptually and methodologically different approaches to the study of emotions in education. For instance, many studies are inspired by psychological and sociological perspectives. From the psychological perspective, emotions are primarily conceptualised as private components of the personality structure of an individual. Consequently, psychological research focuses on the internal, individual (intrapersonal) characteristics of an individual's emotional responses (e.g. see Sutton and Wheatley 2003). This perspective frequently reduces emotions to little more than internal personality dynamics most often divorced from social and cultural contexts. In contrast, the sociological perspective conceptualises emotions as socially or culturally constructed. Sociologically based studies, then, focus on how teachers and school leaders' emotions are socially constructed in the group dynamics of social situations and how those situations uni-directionally shape individuals' emotional experiences and expressions (e.g. see Hargreaves 2001; Beatty 2002). Often ignored in this perspective are both the individual aspects of emotion and the reciprocally shaping interactions of emotion and socialisation (Zembylas 2005).

While both psychological and sociological perspectives offer important insights, claiming that emotions are simply a matter of the individual or group, does not sufficiently address the complex role of emotions in education. Rather, a more useful approach locates emotions in the liminal space between individual and social constructivist approaches, challenging the divisions between individual versus social, private versus public, and emphasising that emotion operates as a constitutively reciprocal component in the interaction/transaction of the *individual* and the *social* (Leavitt 1996). Support for this approach is found by applying feminist thinking and critical theories to the study of emotion (e.g. Campbell 1997; Lupton 1998; Lutz and Abu-Lughod 1990). Without simply dismissing either the social constructivist or the individual approaches, feminist and critical thinking challenge both around two central issues.

First, feminist thinking provides the necessary challenge to the dichotomies of emotion versus reason and individual versus social, considering them remnants of patriarchal thought and historical power relations. For example, from the feminist perspective, the distinction between rational (usually identified with the masculine) and emotional (usually identified with the feminine) is by no means natural; rather, that distinction has been historically constituted in the expression and enactment of hierarchies of power (Zembylas and Fendler 2007). Similarly, privileging either the individual or the social is also the product of historical power relations. Consequently, by perpetuating an assumed divide between the rational and the emotions as well as between the individual and the social, the existing power hierarchies and the status quo of stereotypes about how emotions operate are reinforced.

Second, critical theories reconceptualise emotions as a public, not exclusively private, object of inquiry that is interactively embedded in power relations; thus they historicise the ways in which emotions are constituted. This perspective challenges an ahistorical conception of the subject as a site of emotional resistance, a conception which blinds the subject to the ways power relations work to constitute *feeling subjects.* With this challenge, critical theories analyse the *transaction* between larger social forces (macro-political) and the internal psychic terrain of the individual, highlighting the ways this historicisation can draw out changeable aspects of reality, thus allowing the possibility of ruptures and discontinuities of power differentials at the micro-political level (Boler 1999; Zembylas 2005; 2007).

Drawing on feminist and critical perspectives, then, foregrounds the social, political, and cultural context in which emotions are constituted. Socialisation practices, including corporeal and discursive signs and hierarchies of power and position, are critical to this repertoire, shaping the presence or absence as well as the intensity of any given emotion. The presence and intensity of emotions, in turn, shape the social context in which they occur. Within critical and feminist thinking, then, social constructivist and individual approaches converge around the notion that socialised individuals exist in transaction rather than as isolated entities, and they participate in this transactional socialisation process by adopting or resisting particular meanings, discourses, and expressions of emotions. Within this transactional process emotions are understood as embedded in culture, ideology, gender, and power relations. They are not private; neither are they merely the effects of outside social structures. Rather, drawing on feminist and critical thinking helps us theorise emotions as *trans-formative.*

Emotions are trans-formative in that they are not peripheral by-products of events, but rather they are constitutive forces for (trans)forming individuals, social interactions, and power relations. As such, emotions are constitutive of the power relationships of political and cultural exchange among individuals. The allocation of power is manifested in who gets to express and who must repress various emotions. As Abu-Lughod and Lutz write,

> Power relations determine what can, cannot, or must be said about self and emotion, what is taken to be true or false about them, and what only some individuals can say about them.... [E]motion discourses establish, assert, challenge, or reinforce power or status differences.
>
> (1990: 14)

In other words, there is a reciprocal transaction between the individual and the social where emotions also contribute to the formation of particular relationships and power dynamics. As feminist and critical thinking emphasises, emotion practices are not simply sites of social control but may, in fact, constitute political spaces for transforming existing power relations – such as re-claiming anger as a site of struggling for recognition and redistribution of power relations (Burrow 2005; Holmes 2004).

A *politicised analysis* (Holmes 2004) of emotions, then, foregrounds and interrogates the traditionally held cultural and historical norms about emotion such as what emotions are, how they are expressed, and who gets to express them and under what circumstances. From this perspective, teachers, students, and school leaders are always engaged in political transactions as they relate emotionally to one another across classroom and school spaces. For example, a school principal may feel uncomfortable expressing his or her opposing views to a district or state policy because it is a highly politicised issue in the community. A politicised analysis of emotions would help school leaders analyse and sort through various discourses about emotion, and understand how those discourses operate to fabricate particular meanings for emotion that are circulated through leadership practices.

Affective economies, emotional ambivalence, and power relations

In this part of the chapter, I explore the role of emotions using the theoretical concepts presented earlier to show how affective connections (e.g. in school culture) are formed and trans-formed over time. In particular, I argue how emotions play a crucial role in the ways that individuals come together and constitute collective bodies and emotional cultures in schools – that is, affective connections are not individualised but work to bind together a whole community. Such an argument clearly challenges the assumption that emotions are 'individual' and 'private' phenomena and supports the position that emotions are crucial to politics, in the sense that power is an inextricable aspect of how individuals come together, move, and dwell in schools (see Ahmed 2004). In other words, this idea reiterates the view that emotions are not only considered private reactive responses to events but are also socially organised and managed through 'social conventions, community scrutiny, legal norms, familial obligations and religious injunctions' (Rose 1990: 1).

Ahmed's (2004) notion of *affective economies* maintains that emotions do not reside in a subject but rather circulate involving relations of difference. Affective economies may establish, assert, subvert or reinforce power differentials, because affectivity separates us from others as well as connects us to others; this is why it functions as an economy. For example, an economic understanding of resentment in a school denotes that these emotions do not reside within an individual but are circulated and draw other bodies together. This circulation happens precisely because individuals do not live in a social and political vacuum but move and thus emotions become attached to individuals united in their feelings for something. This economy of affect works to differentiate some individuals from others, emphasises Ahmed, a differentiation process that is never over.

Based on the idea that this differentiation never ends, Harding and Pribram (2004) explain that the notion of affective economies links the individual with the social formation through the practices and energies of affect. Thus, affect becomes an important force and intensity that motivates power relations among individuals. Things that matter affectively can be taken up as sites of political struggle (Grossberg 1992). Political positions can be claimed through and constituted by modes of felt experiences. However, these felt experiences indicate the ambivalence of emotion by showing that 'positive' and 'negative' are not attributes of emotions or of bodies, but represent provisional readings and judgements that have profound effects (Ahmed 2004).

In particular, *emotional ambivalence* refers to the coexistence of two opposite attitudes or feelings (conscious or unconscious), 'positive' and 'negative' (e.g. anger and joy), towards someone or something. Anger, for example, may be ambivalent because it is not only 'destructive' (which is how anger is mostly perceived), but also 'constructive' as it can be directed towards achieving social justice, a change for the better. The ambivalent emotions related to school leadership – such as positive feelings about being a school leader and making a difference, and angry feelings for being unable to get past government bureaucracy, are not entirely private, either, but are also public and political terrain. Often these ambivalent emotions may be related to school leaders' evaluation of their experiences prompted by a desire for a better leadership performance, a process noted for producing a particularly profound effect on the emotional experiences of school leaders (Beatty 2005). Other times, school leaders' emotional responses may result from and further reinforce the levels of power present in school context. These ambivalent emotions exist simultaneously and expose the importance of further exploring the varied emotional responses of school leaders and their struggles to manage them. In particular, the effects of the intersection of emotional ambivalence and the accompanying emotional management on the school leaders' ability to further the goals of change in their school are vastly understudied in school leadership literature.

While Ahmed's position draws on psychoanalysis and focuses on how emotions circulate, the French philosopher Michel Foucault's (e.g. see 1980; 1983; 1990) analyses of power and politics are helpful in examining how emotions are constituted and managed – that is, how and under what circumstances emotions are considered appropriate or inappropriate, and how they function with/in power relations. Although Foucault did not engage directly with emotions, by examining the ways in which emotions function simultaneously as a sign of power and as one of its effects, we can use Foucauldian ideas to describe emotions as historically and culturally constituted. Because emotions may be described both as a way of knowing and as a distinct realm in which meaning is constructed, we are urged to put our discursive practices about emotions and our discursive practices about power and politics into dialogue with one another (Jaggar 1989).

For Foucault, discourses do not simply reflect or describe reality, knowledge, experience, self, social relations, social institutions, and practices; rather, they play an integral role in constituting (and being constituted by) them. In other words, discursive practices establish what can be felt. In and through these discursive practices we ascribe to ourselves bodily feelings, emotions, intentions, and all the other psychological attributes that have for so long been attributed to a unified self. In this sense, subjects *do* their emotions; emotions do not just happen to them. This is where an examination of how and why subjects are constituted as such opens the possibility of creating new forms of subjectivity.

It is important to emphasise that power in Foucault's work is not repressive. Power, according to Foucault, is dispersed, manifest in discursive practices, and exercised; it is not a possession, but it is unstable and localised. Discourses produce power, which in turn continuously produce and constitute the self (Foucault 1977; 1983). Foucault developed two major ways of describing the formation of subjectivity: one based on discipline and normalisation – *technologies of power* – and the other based on care of the self and the uses of pleasure – *technologies of the self*. The notion of technology refers to 'any assembly structured by a practical rationality governed by a more or less conscious goal' (Rose 1998: 26), such as the school, the prison, and the asylum. Technologies operate in terms of a detailed structuring of space, time, and relations among individuals, through hierarchical observation and normalising judgements that the individual uses to conduct his or her own conduct (Foucault 1977).

Technologies of power focus on the relationship between discourses and regimes of power/knowledge and are internalised and self-regulating. Technologies of the self 'permit individuals to effect by their own means or with the help of others a certain number of operations on their own bodies and souls, thoughts, conduct, and way of being' (Foucault 1988: 18). Thus, individuals play a large part in their own control and take the form of techniques for the conduct of one's relation with oneself.

Discursive production of the self is both constraining and liberating; thus, subjectivity is understood through resistance and domination. Foucault maintained that 'where there is power there is resistance' (1990, vol. 1: 95). Attending to the local manifestations of power allows one to track resistances, be critical, and develop strategies for (re)constituting one's power relations: 'The problem is not changing people's consciousness – or what's in their heads – but the political, economic, institutional regime of the production of truth' (1990, vol. 1: 135). In other words, people choose among various discourses that are available or act to resist them.

Implications for school leadership

The preceding analysis of emotions and power relations can contribute to a critical understanding of emotionality in school leadership. For example, technologies of power can serve as a conceptual tool to investigate the role of emotions in the constitution of power relations in the school, how emotion discourses are formed and mobilised and what their political implications are. The focus on the notion of power informs a study of emotions in school leadership because it turns our attention towards examining dominant and/or resistant discourses and leadership practices and their effect on school leader–teacher–student–parent relationships. Thus, an analysis of the reciprocal relationship between emotion and politics identifies the possibilities for affective connections and reminds us of the potential to subvert normalising practices in school culture.

To study emotions in school leadership within the theoretical framework described here allows the exploration of spaces that move beyond theories that psychologise emotions and treat them as internalised (e.g. psychoanalysis) or structural theories that emphasise how structures shape the individual (e.g. Marxism). In this sense emotions are neither private nor merely effects of outside structures. The role of power relations in how affective economies are constructed directs attention to an exploration of emotion discourses and the mechanisms with which emotions are 'disciplined' and certain norms are imposed and internalised as 'normal'. This kind of theorisation allows school leaders first to identify such discourses and then to destabilise and denaturalise the regimes that demand certain emotions be expressed and others disciplined.

For example, many contemporary calls for emotional intelligence in management and organisation (including school leadership and administration) aim at adapting individuals emotionally to the imperatives of *performativity* – that is, how school leaders should perform emotions in 'appropriate' and 'normal' ways (Hartley 2003). This is in line with business and management discourses packaging 'marketable solutions for success and self improvement' (Boler 1999: 65). Hartley warns us to beware of the marketisation of educational management due to the 'rationalization of the emotions for performative purposes' (1999: 309) and where emotions 'are being appropriated for performative and instrumental purposes' (2003: 11).

I also argue that many contemporary discourses about emotional intelligence in school leadership are caught in the obsession for performativity, efficiency, bureaucratic rationality, cultural assimilation, moral self-control, and normalisation of 'emotional skills' (Zembylas 2005). In view of the theoretical framework presented in this chapter, such descriptions of emotional intelligence are largely framed as a set of 'competencies' and thus lack a critical transformative aspect. Engaging with a framework that recognises the politics of emotion discourses prompts us to imagine the possibilities within an alternative discourse, one that could begin to employ criticality in emotional practices; the need for school leaders to create such cultures is clearly important (Beatty and Brew 2004). The dialectics of emotions and power relations in school leadership focuses on the often neglected political implications of emotional aspects. Thus, the ways in which affective connections are used to subvert prevailing emotional rules in the schools reveal the intersections between macro- and micro-political aspects of school leadership and culture.

What is missing from discourses suggesting an appropriation of emotion to the demands of emotional intelligence – along the lines of bureaucratic rationality as a way of creating more successful schools and businesses – is an explicit emphasis on engaging school leaders in a critical analysis of the emotional investments they experience in relationship to particular ideologies. For example, what emotions and leadership skills are associated with the construction of 'successful schools' in the media and elsewhere? How can school leaders become critically aware of such representations and deconstruct their emotional investments to particular ideas (e.g. successful leadership) or images (e.g. the efficient school leader)? To be able to interrupt an appropriation of emotional intelligence, school leaders need to engage themselves and their faculty in analysis of the unquestioned values learned through popular management and the emotions associated with these values – such as liberal individualism and the myth of objectivity and rationality in decision-making.

The ultimate aim of a critical approach on emotions in school leadership is to reshape and expand the terms of emotion discourses, enabling different questions to be asked, modifying the relations among school leaders, teachers, students, and parents, and the rules in the name of which they govern or are governed. The contribution of the political implications of emotions in school leadership amounts to an intervention in a much larger debate about subjectivities in school culture, in which concepts of affective elements of consciousness and relationships, community, and reform are slowly being re-examined. This socio-political character of emotions in school leadership creates the difference between possible and real transformation, and it is this difference that constitutes the power of the theoretical framework presented here as a critical tool to subvert existing conditions. The need for a deeper conceptualisation of this socio-political character can guide research on emotions in school leadership in whatever locality, research informed by a genuine search to understand the power and the limitations of the political merits or demerits of any emotional economy within a school culture.

In light of these considerations, investigation of the politics of emotions in school leadership has two implications. First, there is no school leadership that does not create an affective economy; the processes and analysis of school leadership would need to take emotions into account. Second, the emotions, like power relations, are always located in the spaces between the individual and social and political contexts. In making these observations, it seems that the emotions of school leadership are profoundly influenced by school leaders' participation in particular forms of affective economies in their schools. As I have argued, there is a great deal at stake in the emotional economies in which school leaders, teachers, and students participate. However, school communities are able to constitute affective economies that have the potential to subvert disciplinary mechanisms and practices.

Conclusion

The framework outlined in this chapter opens up exciting new directions for the study of emotions in school leadership. It draws our attention to those affective economies that power relations (re-)construct in school and allows us to better understand which counter-emotions form different (subversive) affective economies. Asking which organisational and discursive dynamics lead school leadership styles to generate a particular set of emotions and emotional norms constitutes an interesting area of research. Unravelling the different aspects of using feminist and critical thought – both as analytic tools and as points of departures for conducting research on emotions in school leadership – creates useful openings for enriching our perspectives about the dynamics of affective relations in the political landscape of the school culture.

References

Abu-Lughod, L. and Lutz, C.A. (1990) 'Introduction: Emotion, discourse, and the politics of everyday life', in C. Lutz and L. Abu-Lughod (eds) *Language and the Politics of Emotion*, Cambridge: Cambridge University Press.

Ahmed, S. (2004) *The Cultural Politics of Emotion*, Edinburgh: Edinburgh University Press.

Albrecht-Crane, C. and Slack, J. (2003) 'Toward a pedagogy of affect', in J.D. Slack (ed.) *Animations (of Deleuze and Guattari)*, New York: Peter Lang.

Beatty, B. (2000) 'The emotions of educational leadership: Breaking the silence', *International Journal of Leadership in Education*, 3: 331–57.

—— (2002) 'Emotion matters in educational leadership: Examining the unexamined', unpublished thesis, Ontario Institute for Studies in Education.

—— (2005) 'Emotional leadership', in B. Davies (ed.) *The Essentials of School Leadership*, Thousand Oaks: Sage.

Beatty, B. and Brew, C. (2004) 'Trusting relationships and emotional epistemologies: A foundational leadership issue', *School Leadership and Management*, 24: 329–56.

Blackmore, J. (1996) 'Doing emotional labour in the educational market place: Stories from the field of women in management', *Discourse*, 17: 337–52.

—— (2004) 'Leading as emotional management work in high risk times: The counterintuitive impulses of performativity and passion', *School Leadership and Management*, 24: 439–59.

Boler, M. (1999) *Feeling Power: Emotions and Education*, New York: Routledge.

Burrow, S. (2005) 'The political structure of emotion: From dismissal to dialogue', *Hypatia*, 20, 4: 27–43.

Campbell, S. (1997) *Interpreting the Personal: Expression and the Formation of Feelings*, Ithaca: Cornell University Press.

Davies, B. and Brighouse, T. (2008) *Passionate Leadership in Education*, London: Paul Chapman.

Deal, T. and Peterson, K. (1994) *The Leadership Paradox: Balancing Logic and Artistry in Schools*, San Francisco: Jossey-Bass.

Foucault, M. (1977) *Discipline and Punish: The Birth of the Prison*, trans. A.M. Sheridan, New York: Pantheon Books.

—— (1980) *Power/Knowledge: Selected Interviews and Other Writings 1972–1977*, trans. C. Cordon, L. Marshall, J. Mepham, and K. Soper, New York: Pantheon.

—— (1983) 'The subject and power', in H.L. Dreyfus and P. Rabinow (eds) *Michel Foucault: Beyond Structuralism and Hermeneutics*, Chicago: University of Chicago Press.

—— (1988) 'Technologies of the self', in L.H. Martin, H. Gutman, and P.H. Hutton (eds) *Technologies of the Self*, Amherst: University of Massachusetts Press.

—— (1990) *The History of Sexuality*, 3 vols, New York: Vintage Books.

Grossberg, L. (1992) *We Gotta Get Out of This Place: Popular Conservatism and Postmodern Culture*, New York: Routledge.

Harding, J. and Pribram, E.D. (2004) 'Losing our cool? Following Williams and Grossberg on emotions', *Cultural Studies*, 18: 863–83.

Hargreaves, A. (1997) *Rethinking Educational Change with Heart and Mind*, Alexandria: Association for Supervision and Curriculum Development Yearbook.

—— (2001) 'The emotional geographies of teaching', *Teachers College Record*, 103: 1056–80.

Hartley, D. (1999) Marketing and the re-enchantment of school management in press', *The British Journal of Sociology of Education*, 20: 309–23.

—— (2003) 'The instrumentalisation of the expressive in education', *British Journal of Educational Studies*, 51: 6–19.

Holmes, M. (2004) 'Feeling beyond rules: Politicizing the sociology of emotion and anger in feminist politics', *European Journal of Social Theory*, 7: 209–27.

Jaggar, A. (1989) 'Love and knowledge: Emotion in feminist epistemology', in S. Bordo and A. Jaggar (eds) *Gender/Body/Knowledge: Feminist Reconstructions of Being and Knowing*, New Brunswick: Rutgers University Press.

Leavitt, J. (1996) 'Meaning and feeling in the anthropology of emotions', *American Ethnologist*, 23: 514–19.

Lupton, D. (1998) *The Emotional Self: A Sociocultural Exploration*, London: Sage.

Lutz, C. and Abu-Lughod, L. (eds) (1990) *Language and the Politics of Emotion*, Cambridge: Cambridge University Press.

Reddy, W.M. (1997) 'Against constructionist: The historical ethnography of emotions', *Current Anthropology*, 38: 327–40.

Revell, R. (1996) 'Realities and feelings in the work of primary heads', *Cambridge Journal of Education*, 26: 391–9.

Rose, N. (1990) *Governing the Soul: The Shaping of the Private Self*, London: Routledge.

—— (1998) *Inventing Ourselves: Psychology, Power and Personhood*, Cambridge: Cambridge University Press.

Sachs, J. and Blackmore, J. (1998) 'You never show you can't cope: Women in school leadership roles managing their emotions', *Gender and Education*, 10: 265–80.

Sutton, R. and Wheatley, K. (2003) 'Teachers' emotions and teaching: A review of the literature and directions for future research', *Educational Psychology Review*, 15: 327–58.

Zembylas, M. (2005) *Teaching with Emotion: A Postmodern Enactment*, Greenwich: Information Age Publishing.

—— (2007) 'Theory and methodology in researching emotions in education', *International Journal of Research and Method in Education*, 30: 57–72.

Zembylas, M. and Fendler, L. (2007) 'Reframing emotion in education through lenses of *parrhesia* and care of the self', *Studies in Philosophy and Education*, 26: 319–33.

8 Measures of hope and despair

Emotionality, politics, and education

Jill Blackmore

Much has been written about emotions from the perspective of individual educators and students, as well as the politics of emotional management in teaching and leading within specific organisational contexts. Little has been written, with some notable exceptions (Boler 1999), of how emotions provide connectivity between individuals and groups as manifestations of the cultural relations and political economy in specific historical contexts. Denzin uses the term 'emotionality' rather than 'emotions' to argue the case for a more contextualised, relational, and socio-cultural perspective. 'In every day life the emotions that people experience and establish can be as basic to their joint actions as are their claims to power, influence and status ... Individuals are connected to society through the emotions they experience' (1984: 24).

In this chapter, I explore the various trajectories of emotionality with regard to collective notions of 'structures of feeling' (Williams 1975) and 'economies of affect' (Grossberg 1988) in education as a 'field' of research and professional practice (Bourdieu 1990). I argue for the need for 'analyses of emotions in the production of knowledge, culture, individual *and* collective identities and power relations' (Harding and Pribram 2004: 864) within wider sociological, cultural studies, socio-psychological discussions about the nature of the post-modern condition and inter/subjectivity in historical contexts characterised as high risk and low trust (Bauman 2001; Beck 1992; Sennett 2006). Considering how teachers, parents, and students 'feel' about education means that we begin to recognise socio-cultural and political influences in attitudes to education in society in terms of collective as well as individual identity formation and socio-cultural emotionalities.

Emotions and education

Sociology has until recently viewed emotions to be the domain of the cognitive or 'psych' disciplinary fields, which have in turn treated emotion as the display of inner individual psychological dispositions. This exclusion perpetuated the rationality/emotionality and public/private binaries embedded in Enlightenment thought long criticised by feminist theorists (Jaggar 1989). Renewed sociological interest in emotions now recognises emotions as social constructs situated within cultural and organisational contexts (Lupton 1998).

Similarly in education, emotions have historically been treated as individual psychological manifestations premised upon a rational/emotional binary, one most evident in the privileging of rational (equated to masculine) leadership in education (Blackmore 1989; Kerfoot 1999). Recently, the need for innovation in the production of learner identities for knowledge-based economies as well as advances in neuroscience that have informed management and learning theory have repositioned emotions as central to the educational experience *and* worker productivity. Emotions are the next resource to be 'tapped' by post-industrial economies and in the production of lifelong learners and learning organisations in Bernstein's (2000) notion of a 'totally pedagogicalised society': the 'crucial regulator and legitimation strategy to translate uncertainty, risk and precariousness into a socialisation characterised by endless learning' (Bonal and Rambla 2003: 169).

In education, emotions have been foregrounded in feminist and critical pedagogy (Bartlett 1998; Kenway *et al.* 1998; McWilliam 1999), teachers' work (Dadds 1995; Nias 1996; Woods and Bagley 1996; Zembylas 2005), teacher identity (Schmidt 2000), leadership (Beatty 2000; Blackmore 1995; 1999; Sachs and Blackmore 1998), organisational change (Hargreaves 2004), and resistance theories (Boler 2004; Cooks and Sun 2002). The recent convergence of school improvement and effectiveness research has incorporated this earlier literature, recognising that the affective is critical to the sense-making process of educational change in terms of how teachers' emotions are a product of their working conditions and teaching and learning relationships and leadership practices (Leithwood 2006).

Much of the literature on emotion in education draws from the work of Hochschild's (1983) 'emotional rules' and 'emotional labour' of teaching and leading and Goleman's (1998) 'emotional intelligence' with regard to pedagogy and leadership (e.g. Ackerman and Maslin-Ostrowski 2004; Ashkanasy and Dasborough 2003). Emotional literacy is now promoted in teacher and leader professional development programs (Power 2004). By contrast, emotions are rarely mentioned in the university reform literature, other than around student subjectivity, feminist pedagogy and academic identity re-formation and the re-positioning of women academics as emotional managers, pedagogical nurturers, and in-house quality assurance workers in the corporatised university (Morley 2003).

Less evident is how structural and cultural relations inform power inequalities and what that means in terms of the affective, with notable exceptions (Boler 1999). Furthermore, culture is usually in teachers' work and educational reform treated as 'an aggregate' of individual dispositions and interactions, and schools and universities are treated as discrete sites responding to external pressures as though there is some clear-cut external/internal divide where educational institutions are impermeable to wider socio-cultural influences (Zorn and Boler 2007). Teachers are viewed as conforming to, accommodating or resisting institutional cultures and organisational objectives, with little regard to their politics, past histories, or wider professional allegiances to education as a field of professional practice (Blackmore and Sachs 2007). Context (education systems, education politics, social structure, and the relations of work, family, and education) continues to be treated as a backdrop presenting challenges to which teachers and leaders respond, rather than producing conditions and relations informing the emotionalities of teachers and leaders and their students. While there is recognition of how race, culture, and gender inform the emotional relations between teachers, students, and communities, the analysis rarely ventures into wider social, economic, and structural analyses that address the emotional investments teachers and parents have as social groups in rejecting and protecting shared privilege, or collective 'feelings' of marginalisation (Oakes and Lipton 2002; Stronach *et al.* 2002).

Zorn and Boler argue that mainstream perspectives fail to see schools and universities 'as constructed realities as opposed to systems or structures that operate independently of the individuals in them' (2007: 140). The micro (personal), mesa (organisational), and macro (structural and cultural factors) are separated out like onion shells that can be peeled away, rather than seen as intermeshed social relations that stretch out into extra-institutional communities of practice (e.g. unions) or transnational social fields that have a shared logic of practice (Bourdieu 1990). Few studies view educational reform as a social movement, an alliance rather than an antagonism between teachers and parents, in association with environmentalist, multiculturalist, and anti-racist movements, themselves 'collective expressions of frustration, of cultural change' (Oakes and Lipton 2002: 396). Opposition and resistance are positioned within the mainstream as negative emotions that have to be 'managed'. The few studies that consider the darker emotional side to teaching and leading, for example bullying and discrimination (Blasé and Blasé 2003), mostly come from political economy, labour process, or neo-Marxist perspectives such as critical organisational theory (Carlyle and Woods 2002). Multiple restructurings, the de-professionalisation of teaching and academic work, and the intensification of labour during the 1990s' neo-liberal reforms, with consequent collective emotional manifestations of alienation, stress, and burnout, have produced 'general occupational stress' (Vanderberghe and Huberman 1999; Zembylas 2005).

Post-structuralist perspectives such as Hartley's identify how the move from government (which exercises rule) to governance (which exercises power) through devolution and partnerships have produced new disciplinary technologies that are the non-bureaucratic invisible aspects of 'emotionality, empowerment, internal marketing, networks, and flexibility' (2003: 441) producing performative aspects of a subjectivity refusing any emotional/rational binary.

> This individualisation of emotion is one aspect of the move towards self management of organisations, but also in the management of the self

> through new therapeutic technologies (from student disciplinary procedures through to performance appraisal and team work) ... emotion is viewed in highly instrumental ways because the value systems and emotional connections that bind groups together are missing.
>
> (Blackmore 1995: 338)

These 'modernist makeovers' or re-enchantments encourage 'greedy' organisations to appropriate the intellectual, physical, and emotional energies of teachers and leaders for organisational gain through the technologies of quality assurance, outcomes-based education, performance management, and innovation economies (Blackmore and Sachs 2007; Gleeson and Husbands 2001; Morley 2003).

> Despite all the talk of the need for social capital – for trust in economic relations, for social inclusion – networks (a feature of governance), they tend to be calculative and ephemeral, not lasting and emotional. Emotions are managed for performative purposes ... as global capitalism is seeking to change the form and function of education on its behalf.
>
> (Hartley 2003: 447)

Cultural studies perspectives similarly see emotions as central to the shift from production to consumption that has mobilised libidinal economies around desire and pleasure (Du Gay 1996). Emotions are seen to be produced, felt, expressed, appropriated, managed, mobilised, and mediated discursively in ways that meet the performative needs of post-modern governmentalities, another element in the commodification of everyday life of post-modern subjectivities. This is a new form of appropriation of labour, part of a wider move in service occupations to 'the presentation of aestheticised selves' and the performative structuring of labour (Adkins and Lury 1999: 605).

Emotionality is also ethical work. While performativity may signify that image counts more than substance and that efficiency is paramount over ethics or equity (Lyotard 1984), the everyday performances required substantively change practices (Butler 1997). Regimes of surveillance stressing out teachers and leaders not only are features of the subordination of education to the needs of the nation state and global capitalism but indicative of contestation over what constitutes a good teacher and academic and education professionalism itself within what is now a highly politicised field of educational research and practice (Gleeson and Husbands 2001; Mahoney *et al.* 2004). The effects of this technologisation of educational work are forms of cognitive and emotional dissonance, between teachers' and leaders' passion for their work and desire to 'make a difference' (doing good) (Nias 1999), and the demands of performativity which is about compliance (being good), thus producing competing 'mindscapes' (Blackmore and Sachs 2007; Sergiovanni 1999). Nussbaum (2001) elaborates on this cognitive/evaluative notion of emotions as 'appraisals or value judgements'.

Emotionality has spatial and temporal as well as a relational dimension. Emotionality is not just a response to an immediate incident, but can arise from long-term unequal relations of power. Those who experience discrimination are fully aware throughout their lives of the shame of powerlessness, which, while 'felt' as an individual, is shared feeling with 'like' others, just as pride is felt as a shared experience in dominant groups (Fortier 2005). Collective experiences of anger and fear arising from domination and discrimination also lead to political activism displayed in social movements and protests, although not necessarily progressive (e.g. terrorism). Anti-racist literature, narratives of marginalised groups, and white middle-class educators' reflections on the racialisation of everyday relations are exploring how emotions circulate between individuals and across groups within particular structural and cultural arrangements of power (Trifonas 2003). Boler (1999) and Boler and Zembylas (2003) refer to the 'pedagogies of discomfort' central to the type of reflexivity required, for example, to promote anti-sexist, racist, and homophobic teaching, and the ethical and moral tensions this produces for individuals.

Epidemiological studies on quality of life, health, and well-being now connect collective feelings to poverty. For the working-class poor stress is a major feature of chronic under- and un-employment – with a range of associated health problems – often concentrated in local communities where there is usually less engagement with education (Wilkinson and Marmot 2003). Stress derives from individuals and groups feeling a sense of hopelessness. Emotions 'underpin the phenomenological experiences of our bodies in sickness and health' providing the 'basis for social reciprocity and exchange' and the link between 'personal problems and broader public issues of social structure' (Carlyle and Woods 2002: xvi). Rather than being a 'natural attribute' of a specific social group, emotions such as 'a sense of desperation, anger, bitterness, learned helplessness or aggression' are 'wholly understandable responses to various social, economic and material difficulties' (Carlyle and Woods 2002: xvi).

The assumption that emotions are largely individual and not social phenomena leads to the assumption that 'social entities at national, governmental and corporate levels of operation' are rational (Harding and Pribram 2004: 865) and only political minorities and particular social groups (e.g. women) are emotional. But emotions are linked to status within specific fields of practice within and across organisations and societies (e.g. the military, bureaucracies, and the professions) (De Botton 2004). Organisations are now seen to be sites of emotional investments of individuals and groups around status hierarchies (Fineman 2003). Feminist and post-colonial theorists argue that emotions are gendered, racialised, and classed in that they are premised upon public/private, rationality/emotionality, male/female, and black/white binaries that have become culturally normalised, classifying emotional displays according to stereotypical emotional attributes of social groups and thus 'naturalised'. Emotionalities associated with teaching and teacher relationships with diverse student and parent populations are likewise marked by what Hargreaves (2001) refers to as 'emotional geographies': the spatial or material closeness or distance in human interactions arising from cultural and class-based stereotypes and moral codes. Emotion, how it is managed and displayed, is now seen to be another differentiating process within organisations (Newton *et al.* 2001).

But, overall, during the twentieth century, the assignment of reason with the dominant, the white, the elite, and the masculine, has served some political interests more than others, creating an 'emotional hegemony' that is portrayed as not emotional but contingent on significant emotional investments in status, hierarchy, and the way things are (Jaggar 1989).

'Generalised anxiety' as a condition of new times

Emotions, therefore, are learned, contextual, and intersubjective; they are historically, socially, and politically contingent, produced by, and productive of, social and political affects at a macro as well as micro and meso levels (Lupton 1998). Social theorists such as Beck (1992), Bauman (1996), De Botton (2004), and Sennett (2006) have argued that we are in 'new times' and 'new economies'. This fast capitalist phase of globalisation is characterised by intensified and rapid flows of people, goods, images, ideas, and money as well as a temporal/spatial collapse with greater interdependence globally (e.g. global warming) producing 'perceptions' of increased uncertainty and risk (Beck 1992). The media and migration have let loose collective imaginations about the future with 'diasporas of hope, diasporas of terror and diasporas of despair' (Appadurai 1997: 6). Rizvi sees discourses of globalisation have mobilised specific fears and desires, producing for some 'a sense of progress, prosperity and peace' and for others 'deprivation, disaster and doom' (2003: 157–8). 9/11 generated a sense of widespread despair, which for the West reverberated as a fear of terrorism conflated into a fear of 'the other' and a feeling that the world has changed forever (Rizvi 2003: 161).

Bauman refers to the 'climate of ambient fear' distinguished by a new world disorder marked by universal deregulation in which the market determines value, a new style life politics with the collapse of familial and state safety nets, and radical uncertainty produced by lack of agency in the light of the all-consuming image industry (1996: 22–4). Whereas the twentieth-century welfare states and bureaucracies of Western social capitalism protected the individual, neo-liberal reforms have produced a post-welfare state that has made the most vulnerable more open to risk as it has stripped away minimal protections. New capitalism is premised upon uncertainty, de-bureaucratisation, and fluidity within as well as between organisations. 'But the fragmenting of big institutions has left many people's lives in a fragmented state … with … a move away from stable unions, big corporations, and relatively fixed markets' (Sennett 2006: 9). These mutual vulnerabilities give rise to a collective sense of fear and grief circulated in the media and on the Internet.

Cumulatively, these factors produce a sense of 'generalised anxiety' even amongst those in more secure positions as a dominant emotionally of contemporary times (De Botton 2004). Denzin argues that 'emotionality draws the person to others, for emotions are felt in relation to other interactants. While emotional experiences are purely private, many emotions are ritually inspired by groups or larger social structures' (1984: 5) (i.e. class or ethnic identification as well as commitment to social movements such as feminism, environmentalism, or nationalism). Key sociological traditions have argued that human emotions and consciousness are shaped by structurally situated conditions: Marx refers to alienation, estrangement, and the forms of disenchantment arising from the reduction of individuals down to exchange value; Weber saw capitalism as 'anchored deeply in religious and emotional attitudes' (Denzin 1984). From a cultural studies perspective, Raymond Williams refers to 'structures of feeling' as 'the felt sense of the quality of life at a particular place and time'; a 'pattern of impulses and restraints' through which the lived experience differs from the 'official consciousness' of prescribed ideas and values of a particular social group (1975: 47). These structures emerge, dominate, and then dissipate over time. Thus there can be a generalised 'anxiety about economic instability as a culturally pervasive emotion, felt or experienced by individuals, but in response to contradictions and constraints in the larger social formation' (Harding and Pribram 2004: 870). Experience is mediated through these structures of feeling, hegemonies of popular commonsense, and individual beliefs, thus integrating the affective and the cognitive. Emotions 'act simultaneously as structures of meaning and structures of power ... intimately connected to larger social operations', and the 'means by which social and cultural formations affect us' (Harding and Pribram 2004: 871).

The contemporary structure of feeling of reflexive modernisation could be characterised by a sense of risk, insecurity, lack of trust, and fear of 'the other' (Beck 1992). Contradictions are emerging between normative standardisation and the crumbling traditions of class culture, gender relations, family, and science. While risk is produced systematically in ways that are incalculable, individuals have increased choices. Intensified feelings of insecurity are exacerbated by post-welfarism characterised by self-help, and processes of responsibilisation and individualisation (Bauman 2001). 'Only a certain kind of human being can prosper in unstable, fragmentary social conditions', with the capacity to 'manage short term relations and oneself' while 'improvising a life narrative' and a 'sustained self of self' in the context of transient relations and multiple jobs where 'no one owns their place in her organization', and there is no guarantee (Sennett 2006: 3–5). 'Durability of persons and objects has been replaced by disposability' (Sennett 2006: 5), whether it is professional skills or education. This fear of disposability is new to many. Emotional insecurity arises because 'most people are not like this; they need a sustained life narrative, they take pride being good at something specific, and they value the experiences they've lived through', and desire 'a rightful and secure position in society' (Sennett 2006: 24, 5).

This is, then, the foreseeable fear-filled future imagined by the middle class, many working at the edge or within the new economy. Pusey (2003) identifies how Australian economic restructuring after 1989 marked by market liberalisation, deregulated industrial relations, and reduced public expenditure on health, education, and wealth, impacted the collective psyche of the middle class. Middle Australia, on the whole, wanted to see a more equitable distribution of income and a fairer society, with higher levels of trust in institutions and no sense of weaker commitment to solidarity such as unions. The majority saw wage and salary earners as losers in the reforms and big business as winners, with society now more unequal and unfair, favouring elites, and more hierarchical.

For the working class, the new work order produced a sense of desperation about changing rosters, irregular hours, and unpaid overtime. In a politics of resentment cultivated by a neo-conservative government, women, elites, welfare freeloaders, and refugees were blamed, or perceived as advantaged. Overall, upper and lower middle class felt 'anger over the precariousness and scarcity of jobs and the consequences of labour market reform' (Pusey 2003: 59). This led to a retreat into the private and alienated, not because of 'moral laxity', but due to economic dislocation underpinned by anxiety about the degrading of civil society.

Arguably, the first decade of the twenty-first century is one that can be characterised by a generalised anxiety, an ontological insecurity, and a fear of being made redundant that is not fully explained away by individual experience, workplace cultures, or stressors. The issue, of course, is whether this generalised anxiety is like a 'disease', moving through and within networks, within communities and societies, and manifest in particular communities of practice such as education.

Education as a field of emotionality

In this context of generalised anxiety, education is more than ever a field of contestation over values and beliefs, individual and collective desires, hope (of success), and fear (of failure). Education has historically been linked with individual advancement and collective improvement for marginalised social groups, promising progressive social change. Britzman argues that anxieties about education, teacher education, and teaching flow over and 'mirror larger public anxieties over the education of children, youth and university students' (2007: 3). Education also sits within a wider social and political frame, prone to crisis in itself and also externally to other crises (e.g. Sputnik, globalisation). What is essential is 'the crisis in education' re-producing a more generalised 'psychoanalytic psychology of uncertainty' (Britzman 2007: 7).

Bourdieu (1990) argues that education, as a cultural field with its own rules, languages, logics, and practices constitutes an objective hierarchy that is 'bounded', subordinated to other fields such as economics, politics, and journalism in the past decade. The penetration of the logic of managerialism and the market has challenged and transformed dominant values and discourses in the field of education. As a cultural field, education has a hierarchy of sub-fields – universities, schools, and technical education – in which universities claim authority over other sub-fields. Despite this, there are shared understandings, discourses, and belief systems as well as rules of engagement about the nature of education and its purpose. Education during the twentieth century was seen by politicians, activists, and professionals alike as a site of social change as well as social reproduction – a means of individual and collective mobility and equity for the marginalised – and as a public good in educating citizens and workers. While the division of labour was racialised and gendered, the massification of educational and bureaucratic systems did allow inclusion. Individuals largely knew their place, but long-term careers provided a 'psychological home', with some discretionary space for 'interpretive modulation' locally that 'gave individuals a sense of agency' (Sennett 2006: 36). Unhappiness with an institution coexisted with social bonding. Therefore nurses and teachers stay in underfunded and dysfunctional organisations because they feel they can make a difference.

Neo-liberal reforms based on parental choice, marketisation, managerialism, privatisation, and vocationalisation means that education has now been tightly coupled to national economies (Blackmore and Sachs 2007; Connell 2006). There was a shift from welfarism to post-welfarism in England as in Australia towards an 'enterprise culture' as a 'deliberate attempt at cultural restructuring and engineering based on the neo-liberal model of the entrepreneurial self – a shift characterised as a moving from a "culture of dependency" to one of "self reliance"' (Peters 2001: 58). These reforms have produced fundamental shifts in the nature of work, the role of the state, and the state's relationship with the individual and education, effecting a cultural shift in attitudes to education through its commodification (Blackmore and Sachs 2007). Education is now viewed increasingly as an international commodity, an individual positional good, imparting to individual students or nation states competitive advantage over others in a magnified instrumentalism. As work becomes central to identity, education is critical to improving life chances as the means to manage individual and collective risk through choice (Pusey 2003). Education promises to guarantee futures and gain advantage in ways that gender, class, and nationality provided in the past. Thus discourses of parental choice found fertile ground amongst the middle class who fear loss of status as well as the desires of marginalised groups to gain recognition, an anxiety intensified by reduced employment and educational opportunities with increased competition. To add to this, as lifelong learning has become the mantra, education increasingly requires increased personal and familial investment. Yet choice is contingent on personal, cultural, and financial capital.

This value shift evident in the Anglophone nation states indicates a move away from social democratic values of cooperation, participation, and collectivism to market-driven values of competition, advantage, and individualism in and through education (Blackmore and Sachs 2007; Gewirtz *et al.*

1995; Wells *et al.* 1997). The social democratic covenant of twentieth-century public systems has been replaced by a new contractualism in employment relations, relations between schools and families, and between the individual and the state. Individuals now relate to organisations more on a basis of fear of being made redundant than trust based on a shared commitment, voluntarism, and mutuality. Cooperation is coerced to produce superficial conformity via the disciplinary technologies of performance management standards. The new contractualism repositions teachers as technical experts required to service the state and clients rather than a professionalism characterised by judgement, recognition, and authority (Carlyle and Woods 2002: 142–3). This repositioning has been accompanied by intense media scrutiny around the education in crisis discourse requiring teachers to defend themselves *as a field* in terms of the rules of the game and value positions.

The interpellation of market and media relations in education and the move towards more competitive social relations in education both exploits and mobilises parental anxiety and emotions (Blackmore 1996): 'You are not a good parent if you do not pay for schooling.' Markets as socio-cultural constructs tap into emotions and are premised upon the emotions of desire, fear, greed, and envy (Woods and Bagley 1996). Emotionality about education is also mobilised and channelled through the media. Within a market context where image and reputation means survival, governments have 'mediatised' strategies to control the professions and divert attention from failed policies (Blackmore and Thorpe 2003) by shaming and blaming of individuals and particular families (e.g. single parents) and low-performing schools, thereby silencing teacher opposition to neo-liberal reforms in what Hargreaves refers to as the emotional politics of school failure, and how in 'intergenerationally unequal societies, distributions of dignity create emotional economies of distinction and disgust … the basic emotions of social exclusion' that 'demarcate success from failure' (2004: 34–5).

The contractualist state now steers through policy and regulates through financial agreements and accountability a range of self-managing public and private providers competing to offer educational services. Schools and universities have become 'service' providers and students and parents 'clients'. In turn, the disciplinary technologies of market and managerial accountability penetrate into the emotions and the soul of educational workers. While there is some autonomy locally, the centre keeps control by setting the tasks, encouraging individual units and teams to compete on a winner-takes-all basis, leading to high levels of stress and anxiety for workers. Internal markets within organisations raise the 'anxiety stakes' as 'the line between competitor and colleague becomes less clear' (Sennett 2006: 52). 'Anxiety arises in ill-defined conditions, dread when pain or ill fortune is well defined. Failure in the old pyramid [of workplaces] was grounded in dread, failure in the new institution is shaped by anxiety' (Sennett 2006: 53).

Educators are, therefore, as a field experiencing a shared sense of a fundamental shift in the nature of their work and relations with their colleagues, students, and communities as well as in their profession. Multiple studies have mapped their sense of despair and anger at the inability to undertake the type of educational work that is required to make a difference at a time when these reforms have increased educational inequality (Blackmore and Sachs 2007; Carlyle and Woods 2002: 138–9; Gleeson and Husbands 2001; Hargreaves 2004). They express feelings of alienation from their work due to capture by the performative exercises demanded of them. These standardised outcome-focused and performance management-driven systems not only undermine collegial cultures but also denounce progressive education, reject principles of social justice, and reduce professional autonomy. Educators across sectors, systems, and nations express an increased sense of powerlessness, greater sense of control being exerted and less agency than within the 'iron cage' of bureaucracies producing widespread feelings of disengagement, alienation, resistance, anger, and distancing:

> ... there is a basic clash of values. And it is a conflict where teachers are in a weaker position. They are under examination in a disciplinary exercise, where their humanistic morality has been replaced by one centred on rational-technician. We have seen a number of comments here about teachers feeling that they were losing control of their own classrooms, and their very selves.
>
> (Jeffrey and Woods 1998: 83–4)

The passion for education

The field of education is infused with a particular articulation of the dominant structure of generalised anxiety arising with new capitalism. Grossberg (1997) refers to the 'economy of affect': the material conditions, distribution, and consumption of the affective as one of several economies – capital, money, information, representations (Harding and Pribram 2004: 872). Thinking of affect as investment provides a range of possibilities: 'producing dependencies, responsibilities', 'connection' as a 'basis of social processes of recognition and difference' as 'integral to the notion of individuality' and as a means of communication in the circulation of feelings amongst people and the exertion of power and influence. The affective economy (communication, recognition, etc.) produces and reproduces its own complex network of power and meaning relations in conjunction with other economies (capital, etc.) such that emotions 'may be part of the constitution of culture and collective identities' (Harding and Pribram 2004: 878).

> The circulation of emotion produces in and between people connection, ruptures, dependencies, responsibilities, accountabilities and so on ... people care – they are invested. If people care, certain effects are produced: they feel and act in certain ways.
>
> (Harding and Pribram 2004: 879)

Economies of affect get beyond representation that often neglects the affective or reduces it to sub-functions of ideology or the 'libidinal economies' of desire. Affective economies have their own organisational characteristics such as, in education, belief in meritocracy but also that education has transformational capacities. Plato, Aristotle, Dewey, and Friere articulated a desire to use knowledge to effect social change. People teach because 'there is an intangible, effable quality to our goal, for the kind of desire we aim to teach is about love, passion and commitment' (Todd 1997: 5). 'Affect here is a form of energy and motivating force or intensity rather than a system of interpretation' (Harding and Pribram 2004: 873), a 'psychic energy' that is the 'coloration or passion within which one's investments in or commitments to the world are made possible' (Grossberg 1988: 285). Affect determines or constitutes what matters to people in ways that 'identify the strong investments people have in their experiences, practices, identities meanings and so on...' (Grossberg 1992: 82). Desire should not be understood only within a negative or libidinal framework – the desire to teach and the desire to learn are critical to every educational moment. Desire, ethics, and 'affect' are productive political forces that create new assemblages that organise desire, affections, and power (Zembylas 2005).

Education as a field 'assembles' the affective in ways that function within power relations. Affect is central to education because it fuels the social imaginary about what education offers in terms of identity and culture (Todd 1997: 5), an imaginary associated also with a particular politics. The passion for teaching is imbued for many teachers with a desire to make a difference. This moral imperative fuels an imaginary that challenges existing power relations (Liston and Garrison 2004; Nias 1996). Pusey (2003) in his studies refers to the 'improvers', the public sector professionals including teachers, who were in despair about society in general and managers who did not care. Their concerns were about the destruction of the public sector through downsizing, privatisation, increased hierarchy, degradation of professional work, and toxic and more socially abrasive work cultures (Pusey 2003: 60). Likewise, in a study of women leaders in schools, technical institutes, and universities, Blackmore and Sachs (2007) found educators angry and in despair because of shifts in the relation between the political and affective economies that had transformed educational work in ways antithetical to their own beliefs and that of the profession. They struggled within the performative culture between 'care for others' as an expression of doing good as citizens and 'self-care' in terms of maximising self-interest and looking after the survival of oneself and one's own. The socio-psychic economy of education simultaneously coopted teachers' good will but also produced guilt. The pleasure of discovery, of process-driven and student-centred learning, were being undermined by high stakes standardised outcomes focus that routinised educators' work at the very moment when innovation and creativity are most needed.

Conclusion

This, then, is the core dilemma of the field of education that produces a particular economy of affect which is linked to a generalised anxiety of the new times. The socio-psychic economy of education has always meant that teachers are susceptible to emotive pressures (e.g. guilt), but more recently, teachers and academics are feeling increased dissonance between their worldviews, dominant ideologies, desire for social justice, and the lived experience of the restructured field of education along market and managerial lines. Grossberg (1988) argues that 'emotion is the product of affect and ideology' that becomes passion, and is therefore part of the articulation of power relations. How this is felt is manifest in how teachers and academics 'feel' and 'talk' about the dilemmas and contradictions of their work marked by a crisis in trust and a widespread sense of powerlessness. Teachers understand that the relations of power have significantly altered, and thus express a range of emotions – dismay, regret, anger, despair (Blackmore and Sachs 2007).

This argument raises new issues for educators and how they relate to each other within the field of education and across the professional fields of politics, journalism, and economics. Rizvi argues that

> ... resources of hope are thus to be found in the development of a new perspective on cultural and democratic change. What needs to be emphasised now is the urgency of new institutional building across cultural traditions, the acknowledgement of justice issues posed by the polarisation of wealth, income and power and the pursuit of interests common to humanity as a whole ... democratic dispositions exist in all cultural situations, even if expressed in radically different ways.
>
> (2003: 27)

The question is whether current modes of educational governance can do that work. It may be emotional bonds that will provide the basis for collective action in the future to preserve what we value most in the context of the de-institutionalisation and social, economic, and political fragmentation of educational work.

References

Ackerman, R. and Maslin-Ostrowski, P. (2004) 'The wounded leader and emotional learning in the schoolhouse', *School Leadership and Management*, 24, 3: 311–28.

Adkins, L. and Lury, C. (1999) 'The labour of identity: Performing identities, performing economies', *Economy and Society*, 28, 4: 598–614.

Appadurai, A. (1997) *Modernity at Large: Cultural Dimensions of Globalisation*, Minneapolis: Minneapolis University Press.

Ashkanasy, N. and Dasborough, M. (2003) 'Emotional awareness and emotional intelligence in leadership teaching', *Journal of Education for Business*, 79, 1: 18–23.

Bartlett, A. (1998) 'A passionate subject: Representations of desire in feminist pedagogy', *Gender and Education*, 10, 1: 85–92.

Bauman, Z. (2001) *The Individualised Society*, Cambridge: Polity Press.

—— (1996) *Post Modernity and its Discontents*, Oxford: Polity Press.

Beatty, B. (2000) 'The emotions of educational leadership: Breaking the silence', *International Journal of Leadership in Education*, 3, 4: 331–59.

Beck, U. (1992) *Risk Society*, Oxford: Polity Press.

Bernstein, B. (2000) *Pedagogy, Symbolic Control and Identity: Theory, Research and Critique*, London: Taylor and Francis.

Blackmore, J. (1989) 'Educational leadership: A feminist critique and reconstruction', in J. Smyth (ed.) *Critical Perspectives on Educational Leadership*, Lewes: Falmer Press.

—— (1996) 'Doing "emotional labour" in the education market place: Stories from the field of women in management', *Discourse: Studies in the Cultural Politics of Education*, 17, 3: 337–49.

—— (1999) *Troubling Women: Feminism, Leadership and Educational Change*, Buckingham: Open University Press.

Blackmore, J. and Sachs, J. (2007) *Performing and Reforming Leaders: Gender, Educational Restructuring and Organizational Change*, New York: SUNY Press.

Blackmore, J. and Thorpe, S. (2003) 'Media/ting change: The print media's role in mediating education policy in a period of radical reform in Victoria, Australia', *Journal of Education Policy*, 18, 6: 577–95.

Blasé, J. and Blasé, J. (2003) *Breaking the Silence: Overcoming the Problem of Principal Mistreatment of Teachers*, Thousand Oaks: Sage.

Boler, M. (1999) *Feeling Power*, New York: Routledge.

—— (2004) 'Teaching for hope: The ethics of shattering worldviews', in D. Liston and J. Garrison (eds) *Teaching Learning and Loving: Reclaiming Passion in Educational Practice*, New York: Routledge.

Boler, M. and Zembylas, M. (2003) 'Discomforting truths: The emotional terrain of understanding difference', in P. Trifonas (ed.) *Pedagogies of Difference: Rethinking Education for Social Change*, New York: RoutledgeFalmer.

Bonal, X. and Rambla, X. (2003) 'Captured by the totally pedagogised society: Teachers and teaching in the knowledge economy', *Globalisation, Societies and Education*, 1, 2: 169–84.

Bourdieu, P. (1990) *The Logic of Practice*, Cambridge: Polity Press.

Britzman, D. (2007) 'Teacher education as an uneven development: Toward a psychology of uncertainty', *International Journal of Leadership in Education*, 10, 1: 1–12.

Butler, J. (1997) *Excitable Speech*, New York: Routledge.

Carlyle, D. and Woods, P. (2002) *The Emotions of Teacher Stress*, Stoke-on-Trent: Trentham Books.

Connell, R. (2006) 'The new right triumph: The privatisation agenda and public education in Australia', *Our Schools/Our Selves*, 15, 3: 143–62.

Cooks, L. and Sun, C. (2002) 'Constructing gender pedagogies: Desire and resistance in the "alternative" classroom', *Communication Education*, 51, 3: 293–310.

Dadds, M. (1995) *Passionate Enquiry and School Development: A Story about Teacher Action Research*, London: Falmer Press.

De Botton, A. (2004) *Status Anxiety*, New York: Pantheon Books.

Denzin, N. (1984) *On Understanding Emotions*, San Francisco: Jossey Bass.

Du Gay, P. (1996) *Consumption and Identity at Work*, Thousand Oaks: Sage.

Fineman, S. (ed.) (2003) *Understanding Emotion at Work*, London: Sage.

Fortier, A.M. (2005) 'Pride politics and multiculturalist citizenship', *Ethnic and Racial Studies*, 28, 3: 559–78.

Gewirtz, S., Ball, S., and Bowe, R. (1995) *Markets, Choice and Equity in Education*, Buckingham: Open University Press.

Gleeson, D. and Husbands, C. (eds) (2001) *The Performing School: Managing, Teaching and Learning in a Performance Culture*, London: RoutledgeFalmer.

Goleman, D. (1998) *Working with Emotional Intelligence*, New York: Bantam Books.

Grossberg, L. (1988) 'Postmodernity and affect: All dressed up with no place to go', *Communication* 10(3–4): 271–93.

—— (1992) *We Gotta Get Out of this Place: Popular Conservatism and Postmodern Culture*, New York: Routledge.

—— (1997) *Bringing It All Back Home*, Durham: Duke University Press.

Harding, J. and Pribram, D. (2004) 'Losing our cool? Following Williams and Grossberg on emotions', *Cultural Studies*, 18, 6: 863–83.

Hargreaves, A. (2001) 'Emotional geographies of teaching', *Teachers College Record*, 103, 6: 1056–80.

—— (2004) 'Distinction and disgust: The emotional politics of school failure', *International Journal of Leadership in Education*, 7, 1: 27–42.

Hartley, D. (2003) 'Education as global positioning device: Some theoretical considerations', *Comparative Education*, 39, 4: 439–50.

Hochschild, A. (1983) *The Managed Heart: The Commercialization of Human Feeling*, Berkeley: University of California Press.

Jaggar, A. (1989) 'Love and knowledge: Emotion in feminist epistemology', in A. Jaggar and S. Bordo (eds) *Gender/Body/Knowledge*, New Jersey: Rutgers University Press.

Jeffrey, B. and Woods, P. (1998) *Testing Teachers: The Effect of School Inspections on Primary Teachers*, London: Routledge.

Kenway, J., Willis, S. with Blackmore, J. and Rennie, L. (1998) *Answering Back: Girls, Boys and Feminism in Schools*, London: Routledge.

Kerfoot, D. (1999) 'The organisation of intimacy: Managerialism, masculinity and the masculine subject', in S. Whitehead and R. Moodley (eds) *Transforming Managers: Gendering Change in the Public Sector*, London: UCL Press.

Leithwood, K. (2006) *The Emotional Side of School Improvement: A Leadership Perspective*, Toronto: OISE Press.

Liston, D. and J. Garrison (eds) (2004) *Teaching Learning and Loving: Reclaiming Passion in Educational Practice*, New York: Routledge.

Lupton, D. (1998) *The Emotional Self: A Socio-cultural Exploration*, Thousand Oaks: Sage.

Lyotard, J. (1984) *The Postmodern Condition*, Manchester: Manchester University Press.

McWilliam, E. (1999) *Pedagogical Pleasures*, New York: Peter Lang.

Mahony, P., Menter, I., and Hextall, I. (2004) 'The emotional impact of performance-related pay on teachers in England', *British Educational Research Journal*, 30, 3: 435–56.

Morley, L. (2003) *Quality and Power in Higher Education*, Buckingham: Open University Press.

Newton, T., Handy, J., and Fineman, S. (2001) *Stress: Managing Emotion and Power at Work*, London: Sage.

Nias, J. (1996) 'Thinking about feeling: The emotions in teaching', *Cambridge Journal of Education*, 26, 3: 293–306.

Nias, J. (1999) 'Teachers' moral purposes: Stress, vulnerability and strength', in A.M. Huberman and R. Vandenberghe (eds) *Understanding and Preventing Teacher Burnout*, New York: Cambridge University Press.

Nussbaum, M. (2001) *Upheavals of Thought: The Intelligence of Emotions*, New York: Cambridge University Press.

Oakes, J. and Lipton, M. (2002) 'Struggling for educational equity in diverse communities: School reform as social movement', *Journal of Educational Change*, 3: 383–406.

Peters, M. (2001) 'Education, enterprise culture and the entrepreneurial self: A Foucauldian perspective', *Journal of Educational Enquiry*, 2, 2: 58–71.

Power, P. (2004) 'Ethics, values and emotional intelligence', *Teacher*, October: 14–15.

Pusey, M. (2003) *The Experience of Middle Australia: The Dark Side of Economic Reform*, Cambridge: Cambridge University Press.

Rizvi, F. (2003) 'Democracy and education after September 11', *Globalisation, Societies, Education*, 1, 1: 25–40.

Sachs, J. and Blackmore, J. (1998) 'You never show you can't cope: Women in school leadership roles managing their emotions', *Gender and Education*, 19, 3: 265–79.

Schmidt, M. (2000) 'Role theory, emotions and identity', *Teaching and Teacher Education*, 16: 827–42.

Sennett, R. (2006) *The Culture of New Capitalism*, New Haven: Yale University Press.

Sergiovanni, T. (1999) 'Conflicting mindscapes and the inevitability of stress in teaching', in R. Vanderberghe and A. Huberman (eds) *Understanding and Preventing Teacher Burnout*, Cambridge: Cambridge University Press.

Stronach, I., Corbin, B., McNamara, O., Stark, S., and Warne, T. (2002) 'Towards an uncertain politics of professionalism: Teacher and nurse identities in flux', *Journal of Education Policy*, 17, 1: 109–38.

Todd, S. (1997) *Learning Desire*, London: Routledge.

Trifonas, P. (ed.) (2003) *Pedagogies of Difference: Rethinking Education for Social Change*, New York: RoutledgeFalmer.

Vanderberghe, R. and Huberman, A. (eds) (1999) *Understanding and Preventing Teacher Burnout*, Cambridge: Cambridge University Press.

Wells, A.S., Lopez, A., Scott, J., and Holme, J.J. (1997) 'Charter schools as post modern paradox: Rethinking social stratification in the age of deregulated school choice', *Harvard Educational Review*, 69, 2: 172–219.

Wilkinson, R. and Marmot, M. (2003) *Social Determinants of Health: The Solid Facts*, Copenhagen: World Health Organisation. Online at www.euro.who.int/document/e81384.pdf (accessed 21 June 2007).

Williams, R. (1975) *The Long Revolution*, Westport: Greenwood.

Woods, P. and Bagley, P. (1996) 'Market elements in a public service: An analytical model for studying educational policy', *Journal of Education Policy*, 11, 6: 641–53.

Zembylas, M. (2005) *Teaching with Emotions: A Postmodern Enactment*, Greenwich: IAP.

Zorn, D. and Boler, M. (2007) 'Rethinking emotions and educational leadership', *International Journal of Leadership in Education*, 10, 2: 137–52.

9 My head and my heart

De-constructing the historical/hysterical binary that conceals and reveals emotion in educational leadership

Cheryl L. Bolton and Fenwick W. English

Thomas Jefferson, third President of the United States, author of the Declaration of Independence, voluminous letter writer, and collector of books from around the world, was one of the most rational men of his time. Yet even the intellectual and well-read Jefferson found himself at odds when he fell in love with a vivacious, beautiful married woman, Maria Cosway of England. At a traumatic parting in Paris, Jefferson penned to her one of the most famous love letters in the English language entitled, 'My head and my heart' (Brodie 1974: 483). In this dialogue written in 1786, the distraught Jefferson recalls their times together. Battling with his inflamed heart, Jefferson uses his head to remind his heart,

> Everything in this world is a matter of calculation. Advance then with caution, the balance in your hand. Put into one scale the pleasures which any object may offer; but put fairly into the other the pains which are to follow, and see which preponderates.
>
> (Brodie 1974: 488)

Jefferson's head advises his heart to 'not bite at the bait of pleasure till you know there is no hook beneath it' (Brodie 1974: 488). Working up to his theme for the moment, Jefferson's head warns his heart to 'retire within ourselves', and that such a stance reinforces the 'intellectual pleasure' (Brodie 1974: 488). Jefferson's heart roars back that his head's 'virtues of mathematical balance' is a kind of 'miserable arithmetic' unfit to equate the human intangibles. And in a telling bifurcation, the heart advises Jefferson's head that while it is appropriate for scientific matters, the heart is the one designated to determine gratitude, justice, love, and friendship (Brodie 1974: 489).

In a more up-to-date example of trying to balance logic, emotion, head, and heart matters, World Bank President Paul Wolfowitz found himself embattled after the Government Accountability Project, a Whistleblower group, provided information to the *Washington Post* that he had ordered a $61,000 pay rise for his girlfriend, a former World Bank Employee

(Hitt 2007: A1). Even as he had apparently tried to follow World Bank rules by requesting a recusal from salary and job decisions regarding his romantic liaison to Shaha Riza, a specialist in women's issues in the bank's Middle East department, his actions provided ammunition for those inside the institution who were opposed to his managerial style and change agenda to try and oust him from office (King *et al.* 2007: A5). It was claimed that Wolfowitz had violated the bank's Code of Conduct in offering Riza promotions and pay rises and that his relationship with her presented a conflict of interest. As a result of considerable pressure, Wolfowitz resigned from presidency of the World Bank on 17 May 2007 (bbc.co.uk/news 17 May 2007).

So the 'head and the heart' binary is more than a quaint bit of historical writing in a now famous love letter from Jefferson to Maria Cosway, but also represents a flashpoint in professional training still very relevant today as the Wolfowitz embroglio clearly demonstrates. The point is not that leaders experience emotion, but that in the preparation of leaders, the methods, models, exemplars, and training often leave them unprepared for emotional jolts when the total human being is confronted with a problem outside the boundaries of rational technical issues. And these are not solely confined to affairs of the heart.

Lumby and Coleman comment on the dominant approach in management by noting:

> Much normative leadership and management literature assumes a rational approach to assessing situations and in response taking logical actions for the benefit of the organisation and/or its clients. However, numerous writers have stressed that the platform of apparent conscious rationality floats on a sea of often unconscious irrationality.
>
> (2007: 31)

The wounded leader: the price of being unprepared

Ackerman and Maslin-Ostrowski studied educational leaders who had endured professional crises and found that many had suffered a variety of wounds. These hurts came about as leaders found themselves at odds with their personal predilections about decision-making situations and role expectations that required a different orientation. The distance between a person's actual identity and the strains on more fundamental values and needs created a wound. The requirement consists of controlling the definition of one's public self as one of the first challenges of leadership. Ackerman and Maslin-Ostrowski note:

> Beneath the surface tension, wounding is often felt at a deeper and more personal level, where a leader's decision, motives, and integrity are impugned by others. Such a response may be signaled by a critical event or a series of events in leadership practice; it need not have anything to do with the leader's genuine competence.
>
> (2002: xii)

A good example of a wounded educational leader is provided by former US Secretary of Education, Terrel H. Bell (1988). A long time devoted educator, Bell was appointed by President Ronald Reagan to do away with the newly formed US Department of Education. After changing his mind about the Reagan agenda, Bell found himself increasingly at odds with the administration's budget cuts to the Education Department, but required by loyalty to publicly defend them. His recollections are poignant and stark testimony to his personal wounding:

> In all of this [the 1984 Presidential election] I found my behavior spurious and my words tainted with a touch of phoniness regardless of my efforts to present an intellectually honest discussion of the issues. I realized that I had to support a Republican candidate, warts and all. This included speaking after a candidate's remarks had extolled the virtues of actions previously taken that were anathema to me, such as lashing funds for the poor, for student aid, and for health care for the aged.
>
> (Bell 1988: 57)

Commissioner Bell noted that when close political contests degenerated into name calling and 'verbal squalor' he felt 'the deepest revulsion' (1988: 157). Ackerman and Maslin-Ostrowski aver that wounding is not atypical but inevitable. In fact they proffer that, 'it seems virtually impossible to avoid wounding' (2002: 10). They quote a veteran school principal [headteacher] who said, 'The non-negotiable that I come back to most often is being true to myself – heeding the call of the heart, my core, for better or worse' (2002: 10).

Ackerman and Maslin-Ostrowski have developed their ideas around the experiences of school leaders, with their research highlighting the importance of emotional balance in preparing them and in portraying the nature of the work of school leadership in more realistic terms than is normally found in the literature. The concept of wounding can be applied to other areas of leadership within the education field.

Examples of wounding were evidenced in interviews with Further Education (post compulsory) lecturers and managers in the UK (Bolton 2007). All of the interviewees had some management responsibility within their department or teaching programmes but described themselves primarily as teachers, not as leaders. The interviews revealed that the lecturers had been deeply affected, not only by the unexpected demands of their roles which compromised what they viewed as being their primary purpose, namely teaching, but also in the way their role expectations differed from those of management. All expressed views that revealed evidence of tensions and compromises between their own expectations and beliefs and how they were expected to fulfil their roles:

> Teaching is being encroached upon more and more ... I seem to be spending more time out of rather than in the classroom ... I feel very uncomfortable about that.
>
> (Interview B 22 May 2007, Bolton 2007)

> [I feel] deflated. Absolutely deflated, because I feel like I'm not there to do my job because I think I'm there to teach and although I'm having the hours with them I can't give them the extra time they need ... because of paperwork.
>
> (Interview D 22 May 2007, Bolton 2007)

> Their (management) priority is to secure as much funding as possible.
>
> (Interview A 22 May 2007, Bolton 2007)

The issues raised were not simply overload stress, but arose from the very real dichotomy that was perceived between their own professional priorities and those held by management resulting in lecturers having to perform duties and act in ways contrary to their own identities and to adhere to decisions made outside of their locus of control regardless of their own ideologies. An issue repeated throughout several interviews was that of students being accepted into programmes for which they were not necessarily suited. The view was, 'we are setting them up to fail' (Interview D 22 May 2007, Bolton 2007), which was in direct contradiction to the lecturers' own intentions and beliefs of the purpose of education: 'My priority is the students. The manager's, although she wants to improve the students, is just figures' (Interview D 22 May 2007, Bolton 2007).

> We are targeted to death. We've got targets and we've got thresholds and audits and paper trails, and we are swamped by it and I think it is at the expense of teaching.
>
> (Interview B 22 May 2007, Bolton 2007)

The examples of wounding expressed were not those from a sudden event but, as Maslin-Ostrowski and Ackerman suggest, 'wounding, perhaps, is more a state that builds little by little than a big explosion' (1999: 227). Having to support actions taken by management and conform to institutional policies despite some being against their own fundamental beliefs had clearly wounded these lecturers. However, wounding need not be negative and it is what is done with the experience that is of significance – the wounding can provide an 'opportunity' (Maslin-Ostrowski and Ackerman 1999: 227) to question one's own actions and understandings.

Personal identity and the limits of rationality

It should be clear that practising leaders have to develop a sense of identity. Gardner indicates that identity is comprised of two parallel social processes:

the first occurs when a child begins to develop 'an increasingly complex and differentiated sense of self as an individual', the second when 'the child comes to feel an affinity to older individuals in particular, and to one or more social groups in general' (1995: 25).

Gardner also indicates that successful leaders tell stories in competition for potential followers. The kinds of stories leaders tell relate to 'stories about self, stories about the group, and stories about values and meaning' (1995: 50). Behind identity stories are the needs of most humans who 'crave an explicit statement of value – a perspective on what counts as being true, beautiful, and good' (1995: 55).

Medawar indicates that the questions behind such values are ultimate ones that exist in a realm that 'science cannot answer and that no conceivable advance of science would empower it to answer' (1984: 66). The meaning of this dilemma for leaders is that if the stories they are required to tell to become empowered by followers are not scientific questions that can be addressed by social science methods in preparation programmes, then in what context can it be said that they are prepared to lead if the world does not conform to the assumptions of such methods?

Figure 9.1 shows a schematic of rational choice theory (RCT) and within it the notion of the *rational actor* as a decision-maker (derived from Elster 1990).

In this schematic, *actions* are derived from beliefs and as such are couched in forms of *evidence* that have some correspondence to perceived reality. On the other hand, *desires* are recognised as more ephemeral and subjective, but in RCT they must be blocked by screens that filter out the purely whimsical ones. RCT and the idea of the rational actor are embedded normatively

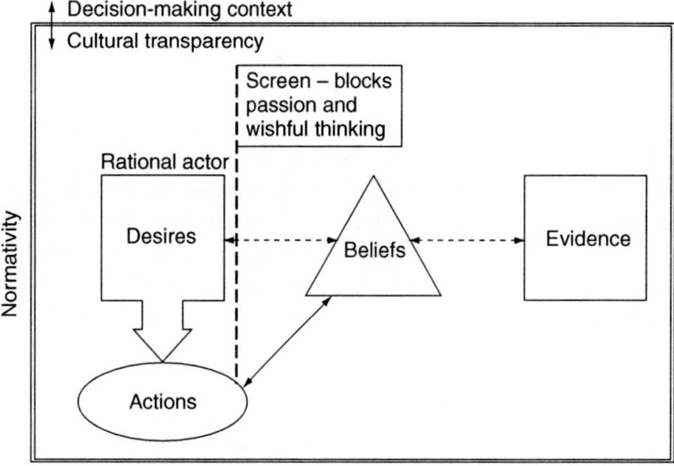

Figure 9.1 Notions of culture and context in Rational Actor (choice) Theory.

forming the basis of the decision-making context. What is not so apparent in this approach to decision-making is that the model and context are deeply embedded in a specific culture and, as Hall has trenchantly observed, 'the natural act of thinking is greatly modified by culture' (1977: 9).

Normative decision theory is centred on the assumption that an individual 'has the authority to make decisions independently of others' (Clough 1984: 23). In turn, a decision is thought to have two parts: an objective and a subjective aspect. The objective is believed to be framed in 'socially accepted standard measures of performance and value' (Clough 1984: 23). This is the normative aspect of engaging in *actions.* The subjective is also uniquely crafted to be rational as opposed to whimsical. Lacking direct social normativity in so personal a realm, the subjective part is hung on the idea of *personal utility*. This concept is believed to represent an individual's personal measure of value.

In the Westernised rational approach to decision-making, personal utility has come to be defined by Daniel Bernoulli's mathematics of probability created in 1738 (Clough 1984: 24), and later extended and expanded to include game theory created by von Neumann and Morgenstern (1944). Game theory is a model incorporating competitive economic behaviour, taught in business schools 'for the study of decision making in situations of conflict, coalition formation, and cooperation among players' (Clough 1984: 305). It is these conceptual hooks that undergird much of the theory taught in university courses in business and educational leadership representing rational choice theory (RCT) in its approach and content.

As such it represents a perspective regarding relationships that are centred on 'transactional cost theory, social exchange theory, and interaction theory' (Flambard-Ruaud 2008: 342). The problems with such theories 'lie in their static nature, when, in fact, relationship building is dynamic, and in the assumption of rational behavior by those involved in the process of negotiation and this too does not always apply' (Flambard-Ruaud 2008: 342). Here is how proponents of rational choice theory handle beliefs and desires, that is, human emotion:

> ... the action should be the best of satisfying the agent's desires, given his beliefs. Moreover, we must demand that these desires and beliefs be themselves rational. At the very least they should be internally consistent. With respect to beliefs we must also impose a more substantive requirement of rationality; they should be optimally related to the evidence available to the agent.
>
> (Elster 1990: 20)

What we see in the context of RCT in Figure 9.1 is that emotion is present in the form of desires, but to be persuasive it must assume properties that may be non-existent in the context in which a leader must perform. Consider, for the moment, the perspective proffered by Starratt that leadership involves drama and that it is a socially constructed, interactive enterprise structured by the culture in which it is exercised. Notes Starratt,

> Every situation is partly unique … hence each performance is guided by the culture which provides a kind of rough draft for action, but each actor has to compose his or her own response to the situation according to the particular and unique chemistry of the time, place and personalities involved.
>
> (1993: 121)

Even the concept of emotional intelligence (EI), introduced by Goleman (1995), is defined to conform to the requirements of RCT. Goleman indicates that EI has five components: self-management skills which include self-awareness, self-regulation, and motivation followed by empathy and social skill in order to manage social relations. Clearly in Goleman's framework emotion becomes very rational and is aimed at the bottom line of a fiduciary relationship centred on profit. Emotion is made to work for maximising a commercial relationship that becomes the centre of exchange.

In terms of rational leadership, then, notions of such things as emotion and culture are simply construed as additional elements meaning that consideration of emotion, for example, becomes a rational behaviour and therefore 'can be subsumed under the rational actor approach as it becomes rational to be irrational' (Rutgers 1999: 31).

Flambard-Ruaud (2008) contrasts this outlook of relationships with that in Asia, that is, the concept of *guanxi. Guanxi* traces its roots to the teachings of Confucius and has multiple interpretations of *wu-lun* or relationships. The first cultural meaning applies generically to relationships. The second pertains to the dictates of reciprocity. The third regards using one's authority to acquire political or pecuniary advantages which may be unethical because *guanxi* represents a way to bypass existing regulations. *Guanxi*'s cultural dimensions include trust and networking within long-established collaborative relationships. Whereas in the West a business relationship is characterised by impersonal involvement and exchange leading to commitment, in Asia, with *guanxi*, the commitment must come first before any other kind of relationship is possible (Flambard-Ruaud 2008: 344–7). Clearly, what is rational in Western culture is not so in many Eastern cultures.

This idiosyncratic portrayal of the context in which leaders work and engage others is hardly the stuff outlined in RCT, in the concept of strategic planning and management based on logic and argument instead of cultural idiosyncrasies peculiar to a specific time, place, and moment in history. Within rational choice theory emotion is acceptable as long as it is, well, *rational*, which seems counter-intuitive to the nature of emotion, especially within unique cultural contexts where culture is not considered dynamic or universal, but distinctively relative (see Paulston 1999).

Hall defines culture as 'the total communication framework: words, actions, postures, gestures, tones of voice, facial expressions, the way he handles time, space, and materials, and the way he works, plays, makes love, and defends himself' (1977: 42). Clearly, rational choice theory would be different within different cultures and be perceived rationally as different since culture is arbitrary and not created along the lines of rationality inherent in any culture's origination. Culture shapes humans in ways that become unconscious after a while, and people within any given culture come to see it as innate. As such, those in a specific culture are:

> Forced into the position of thinking and feeling that anyone whose behaviour is not predictable or is peculiar in any way is slightly out of his mind, improperly brought up, irresponsible, psychopathic, politically motivated to a point beyond all redemption, or just plain inferior.
>
> (Hall 1977: 43)

In a prescient article about doing business in China and India, Gupta and Wang remind business persons who want to take their companies there:

> Given this scale and variety [in geography and linguistic sociocultural diversity] one should abandon any notion of 'an average Chinese customer' or 'an average Indian customer'. In each country, even the middle of the income pyramid consists of more than 300 million people encompassing significant diversity in incomes, geographic climates, cultural habits, and even language and religious beliefs. But because of this diversity, market success in China and India is rarely possible without finely segmenting the local market in each country.
>
> (2007: B4)

Finally, and perhaps most vividly in the world today, the lack of understanding that has come to symbolise the West's failure to comprehend how culture represents what Bozeman has emphasised is the primacy of culture in 'the proper focal point of war research' (1976: 61) is a tragedy of enormous dimensions and consequences. The failure of the West, particularly the US, to fully grasp the lack of universality in its perspective and vision of politics and warfare, has led to failure and frustration, for as Shultz and Dew comment:

> In sum, soldiers and warriors are not the same. They come from different traditions, fight with different tactics, see the role of combat through different eyes, are driven by different motivations, and measure defeat and victory by different yardsticks.
>
> (2006: 6)

In addition, even outside the preparatory curricula of most educational leadership programmes and within or without different cultures, the binary of reason/emotion has strong implications in considering the nature of 'balance' within a leader, not the least which is a negative connotation which has consistently worked against women.

De-constructing the binary that has historically and hysterically discriminated against women

It is the premise of this chapter that the classical binary of head and heart is an ancient one in the human domain, closely aligned with the male/female binary that has portrayed women as emotional and the weaker of the sexes for hundreds of years. Highwater indicates that the ancient Greeks believed that 'women [were] the embodiment of untamed nature, and nature represent[ed] chaos and disorder. Men, on the other hand, embodi[ed] the values of enlightenment and order' (1990: 64). This view of women became a clear sub-text in Greek literature to the point where: 'it became so fundamental an element in our own Western consciousness that we usually read the works of Homer, Hesiod, Aeschylus, Sophocles, and Euripides without noticing that they brilliantly recount history as a vast slander against women' (1990: 64).

When it came to diagnosing medical ailments this chaotic binary mindset prevailed as well. For example, a peculiar malady most often associated with women was that of hysteria. Hysteria means 'womb' and traces its lineage to the religious festival of Aphrodite in Argos in ancient Greece. Renaissance physicians tried to explain women's uncontrollable emotional behaviour by calling it 'hysteria' because they believed the womb became detached from its location in the body and wandered about causing emotional outbursts (Walker 1983: 421).

Porter sheds further light on this aspect of uncontrollable emotion affiliated with women:

> By the eighteenth century, hysteria, which had earlier been judged a somatic malady of women – a disease of the womb – was typically deployed to identify the volatile physical symptoms associated with hypersensitivity, a liability thought especially common in 'the sex', but – significantly, in a culture in which enlightened politeness was blamed for making men 'effeminate' – not exclusively so. The diagnosis signaled superiority in status.
>
> (2003: 401–2)

Ross-Smith and Kornberger (2004) have noted that the linkage between rationality and masculinity continues to sustain gender inequalities, and Schein *et al.* (1996) has indicated that such stereotypes have existed across all ages and continents.

One of the most cherished texts on leadership ever written was penned by Machiavelli (1469–1527) entitled *The Prince.* In this text, he discusses how much *fortuna* (or chance) has played a role in human affairs, and how it may be opposed. First, Machiavelli characterises *fortuna* as female when he comments:

> I think it may be true that fortune is the ruler of half our actions, but that she allows the other half or thereabouts to be governed by us. I would compare her to an impetuous river that, when turbulent, inundates the plains, casts down trees and buildings, removes earth from this side and places it on the other ... and yet men can make provision against it by dykes and banks so that when it rises it will ... not be so wild and dangerous ... So it is with fortune, which shows her power where no measures have been taken to resist her.
>
> (1950: 91)

Then Machiavelli describes how to oppose fortune in a revealing metaphorical vignette:

> ... for fortune is a woman, and it is necessary, if you wish to master her, to conquer her by force; and it can be seen that she lets herself be overcome by the bold rather than by those who proceed coldly, and therefore, like a woman, she is always a friend to the young because they are less cautious, fiercer, and master her with greater audacity.
>
> (1950: 94)

This classic stereotypical metaphorical binary embedded in a pivotal canon in Western literature and politics has cast women into an inferior role because they are deemed emotional and adolescent. This stereotype was commonly held in Europe. For example, in Molière's satire *Les Femmes Savantes*, women were ridiculed for trying to think for themselves (Bodanis 2006: 298). We note with some amusement and sadness that where sex role stereotyping was not present, women often succeeded brilliantly even in these times of overt discrimination. For example, James M. Barry was one of the British army's most distinguished surgeon generals, once having performed a successful caesarean section in seven minutes without removing his full dress uniform. Barry directed that wounded soldiers be placed in disinfected quarters with clean mattresses and invented sterile field dressings. Hanlon recounts that of 462 casualties Barry treated on Corfu in 1857, only 17 died, a record number since the daily death rate at the time was 20 per day (2005: 71). Ironically, when James Barry died it was revealed that 'he' was Miranda Berry.

Whilst we would like to believe that these historical anecdotes are obsolete, there is evidence that gender stereotypes are still very much alive in the workplace (see Josefowitz 1985: 55). Studies by Schein *et al.* discovered that 'sex role stereotyping and "think manager – think male" is a global phenomenon' (Schein *et al.* 1996). In fact, a recent article in the *Wall Street Journal* reported on the Young Women's Leadership School of East Harlem where some 60 eleventh graders were being tutored by successful women in finance on how to brag about their accomplishments as men often do (Knight 2007: B38).

In the UK, an article in the *Guardian* reported that research amongst school children emphasised the difference in self-perception between girls and boys finding that 48 per cent of boys considered themselves to be leaders, but only 18 per cent of girls thought this of themselves. One conclusion was that girls would not consider themselves as 'leaders' for fear of being viewed as 'bossy' (Thomas 2005).

The stereotype is continued, not necessarily through blatant gender distinction, but in how it underlies much of the writing on leadership. Metcalfe and Altman argue that gender should be afforded special attention as leadership discourse is largely constructed from a male perspective (2001: 111).

Fondas (1997) explored aspects of the 'feminine ethos' in standard management texts where a number of these 'feminine' behaviours are emphasised. As an example,

> managers are also 'told' via these feminized cultural messages to focus on helping and developing others in order to demonstrate their responsiveness and sensitivity to people's needs and motivation ... this female culture of 'affiliation and collaboration' is in direct contrast to the male culture of 'competition and hierarchy'.
>
> (Fondas 1997 as cited in Wilson 2001: 117)

Höpfl and Matilial state that 'Notions of contemporary leadership extol the virtues of sensitivity, good communication, emotional management, a sense of community and so forth' (2007: 199). The theme is continued in studies of educational leadership. For example, in the UK, Gray's study of male and female headteachers produced a list of gendered descriptors of men and women that identified some terms as masculine. Their parallels with the norms of RCT are striking: *regulated*, *conformist*, *normative*, *competitive*, *evaluative*, *disciplined*, *objective*, *formal* (1993: 111). These terms are to be contrasted with feminine descriptors which were *caring*, *creative*, *intuitive*, *aware of individual differences*, *non-competitive*, *tolerant*, *subjective*, and *informal*.

It is significant that such so-called feminine traits are now seen as positive in a leader, and it might be assumed that this would perhaps allow more women into leadership. Rosener notes that whilst initially women succeeded in managing by imitating male behaviours that now 'they are succeeding because of – not in spite of – certain characteristics generally considered to be feminine and inappropriate for leadership' (1990).

However, Metcalfe and Altman pose the question as to whether women are placed in leadership positions as a result of their own merit or whether they are permitted to be there 'only because men perceive it as beneficial to patriarchal and organisational systems' (2001: 118). The paradox in this scenario is whether this recent trend towards promoting feminist qualities as important leadership behaviours will be of true benefit in elevating the status of women, or does it mean that men will simply adopt some of these qualities and so 'whereas men will be seen as adding new qualities to those they are already deemed to have, women will continue to be seen as only offering these qualities' (Wajcman 1996).

Education does present an interesting case as teaching has traditionally been viewed as a nurturing role characterised as a 'feminine' trait, representing a 'suitable' job for a woman being in a 'caring' profession and therefore could be presumed to encourage female leaders (Blount 1998: 18). Yet in the UK, government figures show that despite there being more female than male teaching staff, the majority of head teachers are male: 'The disparity is especially stark at secondary level, where women account for only 32 per cent of headships. In the largest secondary schools, around 85 per cent of heads are men' (Department for Education and Skills 2002 cited in NCSL www.ncsl.co.uk, 2004). Cubillo and Brown wonder whether the notion of feminine and masculine traits has adversely influenced women's progression into leadership positions in UK schools and why 'women in middle management roles in education are often assigned pastoral duties; that is, they are cast in the role of the senior mistress while the men are given responsibility for areas such as curriculum and finance' (2003: 279).

In the arena of international business, Daniel Cooper, an event manager for Quacquarelli Symonds, indicates that 'women can be stronger at nurturing and developing staff, and are perhaps less ego-driven than men' (*International Herald Tribune* 2007: 16). Tamara Primakoff, a human resource director for the French postal service has observed that women do have a different approach to management. She notes that women 'are inclined to allow more discussion to convince others and achieve unanimity whenever possible', but, she adds, 'We are still expected to be perfect. Men have the right to make mistakes, but we don't, whether for our peers or our staff. We also have difficulty understanding company codes and conventions that were created by men' (*International Herald Tribune* 2007: 16).

We believe that the emotional/rational binary has worked to the disadvantage of women seeking leadership positions because they have been historically saddled with the label of being 'too emotional' to be effective when leadership is about matters requiring cool calculation and the weighing of 'facts'.

> Women are perceived to lack order, logic, direction and rationality. Consequently, unless they can be converted to reason, in other words, to become homologues of men (Lyotard 1989: 114; Cohen 1989: 31–9), they are thought to lack the necessary leadership skills.
>
> (Höpfl and Matilial 2007: 199)

In education one hardly sees the cultivation or preparation of matters of the heart in curriculum. This is ironic because educational leaders have not only to deal with testing, management matters, and other forms of quantitative analyses, but also with matters concerning human promise, potential, moral growth, and development, issues not purely intellectual nor even rational in the sense that they can be supported factually. Rather, they represent choices, values, and, yes, emotions. By emotion we mean, 'a psychic and physical reaction subjectively experienced as strong feeling and physiologically involving changes that prepare the body for immediate vigorous action' (*Webster's Third New International Dictionary* 1971: 271)

The aesthetic properties of leadership

To more clearly differentiate how the head and heart binary must be altered to more accurately portray a more realistic and gender-neutral perspective in educational leadership, we have constructed Figure 9.2, entitled 'A Fulcrum of the Properties of Leadership'. Here we contrast the historical and gender-biased tenets of rational choice theory (RCT), in which emotions, intuition, and other so-called non-rational elements are filtered out of the locus of decision-making with the realm of educational decision-making centred more on moral as opposed to market issues. RCT, the dominant approach in business schools and most programmes preparing educational leaders, reinforces patriarchal systems of authority in organisational life (English and Bolton 2008). Because RCT is rooted in competitive economic theories and models of profit recognising and rewarding those characteristics typically associated with male exclusivity within most cultures, the attributes that culture usually connects to women are de-emphasised or eliminated because they are labelled non-rational or irrational. We believe this to be especially the case in education where culture, context, and performance are centred on moral dilemmas as opposed to obtaining market dominance, embedded in competitive economics and game theories, in a culture that rewards competition (winners and losers).

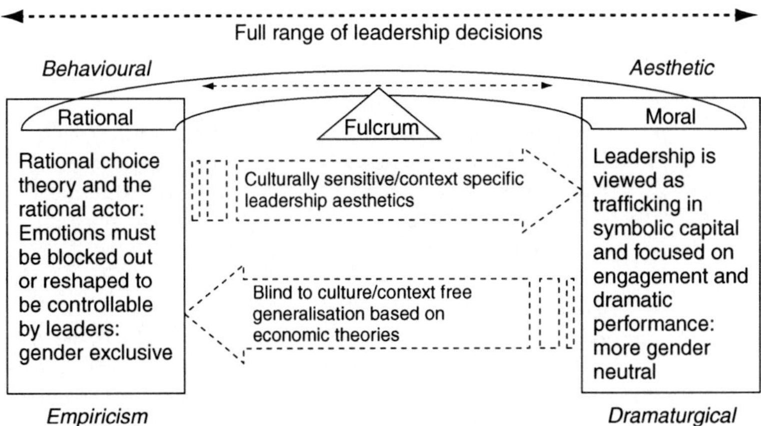

Figure 9.2 A fulcrum of the properties of leadership.

Duke has sketched out the aesthetic properties of leadership. He posits that when a leader points out a direction, a parallelism exists in literature where an author is foreshadowing a desirable end (1989: 353). Leaders traffic in forms of symbolic capital and educational leaders direct institutions that serve as a 'significant mechanism for the production and distribution of such an aesthetic in the larger society' (Bates 2006).

Duke indicates that the aesthetic properties of leadership include *direction*, *engagement*, *fit*, and *originality*. Table 9.1 below illustrates these dimensions compared to the dictates of RCT. This comparison shows clearly how these two views define leadership.

By *direction* is meant that a leader suggests a path along with a reason for travelling it. He notes that while great leaders may not control events, 'they are able to convey a sufficient sense of certainty about the course of events to ally paralytic anxieties and permit energies to be mobilized productively'

Table 9.1 A comparison of Duke's criteria for aesthetic properties of leadership to Rational Choice Theory (RCT)

Leadership dimensions identified by Duke	*Rational Choice Theory*	*Aesthetic properties identified by Duke*
Direction (vision)	Great certainty is required in order to predict market place forces which will result in maximising profits. Culture is generalised and sanitised to conform to measures of certainty	Foreshadowing of the future under conditions of inexact certainty; transformation of vision into reality which is culturally sensitive
Engagement	Emotions are only 'allowed' if they pass certain rational filters which are put into place to block irrational ones	Feelings, emotions, and aspirations are part of the effort to involve people in an enterprise. The full range of emotions is considered legitimate
Fit	The interaction with a leader is defined by market place/probability ratios rooted in the concept of personal utility, an economic as opposed to an emotional connection	A continuing interaction occurs between leaders and followers that is mutually reinforcing and culturally compatible
Originality	Aspects of originality are confined to dimensions which are static because cost theories require stability to maximise return on investment	The capacity of a leader to capture the imagination of the public by his/her actions or framing of the issues

(1989: 363). *Engagement* is a kind of old-fashioned involvement and Duke employs a theatrical metaphor when he says that, 'In a good dramatic production, the playwright and actors are able to involve the audience' (1989: 355). By the idea of fit, Duke is referring to the cultural connection between leaders and followers in 'which the actions of a leader, the actions of his followers, and the traditions of their culture are mutually reinforcing and correspondingly meaningful' (1989: 356). Finally, with *originality*, he is referring to the ability of a leader 'to capture the public's imagination' and he concedes that on this criterion social scientists may falter in trying to define leadership by searching for commonalities and similarities among leaders because, 'Leadership ... defies generalisability and predictability' (1989: 357).

The artistry of leadership, according to Duke, is comprised of dramatics and this term denotes *ritual*, *ceremony*, and *dramatic performance* (1989: 358). Part of *dramatic performance* is the establishment of a particular and distinctive *voice*. Artistry also involves *design*, as 'the transformation of vision into reality'; *orchestration*, bringing people together with diverse talents and abilities so that the sum is greater than parts with the total human effort.

For example, in a recent graduation speech in a medical school, the speaker admonishes fellow classmates to use their hearts in the practice of medicine because:

> Without your heart, you will not feel your patients' anguish and joy. Without your heart, you are replaceable. Let your heart guide you, consult it often in the care of your patients and of yourself ... use your wisdom. Wisdom for knowing when to use logic, when to use intuition, and when to use both.
>
> (Nguyen 2004: 185)

Clearly the speaker is arguing for a balance in the use of logic and evidence and for intuition. Both are critical for success as a medical doctor. We believe both are also necessary for success as an educator and a leader and that by expanding the context of leadership preparation to include the emotional dimensions within the idea of Duke's (1989) leadership aesthetics that: (1) cultural dissonances are less likely to come as a surprise when they are encountered; (2) market place formulas and cost predictive strategies will be tempered by a more realistic appraisal of the uncertainties involved in decision-making; (3) leaders will be more adequately prepared emotionally for the stresses and strains of the job and less likely to suffer 'wounding' as a result; and (4) the historic prejudices against women which are still present in both preparation programmes and the workplace are more likely to be seen as the myths which they are and which if continued work against organisational effectiveness (as defined under the aegis of an aesthetic umbrella).

While we reject the head and heart binary as inappropriate because of its long history of discrimination against women which continues into the present times (Highwater 1990), we believe that emotion must be reinserted into the locus of decision-making because it is part and parcel of humanity itself. And leaders who cannot deal with emotion are also open to being wounded. In summary, no one benefits from a tradition of extending the emotional binary that conceals and reveals a huge chunk of human existence and which places emotion in an inferior position in a decision-making locus.

Even more basic to this conversation between economic and emotionless theories of behaviour is the observation by political scientist Harvey Mann that science requires what the humanities include, that is, the Greek idea of *thumos* which refers to 'a part of the soul that wants to insist on our own importance' (Howard 2007). Mansfield says that literature trumps science because 'literature knows something that science does not: the human resistance to hearing the truth' (Howard 2007: A11). Mansfield acknowledged that, '*Thumos* is one basis for a human science aware of the body but not bound to it, a science with soul and taught by poetry well interpreted' (2007: A11).

We proffer that educational programmes must become infused with curricula that include a humanistic approach that extends knowledge and understanding derived from the arts, humanities, and literature. We note the work of Samier and Stanley (2007) in their explorations of literary representations of Canadian public administration. Samier and Stanley indicate that literature brings to administrative studies an understanding

> ... through the personal and experiential, the emotional, spiritual, and the visceral. Characterisation is more vivid and fully developed including the past history of childhood experience, social class, and early education. The inner world of the administrator is captured through implicit aspects of decision-making, psychology (including 'distorted' personalities like narcissists and sociopaths) and inner sources of behaviour, such as morale, fear, ennui, dependency, despair, powerlessness, isolation and hopelessness. On an organizational level, literary texts tend to emphasise the limits of bureaucracy, its internal contradictions, the dehumanizing effects of control, and the ways that resistance to bureaucracy are practiced, capturing positive forms as more than the product of rational design.
>
> (2007: 3)

Clearly, preparation curricula for educational leaders must reassert a balance of perspectives and traditions than is currently the case because, as Bennis has observed, 'Leaders have nothing but themselves to work with' (1989: 47). And the human self has a logic all of its own which must be treasured, nurtured, and recognised without the binaries that have proven so detrimental to both women and men in the contemporary challenges facing educational leadership today.

References

Ackerman, R. and Maslin-Ostrowski, P. (2002) *The Wounded Leader: How Real Leadership Emerges in Times of Crisis*, San Francisco: Jossey-Bass.

Bates, R.J. (2006) 'Towards an aesthetics for educational administration', in E.A. Samier and R.J. Bates (eds) *Aesthetic Dimensions of Educational Administration and Leadership*, London: Routledge.

Bell, T.H. (1988) *The Thirteenth Man: A Reagan Cabinet Memoir*, New York: Free Press.

Bennis, W. (1989) *On Becoming a Leader*, Cambridge: Perseus Books.

Blount, J. (1998) *Destined To Rule the Schools: Women and the Superintendency, 1873–1995*, Buffalo: SUNY Press.

Bodanis, D. (2006) *Passionate Minds*, New York: Crown.

Bolton, C. (2007) 'Roles and responsibilities of further education lecturers: Standards, aspirations and reality', paper presented at the British Educational Research Association Conference, London, September 2007.

Bozeman, A. (1976) 'War and the clash of ideas', *Orbis*, 20, 1: 61–102.

Brodie, F. (1974) *Thomas Jefferson: An Intimate History*, New York: W.W. Norton.

Clough, D.J. (1984) *Decisions in Public & Private Sectors: Theories, Practices & Processes*, Englewood Cliffs: Prentice-Hall.

Cohen, S.S. (1989) *Tender Power: A Revolutionary Approach to Work and Intimacy*, Reading: Addison-Wesley.

Cubillo, L. and Brown, M. (2003) 'Women into educational leadership and management: International differences?' *Journal of Educational Administration*, 41, 3: 278–91.

Duke, D.L. (1989) 'The aesthetics of leadership', in J.L. Burdin (ed.) *School Leadership: A Contemporary Reader*, Newbury Park: Sage.

Elster, J. (1990). 'When rationality fails', in K.S. Cook and M. Levi (eds) *The Limits of Rationality*, Chicago: University of Chicago Press.

English, F. and Bolton, C. (2008) 'When things of logic are not the logic of things: A second look at leadership preparation in the US and the UK', paper presented at the American Education Research Association Annual Meeting, New York, 2008.

Flambard-Ruaud, S. (2008) 'Relationship marketing in emerging economies: Some lessons for the future', in J.H. Munro (ed.) *Organizational Leadership*, Dubuque: McGraw-Hill.

Fondas, N. (1997) 'Feminization unveiled, management qualities in contemporary writings', *The Academy of Management Review*, 22, 1: 257–82.

Gardner, H. (1995) *Leading Minds: An Anatomy of Leadership*, New York: Basic Books.

Gray, H.L. (1993) 'Gender issues in management training', in J. Ozga (ed.) *Women in Educational Management*, Buckingham: Open University Press.

Goleman, D. (1995) *Emotional Intelligence*, New York: Bantam Books.

Gupta, A.K. and Wang, H. (2007) 'How to get China and India right', *The Wall Street Journal*, 28 April, R4.

Hall, E.T. (1977) *Beyond Culture*, New York: Anchor Books.

Hanlon, T. (2005) 'Only after death was it revealed that the British army's distinguished medical officer was a woman', *Military History*, 22, 4: 16, 70–1.

Highwater, J. (1990) *Myth and Sexuality*, New York: New American Library.

Hitt, G. (2007) 'Wolfowitz memo, dictating raises given to friend, now haunts him', *The Wall Street Journal*, 269, 87: A1–A5.

Höpfl, H. and Matilial, S. (2007) '"The lady vanishes": Some thoughts on women and leadership', *Journal of Organisational Change Management*, 20, 2.

Howard, J. (2007) 'In Jefferson lecture, Harvey Mansfield examines what humanities can teach science', *The Chronicle of Higher Education*, 53, 37: A11.

International Herald Tribune (2007) 'Do female managers have different priorities?' 15 May, 16.

Josefowitz, N. (1985) *Paths to Power: A Woman's Guide from First Job to Top Executive*, Reading: Addison-Wesley.

King, N., Hitt, G., and McCary, J. (2007) 'Wolfowitz stirs World Bank tensions', *The Wall Street Journal*, 269, 92: A5.

Knight, V.E. (2007) 'Teaching young women to brag', *The Wall Street Journal*, 9 May, B38.

Lumby, J. with Coleman, M. (2007) *Leadership and Diversity: Challenging Theory and Practice in Education*, London: Sage.

Maslin-Ostrowski, P. and Ackerman, R.H. (1999) 'On being wounded: Implications for school leaders', *Journal of Educational Administration*, 38, 3: 216–29.

Machiavelli, N. (1950) *The Prince*, trans. L. Ricci, New York: Modern Library.

Medawar, P. (1984) *The Limits of Science*, Oxford: Oxford University Press.

Metcalfe, B. and Altman, Y. (2001) 'Leadership', in E. Wilson (ed.) *Organizational Behaviour Reassessed*, London: Sage.

Nguyen, T. (2004) 'A graduation speech', in K. Takakuwa, N. Rubashkin, and K. Herzig (eds) *What I Learned in Medical School: Personal Stories of Young Doctors*, Berkeley: University of California Press.

Porter, R. (2003) *Flesh in the Age of Reason*, London: W.W. Norton.

Riley, N. (2007) 'Another school dropout', *The Wall Street Journal*, June 22, W13.

Rosener, J.B. (1990) 'Ways women lead', *Harvard Business Review*. Online at www.emerging leader.com (accessed 25 June 2007).

Ross-Smith, A. and Kornberger, M. (2004) 'Gendered rationality? A genealogical exploration of the philosophical and sociological conceptions of rationality, masculinity and organization', *Gender, Work and Organisation*, 40, 1: 16–48.

Rutgers, M. (1999) 'Be rational! But what does it mean?' *Journal of Management History*, 5, 1: 17–35.

Samier, E.A. and Stanley, A. (2007) 'Stone angels & paper airplanes: Literary representations of Canadian public administration', in A. Kubyshkin, R. Timko, and I. Sokov (eds) *Representations of Canada: Cross-Cultural Reflections on Canadian Society*, 4, Volgograd: Volgograd State University.

Schein, V., Mueller, R., Lituchy, T., and Liu, J. (1996) 'Think manager, think male: A global phenomenon', *Journal of Organisational Behaviour*, 17: 33–41.

Shultz, R.H. and Dew, A.J. (2006) *Insurgents, Terrorists, and Militias*, New York: Columbia University Press.

Stanford, J. H., Oates, B.R, and Flores, D. (1995) 'Women's leadership styles: A heuristic analysis', *Women in Management Review*, 10, 2: 9–16.

Starratt, R.J. (1993) *The Drama of Leadership*, London: The Falmer Press.

Thomas, K. (2005) 'Hidden barriers that stall women leaders', *The Guardian*. Online at www.guardian.co.uk/technology/2005/mar/31/businesssolutionsupplement1 (accessed 25 June 2007).

von Neumann, J. and Morgenstern, O. (1944) *The Theory of Games and Economic Behavior*, 2nd edn., Princeton: Princeton University Press.

Wajcman, J. (1996) 'Desperately seeking differences: Is management style gendered?' *British Journal of Industrial Relations*, 34, 3: 333–49.

Walker, B.G. (1983) *The Woman's Encyclopedia of Myths and Secrets*, San Francisco: HarperCollins.

Wilson, E. (2001) *Organizational Behaviour Reassessed: The Impact of Gender*, London: Sage.

Part III

Critical and contemporary issues

10 Accountability and the educational leader

Where does fear fit in?

Michèle Schmidt

Accountability is a seemingly pervasive issue in education affecting almost every aspect of education in the Western world. A myriad of accountability definitions exist in the various professional literatures of different disciplines; however, a widely accepted definition within education seems to remain narrow and bound up with large-scale assessment frameworks that focus primarily, if not uniquely, on testing (Earl and Torrance 2000). This focus has promoted intense scrutiny into the routines of schools, as well as teachers, students, and administrators, riveting our attention to an accountability context that seems to be defined primarily by test scores, raising student achievement ratings, and school rankings that ultimately tend to lead us to either rewards or sanctions, leaving in its aftermath school leaders who experience a wide range of emotional vicissitudes from satisfaction, pride, exhilaration, and debilitating anxiety, shame, blame, and guilt – emotions often exacerbated by fear. Neither novice nor veteran leaders are immune from being publicly identified and/or alternatively humiliated or extolled with the discerning epithet of 'poor performing' or a 'high performing' school as the media, parents, and the community increasingly reify the power of test data into a valid criterion of judgement. Such public announcements leave school leaders the unexpected victims or heroes of an accountability system they had little say in constructing, and within which emotional involvement is often one of the most difficult aspects with which to deal.

This chapter will attempt to theorise the notion of fear and determine its place within an era of a new accountability made up primarily of high-stakes testing. While no one theory of fear exists, its utility remains controversial. This chapter draws on psychological theorists such as Izard, Plutchik, and Rachman; and sociological theorists like Denzin, Hochschild, Hargreaves, and Woods who discuss the sociological, political, and organisational factors that mitigate or accentuate educational leaders' feelings of fear within a context of accountability.

Accountability

Apparently, the most widely known legislation in North America to date is quite possibly the US federal Act entitled, No Child Left Behind (NCLB), the foundation of which seems to be grounded in an accountability system constructed around high-stakes exit exams, a system that is largely premised on evaluating educational progress defined by student success, with rewards or sanctions driving those efforts (Stecher and Kirby 2004).

If we were to focus on this aspect of accountability alone, that is, testing, and compare its usefulness across continents, we would see that reliance on it varies from country to country. But what seems to remain constant is the rhetoric of accountability often depicted as a panacea for improving the quality of schools in general, and, in particular, raising student achievement levels (Schmidt 2008). In a post-Sputnik era, the US has attempted to take the lead in the achievement race with its implementation of mandatory testing. While it is beyond the scope of this chapter to discuss the history of standardised testing in the US, suffice it to say that some scholars believe that 'at the heart of the current vision of schooling is a corporatised model of education that vitiates the democratic impulses and practices of civil society by either devaluing or assimilating them within the logic of market demands' (Giroux and Schmidt 2004: 214). What results is a culture of punishment and fear within our schools, as standardised tests result in either a takeover or closure of schools, probationary status for teachers, loss of funding/accreditation, and dissolution or reconstitution of faculty and administrations.

Unlike other countries that have pulled back somewhat from this approach (e.g. Wales, England, New Zealand, Australia), external standardised testing efforts continue to dominate evaluation policy in the US. This is so despite much criticism from researchers in the field of education (e.g. Berliner and Biddle 1995), and with only moderate evidence of positive policy change. By and large, the new millennium highlights federal accountability legislation under the No Child Left Behind Act that mandates states to administer assessments for grades three through eight; exit exams as part of the diploma requirement; establish sanctions for schools with low passing rates; and grant rewards for those with improved performance results (Peterson 2005; Schmidt *et al.* 2008).

Arguments against testing are numerous, including: evidence that it causes students to dropout; the question of purpose as tests become increasingly simplified to ensure that all students succeed; it does not always align with school curricula; it decreases an emphasis on higher-level skills; it results in less time for curricula beyond exams; and it encourages teachers to teach to the test (Stiggins 1991). Critics also note the difficulty of incorporating the diversity of instructional programmes and skills taught across districts in one test and the problem of conducting reliability and validity tests on the exams (Miller 1992). The high-stakes nature of testing also leads to teachers cheating on tests to increase students' scores and retention rates in the first year of high school (Roderick *et al.* 2002). Finally, there is a disturbing trend indicating that low-income, minority, and immigrant students fail at higher rates than white and Asian students, widening the gap between middle-income and low-income minority students, and intimidating students, causing negative attitudes, alienation, anxiety, apprehension, disengagement from school, and stress, thus reducing students' performance, especially among low-income, disabled, black and Latino students (Roderick *et al.* 2002). Many of these students attach little value to educational achievement because they believe they cannot meet state standards resulting in students being absent on testing day or apathetic in their test-taking efforts (Roderick and Engel 2001). Even when students have several opportunities to take the exit exam, they often became discouraged and drop out (Jacobs 2001).

Alternatively, advocates seem to have equally compelling claims supporting high-stakes testing. The benefits, according to some, expose the achievement gap between low-income, minority students, and other students providing the impetus for remedial and tutorial assistance to meet the test requirements, extra resources, and opportunities to re-take the test (Peterson 2005). Additionally, when student course-taking patterns indicate poor performances on standardised tests, a basic curricular focus on the tests may benefit students, particularly those who are low-achieving, indicating that greater instructional time is associated with greater achievement (Berliner 1992; Roderick *et al.* 2002). In fact, schools with a high concentration of at-risk students may be motivated to mobilise an entire community to institute changes in curriculum, pedagogy, or school organisation (Roderick *et al.* 2002; Schmidt *et al.* 2008). Advocates maintain that testing provides the impetus for training teachers and administrators in the use of data for the development of curriculum and instruction guides that align with the test, promote discussion about student performance and cooperation among teachers, and encourage teachers to teach curriculum that aligns with the test (Miller 1992). In short, supporters claim that testing provides incentives to improve student performance, increases the value of a high school diploma, motivates students, teachers, and school administrators to work harder, serves as a good measure of the curricula, and identifies areas for improvement based on test reports (Wiggins 1989a).

Nevertheless, the topic of testing remains controversial. With the debate still raging, one might ask, what emotional costs are attached to these tests and whom do they affect? We have learned about some of the emotional consequences thus far that relate to student anxiety and apprehension, particularly among low-income, minority students, that often lead to devastating results. Equally disturbing is that in an accountability era defined primarily by test scores, a focus on raising student achievement and school rankings that lead to either rewards or sanctions leaves school leaders and teachers to experience a range of emotions – often delimited or defined by fear.

According to Giroux and Schmidt, 'testing has become the code word for training educational leaders in the language of management, measurement and efficiency' (2004: 220) where accountability often translates into, *I need to know whom I should blame when things go wrong.* Houston (2007) reports on the seven deadly sins of NCLB, where accountability relies on fear, coercion, and blame. He notes that current high-stakes accountability agendas motivate leaders, teachers, children, and parents through fear of sanctions and the use of force, threats, and punishments, all of which block the pursuit of excellence for leaders and teachers, impede clear thinking for children, and place parents in situations where they feel they must compare their children to others or worry whether their children will achieve post-secondary schooling.

Giroux and Schmidt (2004) argue that without confronting and analysing how particular forms of authority are secured and legitimised, and without efforts to determine how, what, and whose values construct this authority, accountability systems are in danger of remaining punitive, regulatory, and controlling. Ultimately, these values will shape the definition of leadership at the expense of leaders' emotions as they are subverted from social justice goals of promoting democracy, critical citizenship, and basic human rights. Instead, leaders find themselves working within organisations promoting market values that encourage a competitive ethic among schools and individuals in pursuit of rewards. When unpacking the implications of the shifting educational landscape for school leaders in this chapter, I ask the following question: At what emotional costs must leaders continue if they are expected to keep pace with an ideological discourse that Burbules and Torres (2000) maintain creates an urgency, real or perceived, that is driving change within society?

Where does fear fit in?

Where, then, one might ask, does fear fit into the leadership paradigm for educators working within such an oppressive organisational climate? Research is almost unanimous in finding that the principal's role is the key factor contributing to successful schools, policy implementation, learning, and achievement (Day and Schmidt 2007; Fullan 2004; Hargreaves and Fink 2006; Leithwood and Jantzi 1999), yet the seemingly inevitable progression of global and market changes that have led to increasing demands for accountability in school systems are shifting the educational perspective. More importantly, these global forces are defining, changing, and diminishing the significance of the principal's role. Complicating these issues further, many countries, in particular the US, face the prospect of confronting declining numbers of principals and difficulties with retention and succession (Cowan 2004).

If we dig deeper into the currency a leader really has within the current accountability era, the situation looks bleak. Although teachers are equipped with academic credentials and leadership qualities, only a small percentage of teachers apply for leadership positions (Cowan 2004). Blackman and Fenwick (2000) report that it is not education entirely that becomes a limiting factor in the principal shortage and problems with succession. Rather, conflicting ideologies and emotions make the administrator's role much more precarious, arduous, intellectually abstruse, and challenging to their ability to prioritise responsibilities and their willingness to take on these positions. Scholars note that leaders are working within a role that is becoming increasingly conflicted, complex, and complicated, resulting in role anxiety, emotional stress, and professional burnout (Gronn 2003; Fineman 1993). Principals are increasingly frustrated because they are being forced to manage the marketplace demands, curriculum change, and governance factors as a result of an increased emphasis on accountability. Leaders are carrying the burden of emotional labour in greedy organisations that demand a seemingly excessive commitment from individuals in an effort to reduce the costs of production (Fineman 1993; Hochschild 1979). These conditions typically lead to burnout and early retirement (Fullan 2004; Gronn 2003; Hargreaves 2003).

Bates (1995) highlights not only the structural, relational, resource-based tensions faced by leaders that are a direct result of what he calls fast capitalism being mediated into schools, but also the undemocratic, anti-social, and inequitable means by which traditional schooling is being subverted, particularly with reference to cultural, social, civic, and aesthetic practices. Grace (1995) stresses that schools are increasingly mired in contradictory possibilities, instilling both confidence and doubt in school leaders. According to some critics, neo-liberal agendas have resulted in teachers and administrators becoming deskilled and driven by accountability, surveillance, and measures of performance leading to a counterculture of fear and lower levels of trust in the educational system (Giroux 2000). When leadership is characterised by conflict, change, and ambiguity, intense emotional reactions are often the result. While leaders' varying responses to reform policies in general are due to the usual subjective nuances of human interpretation, other factors of uncertainty or instability due to a pervading culture of fear and punishment in an era of high-stakes accountability often lead to debilitating emotions (Schmidt 2000). When taken in their entirety, the impact of high-stakes accountability highlights key obstructions to the work ethic of education leaders – one of these being emotional pressures, and, more specifically, fear.

Fear

As is evident in this book, there are numerous theories about emotions. This chapter makes note of two main perspectives, that is, psychological and sociological. A psychological perspective of emotions provides one of the most influential classification approaches to analysing emotions. Such classifications include fear as a primary emotion among seven others: anger, sadness, disgust, surprise, curiosity, acceptance, and joy (Plutchik 1980). When viewed from this perspective, fear as a biological emotion is typically used to increase reproduction and triggers behaviour with high survival value (for example, fear brings about a fight-or-flight response). In other words, fear describes feelings about real or perceived danger or threats (Rachman 1990). Behaviourists such as Watson (1924) suggest that fear is an innate trait, such that it literally becomes a survival mechanism, usually occurring in response to a specific negative stimulus. Typical behavioural reactions caused by fear include intimidation resulting from individuals complying with another's wish or leading to violence, an instinctive reaction of fear rather than a consciously thought-out action (Rachman 1990). When kept under control, fear is a powerful motivator for succeeding in our endeavours, treating others civilly, keeping us healthy and out of harm's way, primarily because we fear the consequences. It might be argued that individuals require a healthy sense of fear to survive. More commonly, however, fear has a pejorative result, having a powerful debilitating effect on our lives, particularly when uncontrolled, influencing our ability to cope with stress and real or perceived danger. Fear plays havoc with our self-esteem, prevents us from thinking clearly, feeling hopeful, falling in love, and resolving problems, often paralyses other emotions, as well as leading to anxiety, panic, and debilitating phobia (Rachman 1990).

There seems to be some consensus that fear as a construct is difficult to describe scientifically due to the subjective nature of its aetiology, as illustrated by the wide range of individual responses to threatening situations. According to Rachman (1990), three salient mutually exclusive extant components of fear exist: 1) a subjective experience of apprehension; 2) associated internal psycho-physiological changes; and 3) attempts to avoid or escape from fearful situations. He posits that an individual's ability to control a fearful situation influences the experience of fear. Furthermore, the ability to cope with fear varies with age and experience. In addition, while it is a primary emotion, it is difficult at times to isolate it as the sole, operating emotion. In other words, it is related to an entire emotional complex containing such other components as worry, anxiety, terror, fright, paranoia, horror, panic, and dread (Plutchik 1980). Typical causes of fear can surpass the simple, innate response to stimuli, to include the theory that fear is a learned emotion. Mowrer (1939) calls this fear conditioning. Bandura (1977) maintains that fear can be acquired vicariously, that is, by observing it in others. Goleman (1995) stresses that emotions are highly contagious. Not surprising, while it is most commonly associated with physical conditions or objects, fear can also be inspired by mere abstract phenomena (e.g. losing control, fear of ridicule or of losing social status). While conditioning can cause fear, it can also reduce or extinguish fear through systematic desensitisation or through modelling another individual's behaviour (Bandura 1977; Mowrer 1939).

Alternatively, when discussing fear as a social construct, we know that emotions are comprised of more than just behavioural reactions, since they are also shaped by the contexts in which individuals work (White 1993). Here we begin to see emotions, specifically fear, resulting from contextual, political, and relational phenomena (Hargreaves 1998). In an era of testing and accountability, profound emotions are often a result of purposes that cannot be achieved (because they are unrealisable, unclear, mutually exclusive, or are purposes that belong to someone else's agenda); feelings of power or powerlessness; and relationships that lack trust, all of which may result in anxiety, guilt, frustration or fear (Oatley and Jenkins 1996). Haviland and Kahlbaugh note that 'people ... experience frustration, anger and despair as a result of their failure to achieve their goals which are unrealistic' (1993: 315). James (1990) states that changes in self-esteem are determined not by accomplishment, but rather by the discrepancy between accomplishment and aspiration leading to anxiety and frustration. These problems, when applied to leaders in an era of high-stakes accountability, become especially visible and compounded as they are faced with increasingly politicised roles.

Studies of effective leadership in the early 1980s (e.g. Blumberg and Greenfield 1980) indicate that the quality of a principal's leadership is dependent upon, or is a function of, the amount of responsibility, authority, and constraints to authority. Furthermore, quality leadership is shaped by the factors that create the constraints and boundaries of that role. Indeed, it seems that federal, state, district, and public sector groups have influenced educational governance, affecting the degree of flexibility a principal may have in making decisions about the quality of education (Ueda 1985). Leaders, then, may experience negative emotions due to their experiences with power and politics inside and outside the schoolhouse. Finally, leaders often experience negative emotions and concomitant feelings of loneliness when there is an absence of emotional, or even empathic, understanding (Denzin 1984). Woods suggests that often 'the only relief for some ... [i]s to aim for a measure of role distance, where the individual denies not the role but the virtual self that is implied in the role for all accepting performers' (1983: 110). Like Goffman's notion of managing a role (1959), 'action may on occasions be simply a going through the motions not as a routine but as bitter necessity, and on such occasions [an individual] may detach and reserve his preferred "self" for better times' (Woods 1983: 110). Worse, when leaders feel that they either lack skill or competence, they might dismiss any possibility of supporting, guiding, or reinforcing others out of the fear that comes with uncertainty (Schmidt 2000). Furthermore, 'when conflict cannot be resolved ... individuals will ... abandon both goals and means and withdraw from the situation' (Calvert 1975: 122). While conflict need not always be stressful (it may even be stimulating), conflict in many cases becomes an emotional burden. Hargreaves and Fullan maintain that 'leading is a lonely profession' (1996: 5) particularly when a leader's decisions are constantly under scrutiny. In these situations, interactions between teachers and leaders become strained. As a result, trust and respect for leaders become diminished (Schmidt 2000).

When related to accountability and leadership, emotions in general are often defined by leaders' abilities to achieve (or not) accountability purposes, their experiences of power and powerlessness within an accountability era, and by their relationships with others as they administer accountability mandates within their schools and within the confines of state and district relationships. When examining leaders' day-to-day interactions with accountability issues, we might posit that, while these three contextual foci are profound catalysts impacting emotions, they are often embedded within a culture of fear.

Culture of fear

A number of interpretations define a culture of fear that are historically grounded and beyond the scope of this chapter. More recently, however, there has been much debate around the implications of a culture of fear that has been consciously directed in which it refers to a perceived prevalence of anxiety in public discourse and relationships. Cultures of fear, therefore, are often a result of constructed fear – a phenomenon in which it is consciously manufactured by a deliberate policy or conspiracy, influencing the way people interact with one another as individuals and as democratic agents (Glassner 1999). Many have written about or portrayed this phenomenon in films and documentaries, including linguist Noam Chomsky, sociologist Barry Glassner, political film makers Michael Moore and Adam Curtis, politician Al Gore, educators David Berliner and Henry Giroux, and lawyer Jeffrey Rosen. While presenting their arguments in different ways, what they seem to agree upon is that a culture of fear is driven by motives for deliberate programming of fear, and is intended, by those in power, to inculcate social control onto a terrorised population. In such situations, fears are carefully and repeatedly created through the manipulation of words, facts, news, sources, or data, in order to induce certain behaviours, to justify governmental actions or policies, to keep people consuming, to elect politicians, or to distract the public's attention from allegedly more urgent social issues. The aforementioned authors and film makers speak of techniques that lead to constructed fear, which includes careful omission of news items, distortion of statistics and numbers, substituting generalisations for complex situations, causal inversion, and fabrication of events or claims. The result is that fear becomes an inhibitor, having a devastating effect on individual functioning. Izard describes it as 'the most toxic of all emotions' (1977: 355) influencing social interactions, reducing the brain's capacity to store and process information, and limiting problem-solving ability and learning. In addition, interpreting others' behaviour can be less positive due to fear. Glassner (1999) suggests that the culture of fear in the US, in particular, shows no sign of abating and holds individuals captive, since it is rooted in deep cultural anxieties. Gore states in his book, *Assault on Reason* (2007), that fear is the most powerful enemy of reason. Both fear and reason are essential to human survival, but the relationship between them is unbalanced. Reason may sometimes dissipate fear, but fear frequently vitiates reason. Michael Moore, in his film, *Fahrenheit 911*, explores the origin of fear by suggesting that corporations are manipulating society's fears in order to sell products. Barry Glassner, in *Culture of Fear* (1999), blames the media. Adam Curtis, in his BBC film, *The Power of Nightmares* (2004), places blame on politicians' need to restore power and authority by manipulating social anxiety among the masses. Jeffrey Rosen, in *The Naked Crowd* (2005), addresses it almost entirely from the perspective of the crowd by highlighting our fear of intrusive surveillance. He reveals society's acceptance of security measures and uses Giddens' (2000) notion of risk culture in a society with a heightened preoccupation with risk. Typical of a postmodern society in which individuals must learn to live with increasing uncertainty and complexity, much energy goes into worrying about the future and the potential risk involved in any type of decision or action.

Leadership within a culture of fear

The impact of high-stakes accountability on educational leaders remains understudied, particularly within the affective realm of such a phenomenon. Evidence is emerging, however, showing us that fear in the system is pervasive as public schooling is increasingly being reduced to a fear-driven exercise (McGhee and Nelson 2005). It seems that what might have been a well-intended culture of educational accountability aimed at improving schools has resulted, instead, in a system of unintentional consequences, driven by a culture of fear. In the past, school leaders' performances were assessed using a variety of indicators that reflected the complexity of the job; now their effectiveness is determined in much narrower terms based primarily on how well their schools perform on standardised tests (McGhee and Nelson 2005). Ironically, principals most affected by such a narrow performance assessment are those who serve large numbers of students of impoverished and minority status, those who receive significantly smaller per-pupil expenditure than the district average, and those who work in schools that often employ a higher percentage of novice teachers (McGhee and Nelson 2005). Alarming evidence shows high rates of principal removals from schools as a result of student test scores that are often preliminary and inaccurate (McGhee and Nelson 2005). Such sanctions leave principals feeling demoralised, isolated, humiliated, and damaged, highlighting a disturbing reality that high-stakes accountability systems can have debilitating negative effects on school leaders, particularly when test scores trump other successes principals may be having in their schools. Worse still, such sanctions often occur with no warning. It is no wonder, then, that there exists a principal shortage, with poor succession rates and fear accompanying the principal role. McGhee and Nelson (2005) imply that high-stakes accountability has the potential to poison the culture of public education.

Further to this point, studies indicate that stress on the job ranks as one of the primary inhibitors for educators seeking or maintaining school administrator positions (Cushing *et al.* 2003). Stress comes from many arenas including public criticism, high accountability demands, and high levels of responsibility while authority and flexibility are simultaneously reduced via union contracts and fiscal and legal requirements. Not to be ignored, job stress manifests itself in many ways, but most obviously by causing health issues such as high blood pressure and weight gain as well as psychological symptoms of depression and anxiety disorders (Cushing *et al.* 2003).

When examining more closely the aspects of leadership that seem to generate the most fear and anxiety, researchers (e.g. Schmoker 1999) are finding that data use by principals tops the list since test data provide evidence of weakness in schools and the need for change. While it is often difficult to disentangle what causes more fear, the use of data or change, cumulatively, the results of both instill anxiety for both principals and teachers since change threatens extant routines and practices, and data can result in the termination of jobs and school closures. In these situations, principals often have to placate their faculty's anxieties and fears around the use of data despite their own anxiety over the lack of training when faced with gathering, organising, maintaining, and understanding data. Lortie (1975) concluded in his studies of teachers' work that they lack confidence in their own ability to raise student performance and, instead, rely heavily on the pressure and support of their administrators. Creighton (2001) believes that educators often fear statistical analysis since they have generally not been exposed to courses in statistical methods. Compounding these difficulties is the manner in which schools receive data. According to Holcomb (1999), schools either receive too little or too much data or data reports are complicated, unwieldy, and not user friendly by the time principals receive them, exacerbating the fear and anxiety surrounding data use.

If we delve further into some of the challenges leaders face in an era of accountability that might invoke anxiety, stress, and fear, the situation looks rather bleak. The leadership landscape is changing with the changing expectations for the position, the movement to define new standards for candidates, the complex balance between leadership and management skills, a nationwide focus on school-wide improvement efforts, long hours, high stress, and an imbalance between authority given and the level of accountability expected (Ferrandino and Tirozzi 2000). Further to this, Ferrandino and Tirozzi (2000) state that, overall, principals feel overwhelmed and anxious about not having enough time to develop high-achieving schools when having to 'sell their school' to the public and parents. When taken in their entirety, the impact of accountability and its resultant marketisation highlight key obstructions to the work of education leaders. Indeed, an era of accountability has produced anxieties and a looming crisis of motivation where 'the character becomes corroded, trust is withheld, and commitment is difficult to sustain' (Sennett 1998: 31). Scase (1999) predicts that employee attitudes to work will become more short term, instrumental, and cynical. When individuals do not feel trusted or valued, insecurity results. Within such cultures of compliance that leaders and their school seem to exist in, emotions can either be 'deadly' (filled with fear, anger, apathy, envy, greed) or 'dynamic' (filled with obsession, passion, delight, love, desire, trust).

Managing fear

Bottery (2006) suggests that educational leaders must now frame their work differently than in the past in order to harness prevailing negative emotions, and more specifically, fear. An understanding of fundamental global, market, and accountability issues is needed to comprehend their impact on policy issues, educational issues, and the methods in which they begin to reconceptualise the roles and responsibilities of leaders. In essence, the increasing economic imperatives confronting our schools need to be translated into a moral discourse that takes into consideration notions of equity, justice, and community (Bottery 2006). For example, as ecological leaders, these discussions must become an objective for the entire school community since they influence organisations, pedagogy, and student instruction (Bottery 2006). Along with this is the requirement for leaders to recognise the necessity for research-based decision-making and the promotion of teacher and action research in schools, enabling teachers to contextualise issues of importance in their own schools, all of which should shape professional development agendas. By building the knowledge capacity among their own ranks, leaders are enabling their organisations to critically examine and argue pervading and often unreasonable accountability agendas that have become the foundation of a culture of fear (Bottery 2006).

Within a context of accountability, while low levels of trust pervade the US and other Western countries, what is needed is more emphasis on celebrating aspects of student learning not captured in external, quantitative forms of accountability (Hargreaves 2003). Leaders need to work toward developing reflexive forms of accountability that involve teachers, students, and parents (Earl 1995). This requires them to understand the meanings and forms of assessment and thereby develop alternative forms for school use (Stiggins 1991). In order to manage the knowledge economy and promote its mobilisation, leaders must not only understand and promote sophisticated forms of accountability, but they also need to do so creatively by fostering teamwork and distributing leadership. What our current times seem to demand are transformational leaders despite the irony of role innovation juxtaposed with socialisation processes of leadership that reward conformity, stability, and complacency rather than innovation and creativity (Bottery 2006). Cline and Necochea (2000) argue for strong, courageous, creative, innovative, even maverick, leaders who are able to seek out innovative teachers, diplomatically validate the status quo while implementing innovative education, are comfortable with micro-politics and mediating provincial expectations, can set aside external mandates that are not reasonable for their school context, and even break rules. This requires leaders who are able to create an atmosphere that is conducive to change, mobilise a school community towards a visionary goal, and nurture an environment that fosters dedication, commitment, creativity, and risk-taking, and who are assessment, media, and technologically literate (Akerlund 1988; Sergiovanni 1994). Leithwood and Jantzi (1999) suggest that the role definition should not be so specific as to impede them from using their own principled discretion. Hargreaves and Fink (2006) argue that the leaders of tomorrow must focus on sustainability. Particularly, in an era of quick fixes, what is needed most are long-term values, leaving enough latitude for leaders to put their own personal stamp on the work they do in schools.

While the above may read like an insurmountable and impossible list of leadership characteristics, what seems to be needed is a new form of moral courage in order to over-ride a nascent culture of fear that pervades schools of today. Aristotle (1962) believed that an individual develops courage by doing courageous acts. Indeed, there is current support for the suggestion that courage is a moral habit that is developed through practice (Cavanagh and Moberg 1999). This view is similar to Bandura's (1977) concept of self-efficacy, where successful actions lead to further success. Individuals are more likely to overcome obstacles and cope, manage, or resolve them if they have had prior success in meeting similar challenges. Yet it is almost certainly a fallacy to believe that our leaders alone can, or should, solve problems related to our current societal turbulence without the collaboration of society as a whole. More than ever before, communities, organisations, government, and special interest groups must cooperate to instill democratic and moral values, and inculcate civic engagement in our youth, and, in this way, promote a dynamic of accountability that is sustainable and morally just.

References

Akerlund, P.M. (1988) 'The socialization of first-year principals and vice principals', unpublished thesis, Seattle University.

Aristotle (1962) *Nicomachean Ethics*, trans. M. Oswald, Indianapolis: Bobbs-Merrill.

Bandura, A. (1977) *Social Learning Theory*, New York: Prentice Hall.

Bates, R. (1995) 'A socially critical perspective on educational leadership', paper presented at Flinders University Conference on Educational Leadership, South Australia, 1995.

Berliner, D. (1992) *Educational Reform in an Era of Disinformation*, Washington, DC: American Association of Colleges of Teacher Education.

Berliner, D.C. and Biddle, B.J. (1995) *The Manufactured Crisis: Myths, Fraud and the Attack on America's Public Schools*, Reading: Addison-Wesley.

Blackman, M.C. and Fenwick, L.T. (2000) 'The principalship', *Education Week*, 19, 29: 46–68.

Blumberg, A. and Greenfield, W. (1980) *The Effective Principal: Perspectives on School Leadership*, Boston: Allyn & Bacon.

Bottery, M. (2006) 'Educational leaders in a globalizing world: A new set of priorities?' *School Leadership & Management*, 26, 1: 5–22.

Burbules, N.C. and Torres, C. (2000) 'Globalization and education: An introduction', in N. Burbules and C. Torres (eds) *Globalization and education: Critical perspectives*, London: Routledge.

Calvert, B. (1975) *The Role of the Pupil*, London: Routledge.

Cavanagh, G.F. and Moberg, D.J. (1999) 'The virtue of courage within the organization', *Research in Ethical Issues in Organizations*, 1: 1–25.

Cline, Z. and Necochea, J. (2000) 'Socialization paradox: A challenge for educational leaders', *International Journal of Leadership in Education*, 3, 2: 151–8.

Cowan, J. (2004) 'How can understanding what motivates teachers to become administrators help the recruiting process of School District #62?', unpublished thesis, Royal Roads University.

Creighton, T.B. (2001) 'Data analysis in administrator's hands: An oxymoron?' *The School Administrator*, 4, 58: 6–11.

Curtis, A. (2004) *The Power of Nightmares*. Online at www.archive.org/details/ThePowerOfNightmaresDVD (accessed 8 May 2008).

Cushing, K.S., Kerrins, A.K., and Johnstone, T. (2003) 'Disappearing principals: What is the real reason behind the shortage of applicants for principal positions across the state and nation? It's the job, stupid!' *Leadership*. Online at http://findarticles.com/p/articles/mi_m0HUL/is_5_32/ai_112686943/pg_2 (accessed 8 May 2008).

Day, C. and Schmidt, M. (2007) 'Sustaining resilience', in B. Davis (ed.) *Leading the Strategically Focused School*, London: Sage.

Denzin, N.K. (1984) *On Understanding Emotion*, San Francisco: Jossey-Bass.

Earl, L. (1995) 'Assessment and accountability in education in Ontario', *Canadian Journal of Education*, 20, 1: 45–55.

Earl, L. and Torrance, N. (2000) 'Embedding accountability and improvement into large-scale assessment: What difference does it make?' *Peabody Journal of Education*, 75, 4: 114–41.

Ferrandino, V.L. and Tirozzi, G.N. (2000) 'The principal, keystone of a high-achieving school: Attracting and keeping the leaders we need', *Education Week*. Online at www.naesp.org/ContentLoad.do?contentId=906 (accessed 8 May 2008).

Fineman, S. (1993) 'Organizations as emotional arenas', in S. Fineman (ed.) *Emotion in Organizations*, London: Sage.

Fullan, M. (2004) *The Moral Imperatives of School Leadership*, London: Sage.

Giddens, A. (2000) *Runaway World: How Globalization is Reshaping Our Lives*, New York: Routledge.

Giroux, H. (2000) *Stealing Innocence: Corporate Culture's War on Children*, New York: Palgrave.

Giroux, H. and Schmidt, M. (2004) 'Closing the achievement gap: A metaphor for children left behind', *Journal of Educational Change*, 5: 213–28.

Glassner, B. (1999) *The Culture of Fear: The Assault on Optimism in America*, New York: Basic Books.

Goffman, E. (1959) *The Presentation of Self in Everyday Life*, New York: Doubleday.

Goleman, D. (1995) *Emotional Intelligence*, New York: Bantam Books.

Gore, A. (2007) *The Assault on Reason*, Penguin Press.

Grace, G. (1995) *School Leadership: Beyond Educational Management*, New York: Falmer Press.

Gronn, P. (2003) *The New Work of Educational Leaders*, London: Paul Chapman.

Hargreaves, A. (1998) 'The emotional politics of teaching and teacher development: With implications for educational leadership', *International Journal of Leadership in Education*, 1, 4: 315–36.

—— (2003) *Teaching in the Knowledge Society: Education in the Age of Insecurity*, Milton Keynes: Open University Press.

Hargreaves, A. and Fink, D. (2006) *Sustainable Leadership*, San Francisco: Jossey-Bass.

Hargreaves, A. and Fullan, M. (1996) *What's Worth Fighting for in your School?* New York: Teachers College Press.

Haviland, J. M. and Kahlbaugh, P. (1993) 'Emotion and identity', in M. Lewis and J.M. Haviland (eds) *Handbook of Emotions*, New York: The Guilford Press.

Hochschild, A. (1979) 'Emotion work, feeling rules and social structure', *American Journal of Sociology*, 85, 3: 551–75.

Holcomb, E. (1999) *Getting Excited About Data: How to Combine People, Passion, and Proof*, Thousand Oaks: Corwin Press.

Houston, P.D. (2007) 'The seven deadly sins of *No Child Left Behind*', *Phi Delta Kappan*, 88, 10: 744–8.

Izard, C.E. (1977) *Human Emotions*, New York: Plenum.

Jacobs, B.A. (2001) 'Getting tough? The impact of high school graduation exams', *Educational Evaluation and Policy Analysis*, 24, 4: 305–31.

James, W. (1990) *The Principles of Emotion*, New York: Dover.

Leithwood, K. and Jantzi, D. (1999) 'Transformational school leadership effects: A replication', *School Effectiveness and School Improvement*, 10, 4: 451–79.

Lortie, D.C. (1975) *Schoolteacher: A Sociological Study*, Chicago: University of Chicago Press.

McGhee, M.W. and Nelson, S.W. (2005) 'Sacrificing leaders, villainizing leadership: How educational accountability policies impair school leadership', *Phi Delta Kappan*, 86, 5: 369–72.

Miller, L.P. (1992) 'Alternatives to norm-referenced testing for assessing student achievement', *ERS Spectrum*, 10, 3: 3–9.

Mowrer, O.H. (1939) 'Stimulus response theory of anxiety', *Psychological Review*, 46: 553–65.

No Child Left Behind, US Department of Education. Online at www.ed.gov/nclb/landing.jhtml (accessed 19 October 2006).

Oatley, K. and Jenkins, J. (1996) *Understanding Emotions*, Cambridge: Blackwell.

Peterson, K. (2005) *High School Exit Exams on the Rise*, Stateline.org. Online at www.stateline.org/live/ViewPage.action?siteNodeld==136&languageld=1&contentld=33244 (accessed 8 October 2007).

Plutchik, R. (1980) 'A general psychoevolutionary theory of emotion', in R. Plutchik and H. Kellerman (eds) *Emotion: Theory, Research and Experience: Vol. 1. Theories of emotion*, New York: Academic.

Rachman, S.J. (1990) *Fear and Courage*, New York: W.H. Freeman.

Roderick, M. and Engel, M. (2001) 'The grasshopper and the ant: Motivational responses of low-achieving students to high-stakes testing', *Educational Evaluation and Policy Analysis*, 23, 3: 197–227.

Roderick, M., Jacob, B.A., and Bryk, A.S. (2002) 'The impact of high-stakes testing in Chicago on student achievement in promotional gate grades', *Educational Evaluation and Policy Analysis*, 24, 4: 333–57.

Rosen, J. (2005) *The Naked Crowd: Reclaiming Security and Freedom in an Anxious Age*, New York: Random House.

Scase, R. (1999) 'Employment relations in small firms', in P. Edwards (ed.) *Industrial Relations*, Oxford: Blackwell.

Schmidt, M. (2000) 'Role theory, emotions and identity in the department headship of secondary schooling', *Teaching and Teacher Education*, 16, 8: 827–42.

—— (2008) 'Risky policy processes: Accountability and school leadership', in E.A. Samier (ed.) *Political Approaches to Educational Administration and Leadership*, New York: Routledge.

Schmidt, M. *et al.* (2008) 'Exit exams and organizational change in a vocational high school', in B. Fuller, M.K. Henne, and E. Hannum (eds), *Research in Sociology of Education*, Bingley: Emerald Group.

Schmoker, M. (1999) *Results: The Key to Continuous School Improvement*, Alexandria: Association for Supervision and Curriculum Development.

Sennett, R. (1998) *The Corrosion of Character*, New York: W.W. Norton.

Sergiovanni, T.J. (1994) *Building Community in Schools*, San Francisco: Jossey-Bass.

Starrat, R.J. (2005) 'Responsible leadership', *The Educational Forum*, 69: 124–33.

Stecher, B. and Kirby, S.N. (eds) (2004) *Organizational Improvement and Accountability: Lessons for Education from other Sectors*, Santa Monica: RAND.

Stiggins, R. (1991) 'Facing the challenges of a new era of educational assessment', *Applied Measurement in Education*, 4, 4: 263–73.

Ueda, T.T. (1985) 'The principal's ability to provide effective leadership in various collective bargaining organizational models (teacher union, administrator roles)', unpublished thesis, Seattle University.

Watson, J.B. (1924) *Behaviorism*, New York: Norton.

White, G. (1993) 'Emotions inside out: The anthropology of affect', in M. Lewis and J.M. Haviland (eds) *Handbook of Emotions*, New York: Guilford Press.

Wiggins, G. (1989) 'Teaching to the (authentic) test', *Educational Leadership*, 46, 7: 41–7.

Woods, P. (1983) *Sociology and the School: An Interactionist Viewpoint*, London: Routledge.

11 The political economy of the emotions

Individualism, culture and markets, and the administration of the self in education

Richard Bates

To get the whole world out of bed
And washed and dressed, and warmed, and fed
To school, and back to bed again,
Believe me Saul, costs worlds of pain.
Adapted from 'The Everlasting Mercy' with
apologies to John Masefield (1945)

There can hardly be anyone in the Western world, who, whether they lived through the 60s and 70s or not, is unfamiliar with the image of a young Vietnamese girl running naked towards the camera, her face contorted by pain and shock as her back is burnt by napalm. There can be few of us who do not share a visceral emotional sympathy for her as well as revulsion at such 'collateral damage' inflicted in our name.

However, whether the pain and suffering of Phan Thi Kim Phuc was 'collateral' or not, they can be seen as an outcome of considerable administrative effort. The production processes involved in making the napalm demand both technical and administrative effort. The mining, transport, and processing of the petrochemicals that are the material base of napalm demand further administrative effort. The construction and management of the fleet of tankers as well as the maritime administration that guides their passage to factories are further networks of administrative expertise. The planes that carry the napalm and the navigational systems that ensure effective delivery are both administrative achievements of considerable sophistication. The programmes that trained and disciplined the men who flew the planes and the logistics that supported them in the field also demand considerable administrative effort. The political and economic systems that required that the napalm be dropped in that particular place at that particular time are also articulated through vast networks of administration. And so on.

In short, the burning girl is, indeed, an administrative achievement.

And so, of course, is our emotional response. The camera itself was the product of administrative effort as, indeed, was the presence of Nick Ut of Associated Press in that particular place at that particular moment; as was the circulation of the image to the world's media and its publication through innumerable print and electronic outlets which themselves also involved sophisticated administrative processes of organisation and decision making.

The point here is that administrative processes both *produce* and *communicate* emotions. While administrative structures may demand 'rational' rather than 'emotional' decision making, and while they may well be populated, as Weber suggested, by sensualists without heart who end up in a sort of mechanical petrification, this does not mean that administrative structures and actions do not have emotional consequences.

Traditionally in Western thought the rational and the emotional have been seen as opposites. Classical social theorists, such as Weber (1922/1968), distinguished between 'rational' and 'affectual' action. Parsons (1951) similarly distinguished between action seen as 'instrumental' and that seen as 'expressive'. More recently, however, the development of a sociology of emotions has suggested that such a clear distinction is a mistake. Turner and Stets, for instance, argue that

> All sociological theories ... begin with the assumption of human rationality – that is, people seek to realize profits in the exchange of resources. All sociological theories, however, see individuals as making decisions ... that are guided by and have consequences for emotions. Rationality and emotions are ... so intricately connected at all levels – the biological, the cognitive, and the behavioural – that it is probably not useful to separate them in analysis, as several hundred years of philosophy and a hundred years of sociology have tended to do.
>
> (2005: 22)

This reconnection of rationality and emotions has clear consequences for the study of organisations and administrative processes. For the most part, such study has been focused on the study of '... the emotional lives of persons in their social contexts' (Lutz and White 1986: 427) or organisational culture and 'Cultural forms [that] are a means of expressing emotions in organizations [where] the effective use of cultural forms hinges on their ability to generate emotions' (George 2000: 1046). In particular, the coincidental shift of focus in organisation theory from administration to management and management to leadership has emphasised the role of leaders in symbolic management where 'the success of symbolic management is largely dependent upon the evocation of emotion' (Ashforth and Humphrey 1995: 111).

As a consequence, several theoretical approaches to leadership and leadership research have developed on the basis of symbolic management, among them: *visionary* leadership (House 2004); a revisiting of Weberian concerns with *charismatic* leadership (Gardner 2003); and more broadly with *transformational* leadership (Bass 1998; Bass and Riggio 2005).

Inevitably, such approaches raise the question of the integrity of such symbolic management: its authenticity or inauthenticity. Luthans and Avolio (2003) argue that authentic leaders are guided by values that allow them to operate at higher levels of moral integrity. Price (2003) suggests, however, that inauthentic leaders may also declare such higher moral values but do so simply to exploit their organisations or followers, making espoused values difficult to use in distinguishing between authenticity and inauthenticity. Harter (2002) suggests that authenticity derives from the consistency of thoughts and feeling with actions.

Such positions raise again the supposed conflict between rationality and emotion. Michie and Gooty return to such a position, pointing out the challenge inherent in 'the conflict between behaving effectively and behaving ethically' where effectiveness may be driven by rational, calculative behaviour, and ethical concerns might require moral/emotional concern for organisational members, stakeholders, communities, or other organisations (2005: 443). In each of these cases, the issue is framed by various conceptions of leadership and their emotional effects on leaders and led. Where administrative structures are considered, it is almost always within the framework of a supposed antipathy between the rationality of administration and the emotions of individuals. Seldom are structural effects considered in the administrative production of emotion unless they are considered as a conflict between rational administrative demands for effectiveness and emotional responses to the coercive nature of such demands.

In education, as in the literature more generally, such issues have been taken up largely in the study of principals and their interactions with teachers. Beatty, for instance, has studied 'the emotions of leadership – their provocations, origins, qualities – and some of their effects on the working lives of educational leaders' (2000: 331). Blackmore (1996; 1999) explored the emotional work of female principals faced with the 'rational' demands of market liberal management demands. Leithwood and Beatty (2007) argue that principals' consideration of teachers' emotional well-being can lead to higher morale, self-efficacy, commitment, and motivation among teachers and improved school climate and achievement for students. Hargreaves has focused on understanding 'why teachers' emotions are configured in particular ways in the changing and varying organizational life of schools' (2001: 1075; 2004).

Much current work relating administration to emotions is based on current notions of transformational leadership (Bass 1998; Leban and Zulauf 2004; Tichy and Devanna 1986) and its importation into education (Hallinger 2003; Leithwood and Jantzi 2005a; 2005b; Silins, Mulford, and Zarins 2002). Transformational leadership essentially argues for the exercise of charismatic authority within rational legal administrative structures. But what is missing from most of these analyses is what Weber was acutely conscious of – the fact that these contrasting forms of authority are based upon contrasting forms of power.

Zorn and Boler make this point, emphasising that the traditional separation of private and public, rational and emotional, male and female are cultural constructions that celebrate particular forms of domination. Moreover:

> The cultural and historical legacies that have dismissed or privatised emotion, depicted as feminised weakness, and excluded emotion from the rational political arenas continue to persist as an ever present ghost of cultural disdain.
>
> (2008: 138)

Whilst acknowledging Hargreaves' and Beatty's groundbreaking social and organisational analysis and their recognition of emotions as being socially and organisationally situated, Zorn and Boler argue, however, that

> [Their] views ... are founded on a mistaken assumption about how individuals and social settings interact and how emotions are formed. Unfortunately, emotions and social settings are understood as individual forces that *act upon* each other, rather than *interact with* each other.
>
> (2008: 140, italics added)

The result of this mistake is to consider the role of the principal, for instance, as mediating the public cultural/emotional life of the organisation with the private personal/emotional life of the teacher. In contrast, Zorn and Boler argue that '... emotions are neither public nor private, but rather must be understood as collaboratively formed' (2008: 142).

In order to remedy this theoretical defect Zorn and Boler suggest two important concepts. The first idea, that of 'economies of mind', suggests that emotion and affect constitute part of the currency of social relations that embody and facilitate the negotiation of power relations. The second is that of 'inscribed habits of inattention' which, while avoiding theories of the unconscious, allows the analysis of power relations through the emotional regard (attention) or disregard (inattention) implicit in social relations (2008; Boler 1999). Further, following Bartky (1990) and Campbell (1997), they suggest that emotions can be either recognised through 'social uptake' that accepts them as legitimate, or 'blocked' through dismissal as illegitimate through the exercise of social/emotional power.

It is this incorporation of power relationships into the examination of emotions and the processes of social interaction that allows a significantly new approach to the study of emotions, administration, and leadership.

> It is only by foregrounding relations of power that define emotional experience and communication that new research can resist the tendency to individualize or universalise emotional experiences. It is not enough that educational leaders show consideration for emotions and their social and organizational dimension. Within education, as in the wider

> culture, emotions are a site of control and a mode of political resistance. Emotion matters in educational leadership because leaders, teachers and learners understand and enact their roles of subordination and domination significantly through learned emotional expressions and silences.
>
> (Zorn and Boler 2008: 148)

Harding and Pribram (2002) reach similar conclusions in their study of the power of feeling, where, following Foucault (1991), they argue that the construction of the self is the outcome of cultural processes/regimes of power, through which various definitions of the self are accumulated and through which individuals are positioned (and position themselves) emotionally and socially. Various 'technologies of power' (Foucault 1979), including emotional technologies, are employed and resisted in order to produce, reproduce, and resist particular definitions of the self. Such processes produce a 'structure of feeling' (Williams 1975; 1979), but within conditions of 'emotional hegemony' (Jaggar 1989) through an interactive process that sees

> ... the process of emotional experience in interaction with cultural practices and social relations as the constant construction, solidification and renewal of structures of feeling, just as the ongoing constitution of emotions prescribes and proscribes the construction of cultural practices and social and personal relations.
>
> (Harding and Pribram 2002: 424)

Such structures of feeling are intimately tied both to individual identities and to social structures. For instance, some of these identities are the result of social categories that precede individuals, many of which are defined in contrast to each other (black/white, male/female, principal/teacher, teacher/pupil) and that are endowed with more or less power, prestige, status, etc., along with various emotional valences. Other identities are chosen through identification with particular social groups and realised through acceptance by those groups via the effective performance of particular roles (Stets and Burke 2000). Both ascribed and chosen identities are emotionally laden and are constantly in the process of negotiation as alternative identities are constructed through processes of social negotiation and change. As Taylor suggests, 'my own identity crucially depends upon my dialogical relations with others' (1991: 48). Such dialogue is both socially and historically constructed: a dialogue that provides for sources of the self (Taylor 1989).

Arendt (1958), similarly, argued that power is the result of communicative struggle, mainly directed towards the reorganisation of relations between people and groups. This is a theme taken up by Bourdieu (1989) who argues that 'world-making' is the result of both 'objective' classification and reclassification of social groups (for instance, through official categorisation) and of 'subjective' and individualised processes involving insults, innuendo, slander, and gossip. Such struggle over 'world-making' is both communicative and evaluative: 'At the heart of any struggle is not just communication but a communication that classifies people and things into particular social categories *and provides an evaluation of those categories*' (Fleming and Spicer 2007: 56, italics added)

Struggles over such classifications are not only evaluations of categories, but also evaluations of individuals and the categories that they inherit, choose, and construct and the selves that they negotiate. This is both a political and a frequently highly emotional process, one that is both a struggle over dignity and a struggle over equity, and one expressed through 'selfhood, ethics, identity, self-transformation, re-enchantment and emotions' (Fleming and Spicer 2007: 186, 187).

Fleming and Spicer argue strongly for the notion of 'struggle' over such issues as a key and in-eradicable feature of work organisations, suggesting that struggle is a more frequent condition than harmony.

> ... [W]e ought to approach workplace struggle and political contestation as a *constitutive* feature of work organizations rather than as an aberration that can simply be managed away. The problem with most mainstream management thinking is that it views politics, contestation and resistance as deviations from the default option of a harmonious norm. We are not suggesting that harmony cannot be attained in work organizations. But such a vision of work is merely ideological if it is prescribed within or superimposed upon the current structure of employment relations, domains whereby asymmetrical power relations are taken for granted and the managerial prerogative a natural right. Indeed, work in today's society is fundamentally permeated by differing interests, factions, contradictions and power/resistance relations.
>
> (2007: 184)

Much recent management literature, in education as elsewhere, seeks to resolve such struggles by the manipulation of emotions through charismatic or visionary leadership or through the 'culturing' and 'reculturing' of organisations such as schools (Deal and Peterson 1999; Fullan 2001). The result is a personalising and individualising of struggle, of power, and of emotional relationships in ways that focus on the micro-politics of organisations and ignore broader issues. But the micro-politics of organisations 'are not hermetically sealed off from society when it comes to power, politics and resistance' (Fleming and Spicer 2007: 188).

Stuart Hall makes a similar point:

> Cultural identities come from somewhere, have histories ... [and] far from being eternally fixed in some essentialist past, ... are subject to the continual play of history, culture and power ... [I]dentities are the

> names we give to the different ways we are positioned by, and position ourselves within, the narratives of the past.
>
> (1993: 394)

Currently two major narratives compete as the contexts within which identities can be constructed. Moreover, while these narratives may have been associated historically within the integrated social orders of the nation state, they are currently breaking apart. 'Two worlds are being dissociated: the world of technologies and markets and the world of cultures, the world of instrumental reason and that of collective meaning, that of signs and that of meanings' (Touraine 2000: 25). Touraine argues that the capacity of globalised technologies and markets to break free of the *social* relations of production produces a paradox within which personality and identity are no longer bound together by existing social relations of production, nor by coherent projections of identity into the future, but seek support either in an idealised notion of past harmony or through retreat into communities that provide alternative sources of identity and support.

At a personal and emotional level, therefore, the difficulty of locating oneself securely within a constantly changing market economy produces the temptation to define oneself in relation to a cultural community constructed around pre-determined and 'stable' ideas of race, religion, gender, belief, or a mode of behaviour. The difficulty here is that although cultures built on such foundations may confer a sense of self and emotional identification, they also open up the possibility of authoritarian demands for unquestioning loyalty and belief. This is particularly the case where the communitarian identity is defined in terms of the discrimination suffered by its members (Touraine 2000: 33).

Principals, teachers, and students, no less than parents, are caught both instrumentally and emotionally within this paradox of competing demands. Schools, being mostly subject to the governance of an economically directed state, are predominantly charged with the inculcation of technical knowledge and skills among students, thus privileging the economic identities provided by the market. On the other hand, under the rubric of 'choice', the state is in many cases not only allowing, but also supporting 'faith' or 'charter' schools through which particular notions of 'virtue' can be articulated along with cultural and religious identities of a quite different kind (Beckett 2007; *Guardian* 2001; Gillard 2007; *Times* 2007).

The emotional impact of these conflicting demands for loyalty and commitment, to the instability of markets on the one hand and to authoritarian communities of belief on the other, creates a significant problem for schools, principals, teachers, and students alike. This conflict, which often expresses itself as burn-out among staff and disaffection and alienation among students, cannot be resolved by siding with either economy or community, although schools typically attempt to do so. It is a conflict that reflects both the increasing integration and unity of the market and the increasing fragmentation of communities (Touraine 2000: 166ff).

If there is to be a resolution of this issue at the level of personal identity as well as at the level of social integration, Touraine argues, it must be based upon both recognition of difference and a commitment to communicate across social and cultural difference. This is only possible if ways can be found to develop individual autonomy from both markets and communities, sufficient emotional resilience to manage communication across difference, and an acknowledgement of the importance of the freedom to build a personal life without coercion, for

> The call for freedom to build a personal life is the only universalist principle that does not impose one form of social organization and cultural practices. It is not reducible to *laissez-faire* economics or to pure tolerance, first because it demands respect for the freedom of all individuals and therefore a rejection of exclusion, and secondly because it demands that any reference to a cultural identity be legitimised in terms of the freedom and equality of all, and not by an appeal to a social order, a tradition or the requirements of public order.
>
> (Touraine 2000: 167)

This principle of self-determination within the context of communication across cultural boundaries is fundamental to Touraine's argument. But it demands significant changes in the instrumental, cultural, and emotional order of schools. First, it demands that schools cease to define themselves solely in terms of curriculum, 'the knowledge they transmit to their pupils … and the exams they use to evaluate the acquisition of knowledge' (Touraine 2000: 275). Second, it demands that schools shift from an emphasis on the broadcasting of messages and information towards an emphasis on communication about the real issues facing pupils, parents, teachers, and administrators. Only by doing so can the subject (pupil, parent, teacher, administrator) achieve the conditions that 'will allow him to become the actor of his own history' (Touraine 2000: 56). This inevitably introduces into the school the emotions attached to those issues that are central to subjects' lives and which emphasis on the formal curriculum excludes.

> … [It] is impossible to speak of a school for the Subject unless we defend schools that communicate, and it is at this point that we encounter the greatest resistance. Whenever this topic comes up, both parents and teachers refuse to talk about it. They are afraid that if the uncontrollable disorder of affective relations is allowed into schools, they will be unable to carry out their primary mission, which is to teach children and prepare them for the examinations that open the door to employment.
>
> (Touraine 2000: 275)

A second reason why communication about real issues across boundaries is so threatening is pointed to by Stephen Law in his discussion of *The*

War for Children's Minds (2006): that is, that open communication across boundaries may threaten both the dominant emphasis on skills and vocation on the one hand, and the cultural traditions and authoritarian imposition of values and 'character' (which so many seem to require of schools) on the other. In advocating a critical liberal education, Law suggests that fundamental to such an education is inculcation of 'the habit of thinking carefully and critically about our own beliefs and attitudes' (2006: 129). This, in itself, requires a particular kind of discipline where children get into the habit of listening to different points of view calmly and carefully considering them in ways that respect others before making moral judgements (2006: 128).

While Law deals mainly with the liberal answer to religious authoritarianism, his arguments apply to all kinds of authoritarian imposition of values and beliefs and are entirely consistent with Touraine's advocacy of the communicative school. But such deliberative principles need also to be coupled with a particular, scientific, conception of knowledge. This is necessary in that it allows pupils to distinguish between truth and falsehood (between evolution and creationism/intelligent design for instance) as well as being a defence against arbitrary power and authoritarian communitarian traditions. It also provides the ground upon which to communicate in a 'world that is retreating into private experience' (Touraine 2000: 279).

So, on one hand, we have the demands of the market for the exclusion of emotions from the curriculum and a concentration on skills and aptitudes required by the world of production and consumption. On the other, we have the demands of authoritarian communities for emotional compliance with unquestioned values and beliefs. Both articulate characteristic forms of administration designed to produce particular educational, social, and personal identities. That these conflicting demands are borne out in the daily emotional lives of principals, teachers, and students should be no surprise. That the functionalist requirements of capitalist markets and the authoritarian requirements of communities of belief are sometimes combined in ways that have unfortunate outcomes should also be no surprise. Indeed, in that Western society where fundamentalism in both markets and religions is most highly developed, such conflicting demands are associated with high rates of social disorder (Paul 2005).[1]

This is partly because, as Bernstein suggests, the contradictory demands of such institutionalised messages and identities are commonly kept apart by systems of strong classification – that is, they are separated and insulated from each other by distinct forms of discourse (e.g. different classifications within the curriculum). As the principles of classification are institutionalised and insulated from each other 'the contradictions, cleavages and dilemmas which necessarily inhere in the principle of classification are suppressed by the insulation' (2000: 7). Social order is in part the result of the successful insulation of such categories as market and culture from each other. Where the insulation breaks down, social disorder may increase.

Such dialogical and institutional classifications present individuals with the possibility of assuming multiple, different (and perhaps conflicting) identities as they simultaneously locate themselves and their identities within different, insulated, social positions. The principle of insulation then becomes, inwardly,

> a system of psychic defences against the possibility of the weakening of the insulation which would then reveal the suppressed contradictions, cleavages and dilemmas ... The internal reality of insulation is a system of psychic defences to maintain the integrity of a category.
>
> (Bernstein 2000: 7)

The emotional consequences of a weakening insulation between categories can be quite significant – as, for instance, when the categories of 'good son' or 'macho worker' conflict with the category of 'gay partner' or 'queer' (Morris 2003). They can also lead to public questioning of categories and attempts to redefine the power that maintains such categories and keeps them separate: the 'world-making' that Bourdieu suggested was integral to changes in the principles of social order. This, and the struggle that it involves, is highly emotional work. But it is work that may be fundamental to an alternative pedagogy: that of discomfort.

Boler and Zembylas articulate a pedagogy of discomfort as a way of challenging '... the inscribed cultural and emotional terrains we occupy less by choice and more by virtue of hegemony' (2003: 111). Such hegemony, they suggest, produces for many of us a comfort zone that needs to be opened up to critical enquiry at both cognitive and emotional levels. For some, such hegemony is challenged by the crossing of borders (e.g. immigrants), where displacement challenges existing and available identities, producing an ambiguity in the sense of self. In such situations, what Dewey (1985) saw as 'habits' are challenged when individuals are confronted by alternative ways of thinking and feeling.

Dewey saw such challenges as a fundamental pedagogical process through which habits might be opened up to scrutiny; habits, which are both '... the building up and solidifying of certain desires; an increased sensitiveness and responsiveness', as well as 'an impaired capacity to attend to and think about certain things' (1985: 171). As habits are both cognitive and emotional, a critical pedagogy of discomfort opens up both territories for educator and student alike. They introduce risk and uncertainty into the pedagogical process. But they also open up territories upon which alternative visions of both self and society can be inscribed. In this way

> ... a pedagogy of discomfort becomes an approach to understanding the ways in which something new is created, how difference is introduced into history. A greater sense of comfort and positive emotional labor comes with examining the ways in which this creativity and invention

> arise out of how educators and students engage in discourses and practices that open up new possibilities.
>
> (Boler and Zembylas 2003: 132)

Moreover, such pedagogies are capable of challenging the xenophobias of class, race, gender, religion, and nationality by seeing difference as a point of departure for the exploration of new forms of identity and social organisation, within both schools and the wider society. They are, indeed, fundamental to what Wrigley calls *Schools of Hope* (2003). They are also fundamental to answering the question that Touraine poses: *Can We Live Together?* (2000). As Boler and Zembylas put it:

> A pedagogy of discomfort invites educators and students to engage in critical thinking and to explore the multitude of habits, relations of power, knowledge, and ethics through which the conduct of educators and students is shaped by others and by themselves. Within this culture of critical thinking (which is not separated from feeling), a central focus is the recognition of the multiple, heterogeneous, and messy realities of power elations as they are enacted and resisted in localities, subverting the comfort offered by the endorsement of particular norms.
>
> (2003: 131)

And this takes us back to a question I have asked before: what would a truly educational administration look like? It would certainly not look solely to embrace the competitive academic skills curriculum required by markets. Nor would it solely embrace the (however genteel) authoritarian curriculum of communities of belief. It would not embrace the didactic pedagogy of either system. Neither would it embrace the formal hierarchical and exclusionary tests for compliance offered by the market model; nor the tests of loyalty and obedience demanded by closed cultures. It would not separate rationality from emotion. Nor would it see transformational leadership simply as the engagement of the emotions in the pursuit of compliance with 'rational' organisational goals and cultures. But it might well embrace a curriculum concerned with the variety of sources of the self and their negotiation within a context of respect. It might embrace a pedagogy of discomfort through which alternative identities might be considered, justified, and chosen without coercion. And it might just embrace a form of evaluation that was concerned with the emotional health of both the administered and the administrators. It might, indeed, be an administration that could

> ... recognize that the goal of education is not to train and prepare young people for society, still less to train them for their future economic roles. Its goal is to train and educate them to be themselves, to enable them to become free individuals who can discover and preserve the unity of their

experience throughout the upheavals of life and despite the pressures that are brought to bear upon them.

(Touraine 2000: 284)

By developing such a truly educational administration it might just be possible to reduce the collateral damage that is currently one outcome of our administrative production of emotion in education, as well as the invisibility of the administrative processes involved.

Note

1 That this is the case is pointed out by Paul (2005) whose study of religiosity and indicators of social disorder such as homicide, abortion, sexually transmitted diseases, suicide, life expectancy, and pregnancy in nations across the developed, democratic world, found that such social pathologies generally correlate with 'higher rates of belief in and worship of a creator'. Moreover, in this respect, 'The United States is almost always the most dysfunctional of the developed democracies, sometimes spectacularly so, and almost always scores poorly.'

References

Arendt, H. (1958) *The Human Condition*, Chicago: Chicago University Press.

Ashforth, B. and Humphrey, R. (1995) 'Emotion in the workplace', *Human Relations*, 48: 97–125.

Bartky, S. (1990) *Femininity and Domination: Studies in the Phenomenology of Oppression*, New York: Routledge.

Bass, B. (1998) *Transformational Leadership: Industrial, Military and Educational Impact*, London: Lawrence Erlbaum.

Bass, B. and Riggio R. (2005) *Transformational Leadership*, New York: Routledge.

Beatty, B. (2000) 'The Emotions of educational leadership: Breaking the silence', *International Journal of Leadership in Education*, 3, 4: 331–57.

Beckett, F. (2007) *The Great City Academy Fraud*, London: Continuum.

Bernstein, B. (2000) *Pedagogy, Symbolic Control and Identity*, New York: Rowman and Littlefield.

Blackmore, J. (1996) 'Doing "emotional labour" in the education market place: Stories from the field of women in management', *Discourse*, 17, 3: 337–49.

—— (1999) *Troubling Women*, Buckingham: Open University Press.

Boler, M. (1999) *Feeling Power: Emotions and Education*, New York: Routledge.

Boler, M. and Zembylas, M. (2003) 'Discomforting truths: The emotional terrain of understanding difference', in P. Trifonas (ed.) *Pedagogies of Difference*, New York: Routledge.

Bourdieu, P. (1989) 'Social space and symbolic power', *Sociological Theory* 7, 1: 14–25.

Campbell, S. (1997) *Interpreting the Personal: Expression and the Formation of Feelings*, Ithaca: Cornell University Press.

Deal, T. and Peterson, K. (1999) *Shaping School Culture*, San Francisco: Jossey-Bass.

Dewey, J. (1985 [1932]) 'Ethics', in J. Boydston (ed.) *John Dewey: The Later Works*, vol. 7, Carbondale: Southern Illinois University Press.

Fleming, P. and Spicer, A. (2007) *Contesting the Corporation*, Cambridge: Cambridge University Press.

Foucault, M. (1979) *Discipline and Punish: The Birth of the Prison*, New York: Vintage Books.

Fullan, M. (2001) *Leading in a Culture of Change*, San Francisco: Jossey-Bass.

Gardner, W. (2003) 'Perceptions of leader charisma, effectiveness and integrity', *Management Communication Quarterly*, 16, 4: 502–27.

George, J. (2000) 'Emotions and leadership', *Human Relations*, 53: 1027–55.

Gillard, D. (2007) 'Never mind the evidence: Blair's obsession with faith schools'. Online at http://www.dg.dial.pipex.com/articles/educ29.shtml (accessed 18 May 2008).

Guardian (2001) 'Facts about faith schools', 14 November. Online at http://education.guardian.co.uk/schools/story/0,,593365,00.html (accessed 18 May 2008).

Hall, S. (1993) 'Cultural identity and diaspora', in P. Williams and L. Chrisman (eds) *Colonial Discourse and Post-Colonial Theory*, London: Harvester Press.

Hallinger, P. (2003) 'Leading educational change: Reflections on the practice of instructional and transformational leadership', *Cambridge Journal of Education*, 33, 3: 329–51.

Harding, J. and Pribram, D. (2002) 'The power of feeling: Locating emotions in culture', *European Journal of Cultural Studies*, 5, 4: 407–26.

Hargreaves, A. (2001) 'Emotional geographies of teaching', *Teachers College Record*, 103, 6: 1056–80.

—— (2004) 'Inclusive and exclusive educational change: Emotional responses of teachers and implications for leadership', *School Leadership and Management*, 24, 2: 287–309.

Harter, S. (2002) 'Authenticity', in C. Snyder and S. Lopez (eds) *Handbook of Positive Psychology*, New York: Oxford University Press.

House, R. (2004) *Culture Leadership and Organizations*, New York: Sage.

Jaggar, A. (1989) 'Love and knowledge: Emotion in feminist epistemology', *Inquiry*, 32: 151–76.

Law, S. (2006) *The War for Children's Minds*, London: Routledge.

Leban, W. and Zulauf, C. (2004) 'Linking emotional intelligence abilities and transformational leadership styles', *Leadership and Organizational Development Journal*, 25, 7: 554–64.

Leithwood, K. and Beatty, B. (2007) *Leading with Teacher Emotions in Mind*, San Francisco: Corwin Press.

Leithwood, K. and Jantzi, D. (2005a) 'Transformational leadership', in B. Davies (ed.) *Essentials of School Leadership*, San Francisco: Corwin Press.

—— (2005b) 'A review of transformational school leadership research 1996–2006', *Leadership and Policy in Schools*, 4, 3: 177–99.

Lutz, C. and White, G. (1986) 'The anthropology of emotions', *Annual Review of Anthropology*, 15: 405–36.

Luthans, F. and Avolio, B. (2003) 'Authentic leadership: A positive development approach', in K. Cameron, J. Dutton, and R. Quinn (eds) *Positive Organizational Scholarship*, San Francisco: Berrett-Koehler.

Masefield, J. (1945) *Poems*, New York: Macmillan.

Michie, S. and Gootie, J. (2005) 'Values, emotions and authenticity: Will the real leader please stand up?' *The Leadership Quarterly*, 16: 441–57.

Morris, M. (2003) 'Queer pedagogies: Camping up the difference', in P. Trifonas (ed.) *Pedagogies of Difference*, New York: Routledge.

Parsons, T. (1951) *The Social System*, Glencoe: Free Press.

Paul, G. (2005) 'Cross national correlations of quantifiable societal health with popular religiosity and secularism in the prosperous democracies', *Journal of Religion and Society*, 7. Online at http://moses.creighton.edu/JRS/2005/2005–11.html (accessed 18 May 2008).

Price, T. (2003) 'The ethics of transformational leadership', *The Leadership Quarterly*, 14: 67–81.

Silins, C., Mulford, W., and Zarins, S. (2002) 'Organizational learning and school change', *Educational Administration Quarterly*, 38, 5: 613–42.

Stets, J. and Burke, P. (2000) 'Identity theory and social identity theory', *Social Psychology Quarterly*, 63, 3: 224–37.

Taylor, C. (1989) *Sources of the Self*, Cambridge: Harvard University Press.

—— (1991) *The Malaise of Modernity*, Concord: Anansi Press.

Tichy, N. and Devanna, M. (1986) *The Transformational Leader*, New York: John Wiley.

Times (2007) 'More Faith Schools are Planned in an effort to Integrate Minorities', 8 September.

Touraine, A. (2000) *Can We Live Together?* Stanford: Stanford University Press.

Turner, J. and Stets, J. (2005) *The Sociology of Emotion*, Cambridge: Cambridge University Press.

Weber, M. (1968 [1922]) *Economy and Society*, trans. G. Roth and C. Wittich, Los Angeles: University of California Press.

Williams, R. (1977) *Marxism and Literature*, New York: Oxford University Press.

Wrigley, T. (2003) *Schools of Hope*, Stoke on Trent: Trentham Books.

Zorn, D. and Boler, M. (2008) 'Rethinking emotions and educational leadership', *International Journal of Leadership in Education*, 10, 2: 137–52.

12 'Let's get personal'

Disrupting gender norms in educational organisations

Janice Wallace

Dominant organisational theories that are premised on masculinist meta-narratives (Blackmore 1989) shape practices within the neo-liberal state (Coulter 1998). These theories have shunned affect, which is considered subjective, and therefore suspect, forbidden, emotional, and irrational – all associated with normative femininity – in favour of the instrumental, rational, and measurable – all associated with normative masculinity. However, feminist poststructuralists (e.g. Kenway *et al.* 1994) have argued that such bifurcations – that is, male/female, rational/emotional – obfuscate the complex nuances of human interaction in organisational settings. Indeed, as I will argue in this chapter, it is in the discursive terrain of the emotional in organisations where the fraudulence of this dichotomy is exposed. Further, although organisational technologies, such as bureaucracy, attempt to eliminate the effects of affect, their efficacy is incomplete given the stubborn strength of idiographic influences in organisations. Weber observed that 'the more [bureaucracy] is dehumanised, the more completely it succeeds in eliminating from official business, love, hatred, and all *personal, irrational and emotional elements* which escape calculation' (1968: 216, italics added). Weber's statement infers that the imposition of bureaucratic rationality is always incomplete because, as anyone who has worked in bureaucratic organisations knows, the non-rational is not easily contained. As Hearn and Parkin point out, attempts to eliminate, control, or harness the energy of the non-rational are ultimately futile because 'the reality is that organisations are *places of emotion*, ranging from anger to joy to sorrow, from love to hate, with characteristic emotional climates and cultures', including sexual feelings, which are not so easily 'managed' (1995: 136, italics added).

The 'places of emotion' that are revealed in the tensions and resistances created and experienced by three women who worked as gender equity officers in Ontario education systems[1] during the mid to late 1990s are the focus of this chapter. My research with them[2] occurred during a period of rapid political and economic change that precipitated a progressive shift towards neo-liberal policies in public administration that privileged autonomous individualism and neo-conservative social values. An active, individuated, and rational social actor who thrives in the public realm was the discursive focus of policy that shifted away from communitarian norms held by a minority semi-socialist government that introduced increasingly prescriptive equity policy, to the marketplace values of a neo-conservative government with a huge majority that was free to impose its ideological will. The personal – the realm of private actions, emotions, and the body – became a target for commodification within the rules of the marketplace in this new regime as evidenced by the repeal of Bill 79: The Employment Equity Act and the passage of Bill 8: An Act to Repeal Job Quotas and to Restore Merit-based Employment Practices in Ontario. Bill 8's title is instructive in understanding the abrupt ideological shift in the direction of employment equity policy from that of the previous decade; that is, policy moved from voluntary to mandatory gender equity policy in educational organisations to an individuated competitive model of employment policy premised on a belief in ahistorical principles of merit. This shift signals the complex discursive space occupied by Kate, Linda, and Marg[3] who were hired in response to Bill 79 and then lost their positions as a result of Bill 8. I will turn first to the analytical possibilities of governmentality before taking up a feminist poststructural analysis in order to re/consider the emotional environment in which they did their work.

Govern/mentality and gender equity work

Before exploring governmentality, as taken up in this chapter, I wish to add that I am not using its full analytical range.[4] My focus here will be finding connections between actions of the state as demonstrated in equity policy formation and the experience of enacting those policies by actors in state-governed systems.[5] In particular, I am interested in forms of resistance in and through emotions and the body to gender equity policy in educational workplaces. Unlike notions of *government* that are specific to the actions of formal political authority, I use *governmentality* as an analytic tool to explore links between 'technologies of self and technologies of domination, the constitution of the subject and the formation of the state' (Lemke 2000: 2). In between 'the games of power and the states of domination, you have governmental technologies' (Foucault 1988: 19). The technologies to which Foucault refers are those discursive tools that 'account for the systematisation, stabilisation and regulation' (Lemke 2000: 6) by which subjectivities are formed within asymmetrical relations of power.

Competing discourses are characteristic of gender equity work in educational systems. First, educational systems are a favourite surrogate in neoliberal states (e.g. Wallace 2004) for their readiness to compete within the new rules of competitive global economics. Second, the discourse of rights in Canada's federal and provincial law,[6] as well as the obvious gender disparity in access to administrative positions and under-representation in low-status but well-paid jobs, such as caretaking in educational systems, makes it difficult to dismiss the rationale for gender equity policy. A third confounding factor in the discursive milieu of gender equity work is the circulation of patriarchal privilege that has always been a powerful mediator in access to desirable positions in educational organisations. Thus, Bill 79 and its equity policy predecessors,[7] were supported grudgingly, disappeared altogether, or were commodified as a technique at the service of diverse global markets (Blackmore and Sachs 1999). As a result, Kate, Linda, and Marg occupied a complex discursive space that was fraught with tension as each woman embodied instruments of governmentality (e.g. they were responsible for collecting statistics related to compliance to extant gender equity policy) and were also the object of resistance to the equity 'tapestry of discourses' (Kenway *et al.* 1994) that was woven by neo-liberal discourses of individual meritocratic competitiveness, patriarchal discourses of male privilege, and critical discourses of more broadly conceived notions of social justice. The complexity of their position was further exacerbated by the unequal discursive positions of males and females with regard to access to the technologies of government and the inherently emotional nature of their work.

Foucault's notions of governmentality in conjunction with feminist analysis provide some insights about the emotional location and nature of Kate, Marg, and Linda's work. Boler, building on Foucault's theory that technologies of government lead to internalised control, argues that organisations are inherently 'places of emotion' because bureaucratic rationality 'occur(s) fundamentally through structures of feeling' (1999: 21). Blackmore observes, for example, that postmodern organisations, seeking to respond to rapid and unpredictable change, have commodified 'the intellectual (creativity) and emotional (e.g. personal commitment to a value position or loyalty) energy for their ends through voluntary means' (1996: 338). Women are particularly vulnerable to the commodification of emotional work which added to the complexity of Kate, Linda, and Marg's work in terms of both their position within the board of education as well as what they were required to do in calling into question practices that led to the under-representation of women. For example, women, who are perceived to be more capable of providing 'caring' leadership at a time of great social, economic, and political turmoil, are increasingly being positioned as emotional labourers in restructured organisations. While the notion of 'caring' leadership has been picked up in academic and popular literature that espouses moral leadership, leading with the heart, and so on, neo-liberal discourses are demanding a managerial ethos in which administrative action is subject to the dominant question, 'Is it efficient?' rather than concerns for social justice. In this context, 'the managerial subject in organisational life is a subject working at identity construction, an existential project of becoming, but one constantly exposed to points of discursive interruption – and resistance' (Whitehead 1998: 207). Thus, men and women are positioned differently by gendered discourses within the technologies of neo-liberal governmentality in which emotion is not only taken up instrumentally but is articulated in ways that are normatively prescribed for both men and women. The emotional ambiguity of an increasingly performative ethos in educational organisations for men and women, then, is extremely complex: men are privileged in seeking desirable positions because they are men but are constrained by a hegemonic masculinity which may be uncomfortable for many, while women are seen as a disruptive 'other' whose socialisation may be useful to achieve the ends of the organisation but are constrained by an essentialised femininity that limits their opportunities within bureaucratic organisations.

In this context, then, Foucault's notions of governmentality are a useful analytical tool in drawing connections between technologies of government and technologies of the self, the management of which is the work of Kate, Linda, and Marg as gender equity workers. However, their work was continually challenged by patriarchal and meritocratic tensions that undermined the ideological underpinnings of gender equity policy within each educational organisation, even when the government at the time demonstrated strong commitment to gender equity. I will turn now to theories of emotions in organisations that enable a deeper understanding of the experiences of Kate, Marg, and Linda, which follow.

Exploring 'places of emotion' in organisations

In his anthology exploring emotions in organisational settings, Fineman states:

> Emotion work is the effort we put into ensuring that our private feelings are suppressed or represented to be in touch with socially accepted norms ... Emotional labour is the commercial exploitation of this principle: when an employee is in effect paid to smile, laugh, be polite or 'be caring'. An essential feature of the job is to maintain an organizationally prescribed demeanour or mask. This can be fun: an exquisite drama. It can also be stressful and alienating.
>
> (1993: 3)

Using Fineman's definitions, the scenarios described later in this chapter suggest that many of the administrators, whose good will was essential to Kate, Linda, and Marg's ability to do their work, publicly espoused support of gender equity employment policy but were doing emotion work in the sense that they suppressed private feelings of defensive anger in order to be seen as supportive of these policy initiatives. Linda, Marg, and Kate were also doing emotion work because they felt that they needed to suppress their true feelings in order to maintain credibility so that their work would not be further marginalised. For example, they all believed that if they had responded publicly with the level of indignation they felt, or had cried, or otherwise expressed strong emotion, their emotional expression would have been pathologised as irrational and 'typically female', thus negating their work of resistance. However, the differing discursive positions of men and women in educational organisations minimally constrained men since their private feelings received tacit or even open support from other male, and sometimes female, work colleagues.

Linda, Marg, and Kate were required not only to do emotional work but also emotional labour in the sense that they were positioned within the organisation to deflect administrative responsibility for changing gendered practices and to absorb the anger of some workers towards gender equity employment policy and the frustration of those who were seeking equitable employment opportunities. In Kate's words, she perceived herself as 'a buffer between the people who are seeking equity and the administration'. Because each of the women in this study had a deep ideological commitment to gender equity, their decision to absorb resistance to employment equity with silence on many occasions, while strategic, was also very painful. As Putnam and Mumby argue, 'Emotional labour is experienced most strongly when employees are asked to express emotions that contradict their inner feelings' (1993: 38).

Even though Marg's organisation was formally supportive of gender equity employment policy, she still found herself working to motivate apathetic and sometimes hostile workers and leaders to put the policy into practice.

MARG: Through membership in committees, I represent the advocacy part of keeping women's issues alive in those particular settings which isn't that easy to do. I mean, trying to keep it in front of people, including a lot of union/federation people as well as management who are supportive but are apathetic a lot of the time.

Although all three women strongly emphasised that their commitment to their work as gender equity advocates helped them persist in the face of unpredictable support for their work, they often felt alone and vulnerable as they tried to inform uninterested or hostile stakeholders about various aspects of employment equity policy.

KATE: The thing about this work is you don't know, you never, ever know what the reaction of the people in the room that you're going into – whether it's Executive Council and you're making a case for something, or whether it's at a trustee meeting, or whether it's a parent council meeting at a school, or speaking to a group of teachers – you just never know what the reaction is going to be ... You don't know whether you're going to be personally attacked ... and that is extremely stressful.

During the focus group, I used the phrase 'emotional labour' during our discussion, and, while none of the women knew its academic definition, they responded with an intuitive sense of its meaning in their work.

LINDA: I had to go out and talk to teachers about Bill 79 ... about the need to hire and promote minorities and women and setting up goals and time lines. I almost at the end wanted to wear a t-shirt saying, 'Don't shoot the messenger!' because I really did experience ... what were the words you used? ... emotional labour. Yeah. It was very, very hard work going out and dealing with those presentations and presenting to teachers at staff meetings ... I gritted my teeth, you know. I wore my armour.

Positioned as both subject and object of the employment equity policy, their message was often read as self-interested and was definitely unpopular with the majority of those in their audiences in many organisational settings. All three women spoke of the need for strong administrative support in implementing gender equity employment policy but, even when there was official support for the policy, it was clear that substantive support was unevenly available. For example, Marg relates a story where, despite official and structural support for gender equity, the resistance of two associate directors was revealed.

MARG: I wished them each 'Happy International Women's Day' and they were not amused. One of them refused to acknowledge my remarks and just sort of ignored me. The other one said, 'I'd hoped that I would've gotten through today without having to hear that.'

All three women reported similar incidents and confirmed that constantly negotiating the emotional terrain of advocating for gender equity policy among resistant colleagues was, just as Fineman suggests, 'stressful and alienating'.

An exquisite drama

Despite the toll taken by the emotional labour of doing equity work, it was obvious that each woman had chosen her work because of the emotional attachment she felt to the possibility of transforming sexist practices in educational organisations. Fineman refers to the paradox of concurrently experiencing both the pleasure and pain of emotional labour as 'exquisite drama' (1993: 3).

KATE: The emotional labour, it was intense ... but it was balanced by the fact that you were doing work that needed to be done ... that at times you could assist someone who really needed help, that on occasion you would see real change in a school administrator. You know, someone that at first you could hardly believe that this kind of person still existed – a real dinosaur – and actually see that person change over the course of two years or three years, primarily through, in the case I'm thinking about, his interaction with me and then became involved in things that were going on.

Each woman had similar stories of success in changing individual and systemic practices and took great pleasure in those victories, but every statement was tinged with battle fatigue.

MARG: You may get your victories. I mean, I look at our new standard procedure [for handling sexual harassment cases] and I think of all the energy and the work that went into it. But it's done and it's printed and it's out there ... and you get this feeling of satisfaction, but a lot of stress.

Marg's comment brings together the pleasure and pain of emotional labour and demonstrates what Hearn suggests: 'All knowledge of emotion is intersubjective, is a matter of desire (rather than disinterested cognition) that is structured around power, and is dialectical' (1993: 149, citing Game 1991: 8). In the words of an old television sports show, there is 'the thrill of victory and the agony of defeat' when countering resistance to gender equity policy because the ideological stakes are high, the structural barriers to success are formidable, and gender equity policy is embodied in a way that is lived 'closer to the edge of our skin' (Pratt 1984, cited in Boler 1999: 182) than most other educational policy since it is so closely aligned with a sense of personal and sexual identity.

Embodying gender equity

Kate spoke directly to her embodied position as a gender equity worker by remarking with considerable emotion, 'This is the problem with the way it's been set up from point one ... Kate does equity; Kate IS equity.' Kate's comments point to a fundamental discursive position of not only her work, but also Linda's and Marg's experience; each equity worker in this study embodies a resistant discourse to patriarchal practices that hold gender inequities in place. At the same time, each woman is a target within the organisation for neo-liberal and patriarchal discourses that are resistant to transformation. That is, Kate, Marg, and Linda embodied gender equity policy that, by its very nature, increases 'specific consciousness of gender' (Hearn and Parkin 1995: 139). Thus their bodies became signifiers of an otherwise covert sexual ideology and are, therefore, targets for resistance to transforming that ideology. One particular incident demonstrates this phenomenon in Marg's experience:

MARG: We did a lot of workshops [on gender equity in the workplace for the care taking department]. We have a new head of the department and [a female colleague of mine] and I would open the workshop with the head of the department and then the facilitator – we had a paid facilitator – would do the workshop. We'd only be there for about fifteen minutes to make sure everything was set up, say hello to the people, introduce people and leave. One day our facilitator was sick and we all got to the workshop and got the message that she'd be unable to attend. So we cancelled the workshop but the head of the department said – he must have been to twenty of these workshops already – he said to the group of men (they were all men – chief caretakers) that the facilitator couldn't come but [my female colleague and I] were going to strip for them ... It was just absolutely appalling. [My colleague] and I just ... [she] didn't say anything to him but the look was ... so I just said it was inappropriate.

As this incident demonstrates, gender equity policy is resisted by attention to female equity workers' embodiment as sexual beings. In organisational settings that are presumed to be rational, sexualising women has the effect of drawing attention to their embodiment of the non-rational, their intrusion in the public domain, thus deflecting their message and marginalising their voice as invalid in public discourse. It also disciplines women who have assumed some authority over male actions in public settings in which men have assumed a normative privilege over women's bodies. In other words, organisational rationality is a façade that is frequently disrupted by what Hearn and Parkin (1995) call organisation sexuality.

Revealing organisation sexuality

One way to think about the concept of organisation sexuality is to examine the ways in which divisions of labour are both constituted by and constitute normative constructions of sexuality: masculine and feminine. However, organisation sexuality is also about desire, the body, the biological states associated with the masculine and feminine, and the ways in which female sexuality may be seen as disruptive to organisational efficiency. Organisational rules attempt to rationalise and control organisation sexuality by, for example, controlling physical and emotional proximity, but it still finds expression in the interstices of space (e.g. in out-of-the-way locations) and time (coffee breaks, office parties, etc.) through language and imagery, gaze and touch, and emotions and feelings. Normative expressions of sexuality in the particular culture of organisations that privilege male sexuality is called into question by gender equity policy and is often resisted by the imposition of male sexual power. For example, all of the women in this study reported being constructed by others, even senior administrators, as a 'prude' and 'spoiler'. Linda described one incident at an end-of-year party in June.

LINDA: We had a little party in the courtyard at the education centre and somebody was up at the microphone. They were making speeches, giving out little parting gifts to people and [an administrator] made some [sexist] comment ... but then he said, 'Whoops, can't say that.

Linda's here.' So – it was a sexist comment – his reaction was to say, 'Whoops, can't say that! Linda's here.' What about the fifty other women who were standing around the microphone listening to the comment he made?

Linda had not only been implicitly labelled as a prude but, by constructing her as a spoiler, the administrator making the speech had also differentiated her from other women. That is, Linda was discursively constructed as deviant, whereas his characterisation of other women in his (hetero)sexist comments was imposed on them as 'normal'. Kate responded to Linda's story by describing the same pattern of behaviour exhibited by her supervisor who, in the one and only performance evaluation she had in almost seven years of employment, commented on his perception that since she had come to the board, 'people feel like they can't have any fun any more'. She commented somewhat wearily about this experience, 'I wore a lot of that as personal ... (pause) ... and I don't want to say attacks but, you know, that sort of personal ... (pause) ... I don't know what the word is if not attacks.' As Marg listened to each of these stories, she wryly commented, 'Sexism is such fun.'

Martin observes that 'heterosexuality is itself a compulsory set of relations produced not at the level of the body, but at the level of discourse and social practice, a compulsory sexuality that enables male dominance and refuses autonomy or solidarity among women' (1988, citing Rich 1980: 12). That is, expressing one's (hetero)sexuality in (educational) organisations marks oneself as 'female' and, therefore, less authoritative and capable because of the difference one represents. As Blackmore notes, 'Gender, sexuality and the body are part of the complex "technology of control" within organisations and how women come to be integrated unequally into organizational life' (1999: 171). One technology of control that all three equity agents noted was trading on heterosexist discourses by those who labelled women working towards gender equity as lesbians. Within homophobic school settings, the effect was to discourage, isolate, and belittle the efforts of these women in schools which also effectively disarmed allies for the work Marg, Linda, and Kate were hired to accomplish.

LINDA: [T]here were committed people in our schools, and I'm going to say particularly at the secondary level, that I know are doing some awesome stuff.

MARG: I think that they personally get singled out within school environments and often get subjected to a lot of personal attacks. I mean ... People get accused of lesbianism all the time, and I mean, it shouldn't be a hurtful thing, right? ... But it gets thrown up as an accusation, you know, so you're either prudish, you don't have enough straight sex in your life, or you're a lesbian and that this is a terrible thing in a homophobic world. I mean, women who are lesbians have a terrible time working on these issues and women who aren't lesbians ... they're all 'tainted' in a homophobic world.

Kate, the only woman who was single when she took up her position, made a particular point at the end of our last interview of returning to the theme of the ways in which her work was personalised which was, as she put it, 'what makes the job so hard'. Perhaps, as Blackmore notes, Kate encountered more coercive resistance to her presence because 'single women in particular [are constructed as] deviant, different and dangerous, either because of their implied lesbianism or sexual availability' (1999: 171). On one occasion, for example, Kate found some 'virgin again' pills had been placed on her desk by a 'secret pal' and on another she was publicly reminded that her predecessor had been willing to wear a 'boobie prize' – a hat festooned with large plastic breasts – at an office golf tournament. The implication was that her unwillingness to participate in similar sexual 'play' was at the least prudish and humourless, if not evidence of an alternative sexual preference.

Let's get personal

As Blackmore notes about the resistance that equity advocates faced in Australia, 'One could be passionate about power but not about equality' (1999: 112). While the equity workers in this study found it expedient to contain their passion as strategic emotional work, it was that passion which allowed them to remain hopeful that dominant notions of meritocracy, based on non-rational normative preferences, could be disrupted and transformed. Therefore, while the personal – the emotional – was used as an instrument of resistance against them, it was also a powerful instrument for change.

Kate, Linda, and Marg continue to be aware of the power of neo-liberal discourses to displace public equity policy with discourses of the marketplace, but they are willing to continue the emotional labour of acting as individual subjects working to effect change within shifting organisational locations. As political ideologies have reshaped the discourses around equity practices in their organisation, they have simply repositioned themselves within the discursive territory available to them. For example, following our interviews, Kate's official role as an equity advocate was discontinued following the passage of Bill 8 and the amalgamation of her board with three others, but she was actively pursuing avenues within new committee structures where she could continue to advocate for all forms of equity. She spoke hopefully about her intent to continue advocating for equitable employment practices, especially for immigrant women, in whatever ways she could. While emotions in the domain of the personal were used as an instrument of resistance against the work of the equity advocates in this study, they are also a powerful instrument for change and one that needs to be considered thoughtfully in the work of social justice in educational workplaces.

Notes

1 Kate worked for a largely rural board, Linda for a board comprised of a highly industrialised urban city and surrounding suburbs and rural areas, and Marg for a very large urban board in Ontario with a long history of policy commitment to gender equity.
2 For a more complete discussion of my research, see Wallace 2002.
3 The names used are pseudonyms for the participants in this study.
4 Here I am referencing Dean's (1999) notion of govern/mentality as mentalities of governing by both those who govern and those who are governed. Governmentality has been taken up as an analytical tool very broadly. See, for example, Miller and Rose 1992; Spencer 2001.
5 Canada's education system is governed through a series of acts and bills at the provincial level of governance.
6 *Canada's Charter of Rights and Freedoms* is an example of federal and provincial discourses of rights in Canada.
7 See Wallace 2002 for a fuller discussion of the policies that preceded Bill 79.

References

Boler, M. (1999) *Feeling Power: Emotions and Education*, New York: Routledge.

Blackmore, J. (1989) 'Educational leadership: A feminist critique and reconstruction', in J. Smyth (ed.) *Critical Perspectives on Educational Leadership*, London: Routledge.

—— (1996) 'Doing "emotional labour" in the education market place: Stories from the field of women in management', *Discourse: Studies in the Cultural Politics of Education*, 17, 3: 337–49.

—— (1999) *Troubling Women: Feminism, Leadership, and Educational Change*, Buckingham: Open University Press.

Blackmore, J. and Sachs, J. (1999) 'Managing diversity or managing for diversity in the corporate university', paper presented at the annual meeting of the Australian Association of Research in Education, Melbourne, 1999.

Coulter, R. (1998) 'Us guys in suits are back: Women, educational work and the market economy in Canada', in A. MacKinnon, I. Elgqvist-Saltzman, and A. Prentice (eds) *Education into the Twenty-First Century: Dangerous Terrain for Women?* London: Falmer.

Dean, M. (1999) *Governmentality: Power and Rule in Modern Society*, London: Sage.

Fineman, S. (1993) 'Introduction', in S. Fineman (ed.) *Emotion in Organisations*, London: Sage.

Foucault, M. (1988) 'The ethic of care for the self as a practice of freedom', in J. Bernauer and D. Rasmussen (eds) *The Final Foucault*, Boston: MIT Press.

Game, A. (1991) *Undoing the Social: Toward a Deconstructive Sociology*, Milton Keynes: Open University Press.

Hearn, J. (1993) 'Emotive subjects: Organisational men, organisational masculinities and the (de)construction of emotions', in S. Fineman (ed.) *Emotion and Organisations*, London: Sage.

Hearn, J. and Parkin, W. (1995) *Sex at Work: The Power and Paradox of Organisation Sexuality*, rev. edn, New York: St. Martin's Press.

Kenway, J., Willis, S., Blackmore, J., and Rennie, L. (1994) 'Making "hope practical" rather than "despair convincing": Feminist poststructuralism, gender reform, and educational change', *British Journal of Sociology of Education*, 15, 2: 187–210.

Lemke, T. 'Foucault, governmentality, and critique', paper presented at the Rethinking Marxism Conference, University of Amherst, Maine, 2000. Online at www.thomaslemkeweb.de/publikationen/Foucault,%20Governmentality,%20and %20Critique%20IV-2.pdf (accessed 23 April 2008).

Martin, J. 'The suppression of gender conflict in organisations: Deconstructing the fissure between public and private', paper presented at the Annual Meeting of the Academy of Management, San Francisco, 1988.

Miller, P. and Rose, N. (1992) 'Governing economic life', *Economy & Society*, 19, 1: 1–31.

Pratt, M.B. (1984) 'Identity: Skin/blood/heart', in E. Bulkin, M.B. Pratt, and B. Smith (eds) *Yours in Struggle: Three Feminist Perspectives on Anti-Semitism and Racism*, Brooklyn: Long Haul Press.

Putnam, L. and Mumby, D. (1993) 'Organisations, emotions, and the myth of rationality', in S. Fineman (ed.) *Emotions in Organizations*, London: Sage.

Rich, A. (1980) 'Compulsory heterosexuality and lesbian existence', in *Blood, Bread and Poetry: Selected Prose*, New York: Norton.

Spencer, B. (2001) 'The seduction of the subject citizen: Governmentality and School governance policy', paper presented at the annual meeting of the American Educational Research Association, Seattle, April.

Wallace, J. (2002) 'An equitable organization: Imagining what is "not yet"', *Educational Management and Administration*, 30, 1: 83–100.

—— (2004) 'Educational *purposes economicus*: Globalization and the reshaping of educational purpose in three Canadian provinces', *Canadian and International Education*, 33, 1: 99–117.

Weber, M. (1968) *Economy and Society: An Outline of Interpretive Sociology*, Berkeley: University of California Press.

Whitehead, S. (1998) 'Disrupted selves: Resistance and identity work in the managerial arena', *Gender and Education*, 10, 2: 199–215.

13 The leader and the team

Emotional context in educational leadership

Megan Crawford

The emotional dimension of educational leadership is brought into particularly sharp focus when considering teams. The work of educational leaders is distinct from other forms of leadership because it deals with the hearts and minds of young people and those in the wider community context. Educational leadership is thus deeply concerned with teaching and learning, but it cannot ignore relationships and how adults work and learn together. Law and Glover note that educational leaders 'are expected to help others make sense of a complex world in which there is less predictability and more uncertainty – a major challenge which requires high-level skills, knowledge and understanding' (2000: 263). Educational leadership is, at one and the same time, about a social function, education, and also individuals who perform that function. In other words, educational leadership is contained both in personal roles, such as 'senior teacher', and as a function within a social setting. Ogawa and Bossert argue that: 'leadership flows through the network of roles that comprise organisations ... with different roles having access to different levels and types of resources' (1997: 19). Leadership is related to the distribution of resources through social networks, and it is educational leaders who help create the conditions in which people will want to work to the optimum levels of their energy, interest, and commitment (Whitaker 1997).

This chapter will argue that leadership is reliant on both the emotional quality of those in leadership roles in schools and the quality of the social relationships of the team. There is a synergy between views of leadership as a process, distributed throughout the school, how those in leadership positions manage their own emotions, and how those they lead experience and manage their own emotions. I examine that synergy, drawing primarily, but not exclusively, on the social constructionist perspective suggesting that the stories people tell about emotion not only give substance to the feelings of the participants, but help leaders understand the emotional context within which they work.

Describing emotional context

Currently in England, headteachers (principals) and senior teachers are becoming increasingly more difficult to recruit and retain, leading to a policy emphasis on how to recruit more successfully and how different forms of leadership might address this shortage. In other words, the emphasis is on structure, not people and their needs and concerns. Ten years ago, before the current crisis, Whitaker noted that there was a need to challenge the principle that people and how they are treated is one of the least significant factors for consideration in schools, 'What is so abusive about schools is the appalling waste of human talent they preside over' (1997: 144). My own research into emotion and educational leadership has suggested that problems like recruitment difficulties in schools are much easier to discuss 'rationally' than relating these problems to the more problematic relationship of emotion and educational leadership.

Sugrue maintains that the focus in the literature over the last two decades has been on conceptualisations of school leadership that have evolved from school effectiveness and improvement research, and have therefore 'Unwittingly shaped and circumscribed the discourse on leadership' (2005: 6), mainly to do with the standards agenda. The crux of his argument is that although many types of leadership are advocated, for those who actually practise leadership, these typologies add nothing of any real value. Bottery also suggests that 'the very literature that is intended to provide some signposts can itself begin to look like a bewildering maze' (2004: 13). He argues that if leaders took anything at all from this, it was that leadership is in essence rational. It is the very act of labelling that may add a patina of rationality. Looking at theoretical models of leadership the opposite can also appear. Theories that were described rationally seemed to have emotional connections, while some, such as 'invitational leadership', have more explicit connections to emotion through its emphasis on affirmation, respect, trust, and support. Reading summaries of the main leadership theories with a focus on emotion can be helpful:

> Trait theories, for instance, have suggested that leaders possess certain distinct personal qualities; style theories have suggested that leaders are distinguished by the different importance they place on the management of tasks or the management of relationships; situational theorists have argued that different situations actually require different kinds of leaders; and contingency theories have suggested that the best way forward is through the matching of a particular leadership style to a particular situation.
>
> (Bottery 2004: 13)

It is clear that affect is a thread that runs through them all. In other words, emotion and rationality are interpenetrated. If this view is taken, it leads to a different view of the emotional context of leadership. Sugrue suggests that transformation of schools would be better served by reasserting the importance of 'individuals, their biographies, and their passions, in how schooling has the capacity to work for the advantage of all learners' (2005: 13). A focus on individuals and their passions may seem to be going against the grain of prevalent thinking in educational leadership – the figure of the dominant 'leader' would seem to be old fashioned and out of step with research. Southworth (2004) has suggested that leadership research has moved away from whether heads and other leaders do make a difference, to focus on the ways they have their influence. Emotion is one of those pathways, and a very important one. It is through the organisational perspective that the impact of emotion may be felt, and it is at the organisational level that many research studies have been carried out.

The culture of an organisation is created and sustained at least partly by the emotions of the participants, and it is important that those in leadership roles understand something about how emotion affects the team. Some may be conscious displays, some unconscious, but it may be that the unheralded and unacknowledged aspects of an organisation may be the very parts that help create and sustain culture, and it is important that educational leaders seek to understand them.

Pathways of emotion

In the 1980s Hochschild wrote:

> Emotion functions as a prism through which we may reconstruct what is often invisible or unconscious – what we must have wished, must have expected, must have seen or imagined to be true in the situation. From the colors of the prism we infer back what must have been behind and within it.
>
> (1983: 246)

The prism is a useful metaphor for seeing educational leadership and emotion as transparent and yet deceptively powerful as affective concerns are connected to important areas such as values, principles, and judgements. One way to look at this would be to view feelings as inhabiting people, and emotions inhabiting schools. One is related to the self and the other to the organisation.

As educational leaders work with teams of people, there are insights to be gained from many approaches to the study of emotion. As leaders work with expressed emotion and unknown inner feelings, a psychodynamic approach may be illuminating. Knowledge of other perspectives from the psychological literature may also prove an invaluable aid to the practice of team leadership in education. Research by Haviland-Jones and Kahlbaugh, for example, has shown that emotion may be a central organising feature in some dynamic constructs of identity, because emotions, thoughts, and feelings are the things that are most real to people at any given moment. To find the inner self, they argue, requires a dynamic construction of identity or an 'ongoing construction of connections between emotion and self-knowledge' (2004: 293) to those emotional events that are the 'glue of identity'. They argue that identity itself is 'a product of intersubjective memories, present events, and emotional resonances' (2004: 301), and that one of the functions of emotion is to glue together chunks of experience to provide meaning. So, emotion is linked to leadership in many significant ways, through past events, through talk, through the personal sense of self, and in the culture of schools and schooling. All of this is linked to the part that emotion plays in relational events, and how they are encoded and received in individual memory. Memory is a crucial aspect of teams, whether one is a leader or follower as it helps define the unique personal identity and story of each.

Developing leadership narratives

Elsewhere (Crawford 2008) I have suggested that educational leaders weave their own leadership narrative to explain themselves as they develop. A personal leadership narrative is dependent on emotional involvement and recall. One example of a written version of this is David Loader's narrative of his professional life as an Australian college principal. He suggests that personal revelations in interactions with other school leaders allow conversations to have more meaning for those involved in school leadership (1997: 145).

The leadership narrative, made up of emotional influences and social relationships, has to relate to others' personal narratives, as well as the organisation's 'emotional histories' built up over time from everyday interactions, part of the social construction of reality and the culture of organisation. All these narratives in turn influence the interpretation of events by the participants involved in social interactions. The narratives may be internal or externalised into stories. Stories that are told in teams, or in the organisation more generally, give substance to the feelings held by the participants. But interpretation of them is hermeneutic, and defined both by the pre-understanding of the interpreter, and the pre-socialisation of the other person. Such stories can bring out areas of team work not accessible by other methods, and are part of the way that fundamental meaning structures in a person's life can be affected. What gives such narratives their power is how they touch upon leadership concerns emotionally. Social constructionists suggest that such stories not only represent personal emotions but also actively constitute the emotional form of work life. Fineman argues that although we can express our feelings directly, for example 'I hate these meetings', our feelings often are encased in the stories we tell, and that these stories importantly give legitimacy to our feelings. He even goes so far as to suggest that they are a key mechanism of emotional expression because they allow people to safely express difficult feelings. Stories can help people over any difficulties they may have with professional acceptability in discussing feelings. As Fineman notes, 'The story is not a measure of the objective truth of an event, but is a fine indicator of our feelings and how we wish to present them' (2003: 17). Stories resonate in different ways with different people but also entail diverse and even contradictory meanings for a single person (Gabriel 2000: 90).

Temperament and identity may also play a part in the leadership narrative. Caspi *et al.* (1987) indicate in their research that there are patterns of childhood emotionality that people carry with them into adulthood. For example, they noted (30 years later) that men who were assessed as ill tempered as children were less likely to stay in school and more likely to change jobs, while women were more affected in their home life. Such research is a pointer to links between the headteacher as adult and as child, especially in terms of behaviours and values. Saarni, a developmental psychologist, puts this well when she states:

> Temperament provides some degree of response style consistency over time and across situations, whereas specific emotional reactions yield the variability that comes from the influence of specific contexts, specific appraisals, specific social transactions, and the unique meaning systems that are applied to make sense of emotional experience.
>
> (2000: 312)

This concurs with Fineman's recommendation that, 'Ideally, we require theory that collapses the individual/organizational/social distinctions from the outset and builds explanations interrelationally' (2000a: 4), but this is particularly difficult to achieve. More manageable, perhaps, is theory that has certain main assumptions. Saarni's work on emotional development of children is particularly pertinent for discussing the role of personal histories in the way that educational leaders view emotion, feeling, and leadership because she states an assumption that guides her: 'our emotional experiences are inseparable from our relationships with others' (2000: 319). This is crucial to any understanding of the leader and the team. Our assumptions also permeate any understanding of identity, and the way it interrelates with social experiences. She also states that

> People are motivated to construct a desired identity (which incorporates social categories such as gender) that derives its meaningfulness from others' responses to the self's projected images … and it is in this sense that identity itself constitutes a contextual process that permeates people's emotional and social experiences.
>
> (2000: 319)

Culture and context are the setting for the individual personal history, and if emotions have a function for fulfilling inter- and intrapersonal goals, then the leader's life so far, and how one assumes the identity of an educational leader, will influence the work of the team.

So far, I have suggested that educational leaders frame their practice within a particular narrative which helps them to function as leaders. A personal leadership narrative is holistic because it takes in the whole person. The way that a person conceptualises his or her own leadership will have an impact on the way that that leadership is then practised. The personal leadership narrative is related to the idea of emotions being both inherent *and* socially constructed. The telling of this narrative can pinpoint aspects of both emotion and feeling, and in this respect can be seen to be related to the Johari window, which allows the reflective learner to combine self-examination with feedback from others in order to increase knowledge of the 'unknown self'. Personal narratives also reveal some of the complex relationship between gender and emotion. Hall looked at three female primary heads in her study of six women headteachers, tracing their path to headship. Barbara, Heather, and Susan all shared a commitment to becoming a teacher from early childhood, which was not true of my sample. She did find, however, that

> parental influences (particularly fathers) were significant influences on the women heads' early independence, self-sufficiency and desire to succeed ... although family of origin is by no means an exclusive influence on future values and behaviour, it shapes perception of which resources achieve which results.
>
> (1996: 43–4)

Leithwood (2006) has also suggested that leaders' underlying values are important when choosing headteachers.

The present understandings of emotion in the leadership field are at best partial and at worst a simplification, for example, in the case of Emotional Intelligence (EI). In a piece that lays out how emotion has become a management commodity, Fineman reminds the reader that it has always been known that certain work relationships require emotional skills (2000b: 102), but with EI, what Goleman has succeeded in doing is linking such competences explicitly to business success. He suggests that such management ideas become popular because of 'psychological, cultural and rhetorical factors' (in Fineman 2000a: 103). If EI might just give a business a competitive edge, then it is something that business leaders should take note of. Again Fineman notes:

> Presenting emotional intelligence as a learned competence or set of competences is a key ingredient of the sell ... emotional intelligence is stripped of any 'irrational', 'feminine', even 'feeling' connotations that could worry or alienate managers. It is less a celebration of feeling than a resource to enhance managers' 'intelligent', rational control.
>
> (2000b: 105)

Leading a team is a role that requires emotional skill, and has struck a chord amongst those who lead in schools. EI has been seen as a possible solution to a problem of recruitment and sustainability. It is sobering, however, to bear in mind that success is not so easily defined. As Fineman graphically describes it:

> The search for key, universal, characteristics of managerial success has a long history of futility. If emotionally intelligent managers succeed, so do/have managers who seem to make no conscious choice about how to express their emotions – be they typically kind, charismatic, impassive, volatile, aggressive, autocratic, even ruthless. On this basis it would, at times, be emotionally intelligent to be uncompromising, inflexible, angry or pessimistic.
>
> (2000b: 109)

In the psychological literature, assessment of the claims of EI has been carried out by Matthews *et al.*, who note that much of Goleman's (1995) work demonstrates nothing much new in terms of research as a great deal is already known about emotions and personality; they state that Goleman makes strong claims 'with little (or scant) empirical backing' (2002: 13). The plausibility of EI is due, at least partially, to the fact that it reminds leaders what they probably already knew; that emotion and thinking do work together, and that there has perhaps been too much emphasis on the rational and not enough on the power of emotion and feeling. EI's popularity could also be because rational discussion of emotional competences is emotionally safe, and does not require or suggest a change in internal personal feelings, or a challenge to one's own leadership narrative.

There is an argument for bringing back the personal, inherently emotional approach to the role of the principal: 'Leadership has its highs and lows, its successes and failures. Principals cry, laugh, dream and become suspicious. There are times when principals do want the fairy godmother to come and save them' (Loader 1997: 3). Earlier, I noted that Ogawa and Bossert conceptualise leadership as flowing 'through the network of roles that comprise organisations' (1997: 19). If leadership is an organisational quality, then so is emotion. To paraphrase Ogawa and Bossert, it flows through the network of people who comprise schools, but at the same time, emotion in educational leadership resides not only in the organisation but also in the person of the leader and the lead; the inherent and socially constructed aspects of emotion work together. Both of these make up the emotional context of the school.

Emotional context

Educational leaders have to perform a delicate emotional balancing act most of the time. They have to build a climate of genuine emotion where acceptance and trust are the building blocks of team work, and others not only want to follow them as leaders, but feel able to become leaders themselves. Thus positive emotion could be a necessary condition of distributed leadership. Leaders need to be able to engage themselves and others in the task of emotionalising organisations. Emotionalising schools means that educational leaders need to allow new understandings of emotion to inform leadership, and to begin asking how and why emotions shape these processes. All the richness of the research into emotion from many fields of study, such as described in this book, can add more to educational leadership than a concentration on any one particular perspective.

Those who work in teams might find it useful to look at descriptions of leadership as an art. De Pree, in his best-selling book on how to succeed at leadership, sums this viewpoint up when he states: 'Leadership is much more an art, a belief, a condition of the heart, than a set of things to do. The visible signs of artful leadership are expressed ultimately, in its practice' (1989: 148). This relationship between the rational and the emotional allows leaders to have an emotional side of practical value to them in their many roles. In other words:

> Key to such research are forms of knowledge of practical value to the people involved, ways of knowing Aristotle referred to as phronesis. A primary principle behind this research is that it makes co-researchers of participant and practitioner; and because our curiosity, when shared, can change things, the view is that we might as well work together to make practical changes that are mutually welcomed.
>
> (Strong 2003: 264)

It is Aristotle's suggestion that a man of practical wisdom should be able to deliberate well about the things that are good and helpful for himself that enable an effective team in education.

Whitaker argues that it has been a false start when leadership theorists have tried to see what, in the personality and experience of skilled leaders, explains their skills and abilities. He suggests that a more productive avenue is to ask, 'What is it that enables successful organisations to succeed and thrive?' and that this will lead to an answer that is more complex than simply good leadership from the top. Whitaker proposes 'life-enhancing leadership' which helps people to be as effective as they both want to be, and 'have the potential to be' (1997: 127, 128). By asking what enables successful organisations to succeed and thrive, one of the answers may be that the particular, individual, emotional narrative of the leader will influence team context in a way so that others can be effective. Whitaker implicitly acknowledges this when he notes that:

> It is through the countless interpersonal transactions of the school day that people's lives are changed, organisational improvements are made,

> dreams are realised and needs are met. We need more understanding of those snatched moments in corridors.... Life-centred leadership is essentially a catalytic process, helping others to bring about changes in themselves.
>
> (1997: 140)

In my own research, a very experienced head underlined the 'countless interpersonal transactions of the school day' when he talked about how his relatively new inexperienced staff was developing:

> I've got a newer staff coming in which means that a new culture of working together and openness is beginning to develop. There are still the odd situations where unnecessary problems happen and I ask the staff to ask themselves 'Are we working together?' I still think they could be more open emotionally among one another – I mean, a teacher had gone in for an operation, and the staff didn't know, so I was wondering whether I should have told them. It is a fundamental lack of closeness – it makes me wonder sometimes – am I doing this wrongly? I've been trying to get them involved, as I don't have the best answer for this school, and maybe that some of these things I care too much about!
>
> (Crawford 2007a: 89)

Southworth argues that literature on headship in the UK is far too preoccupied with seeing leadership through the lens of the headteacher, and casting heads as 'pivotal, proprietorial and powerful', whilst in fact the landscape is changing towards distributed and 'learning centred leadership' (2004: 22). The rhetoric of the landscape has indeed changed, but it remains true that headteachers are still an emotional pivot. Their own emotional well-being is vital to creating the conditions in which other sorts of leadership can develop and thrive. All the heads that I interviewed saw themselves in this pivotal position emotionally, and their personal leadership narrative emphasised their desire to make a difference by being in charge. This does not mean in charge and proprietorial. Laura's answer to what sort of head she was gives a better clue:

> Somebody who has clear sense of what they are trying to do and has a firm grip on what's happening and what others are doing. I aim to have open lines of communication – so that staff know what I am thinking and why I am thinking it; a spider in the centre of a web, but not an aggressive one!
>
> (Crawford 2007b: 91)

It is this centrality of the leader emotionally that has come out clearly from this research. Thus headteachers are not dominating and powerful in a masculine, powerful sense, but rather as webs spun from their own emotional bases and that of their staff, forming an emotional context within which the narrative of education is carried out. To put it more simply, their knowledge of their own emotional selves enables them to visualise how they wanted others to relate to each other within the school (staff, parents, and children), within an emotionally coherent context. Hall also notes this in her study of six female headteachers. She suggests that for each, effectiveness 'depended on her sense of self-efficacy combined with support from others which allowed her to be herself' (1996: 186). She also wondered whether men as managers are as concerned to know and manage self as women, and notes that more research is needed 'into the relationship between men's self-concept and their educational leadership practice' (1996: 187). Although this is not within the remit of this chapter, it is nevertheless an important point to note. Of course leadership has changed since Southworth's study in the 1980s and Hall's in the 1990s. Society is more culturally attuned to matters of emotion, and public expression of emotion is more acceptable now for leaders in government as well as education. This still reflects, however, much of Hall's concerns with gender, and, in particular, issues of control and power. The need to deepen knowledge of one's self as a leader emotionally needs to relate to such outward expressions of feelings, at the same time as this self-knowledge generates a powerful emotional context for team working within an educational organisation.

Conclusion

In this chapter, I have argued that an individual's complexity is not adequately served by competency approaches to emotion, and thus neither is the team or group best explained by studying such approaches. The leader forms and makes manifest an emotional context within which the other important narrative, education, is carried out. To put it another way, the leaders' knowledge of their own personal leadership narrative enables them to visualise how they want others in the organisation to relate to each other. Their concentration is upon providing an emotionally coherent context within which others can thrive. The role of 'the leader', and his/her interrelationship with leadership throughout the organisation, can be effectively re-conceptualised through emotion and the personal leadership narrative. By giving more voice to the personal leadership narrative, further questions are raised about the way educational leadership is shaped by personal emotional experience. As suggested in the last section, more work could be done on the interaction between biological, social and cultural past, gender, and the emotional context of a particular educational leadership context. Using the personal leadership narrative could uncover relationships with other studies, such as Hall's (1996) and Coleman's (2002) which signpost the links between life history, relationships at home and work, and socialisation into teaching.

The recurrent difficulty with emotional matters is that emotion and leadership can be viewed as difficult territory where the knowledge base in educational leadership is only now developing fully, beginning to draw much more consistently on other disciplines as I have shown in this chapter. For the educational leader, and the team member, in an accountability climate such as exists in many Western nations, it is often difficult to argue rational reasons for exploring the emotions of oneself and others. This requires an in-depth understanding of how affects are often more significant as rationales for, and outcomes of, actions rather than cognitions. So, although there may be a cognitive rationale for actions, there is usually an underlying and probably stronger affective rationale. In a fundamental sense educational leaders are moved to action by their feelings. Dillard (1995) also argues that educational leaders, and those they work with, not only use their experiences to lead, but they lead from themselves as people, their past experiences and their personalities and life experiences. Bringing these other experiences to the fore can enhance not only the leader, but also the team.

References

Bottery, M. (2004) *The Challenges of Educational Leadership*, London: Paul Chapman.

Caspi, A., Elder, G.H., and Benn, D.J. (1987) 'Moving against the world: Life course patterns of explosive children', *Developmental Psychology*, 23, 2: 308–13.

Coleman, M. (2002) *Women as Headteachers: Striking the Balance*, Stoke-on-Trent: Trentham.

Crawford, M. (2007a) 'Emotional coherence in primary school headship', *Educational Management Leadership and Administration*, 35, 4: 521–34.

—— (2007b) 'Rationality and emotion in primary school leadership: An exploration of key themes', *Educational Review*, 59, 1: 87–98.

—— (2008) *Getting to the Heart of Leadership: Emotion and the Educational Leader*, London: Sage.

De Pree, M. (1989) *Leadership is an Art*, New York: Doubleday.

Dillard, C.B. (1995) 'Leading with her life: An African feminist (re)interpretation of leadership for an urban high school principal', *Educational Administration Quarterly*, 31, 4: 539–63.

Fineman, S. (2000a) 'Emotional arenas revisited', in S. Fineman (ed.) *Emotion in Organizations*, London: Sage.

—— (ed.) (2000b) *Emotion in Organizations*, London: Sage.

—— (2003) *Understanding Emotion at Work*, London: Sage.

Gabriel, Y. (2000) *Storytelling in Organizations: Facts, Fiction, and Fantasies*, Oxford: Oxford University Press.

Goleman, D. (1995) *Emotional Intelligence*, New York: Bantam.

Hall, V. (1996) *Dancing on the Ceiling: A Study of Women Managers in Education*, London: Paul Chapman.

Haviland-Jones, J. and Kahlbaugh, P. (2004) 'Emotion and identity', in M. Lewis and J. Haviland-Jones (eds) *Handbook of Emotions*, New York: Guilford Press.

Hochschild, A.R. (1983) *The Managed Heart: Commercialization of Human Feeling*, Berkeley, University of California Press.

Law, S. and Glover, D. (2000) *Educational Leadership and Learning*, Buckingham: Open University Press.

Leithwood, K. (2006) Discussion with author, British Educational Leadership, Management & Administration Society Conference, Milton Keynes.

Loader, D. (1997) *The Inner Principal*, London: Falmer Press.

Matthews, G., Zeidner, M., and Roberts, R. (2002) *Emotional Intelligence: Science and Myth*, Cambridge: MIT Press.

Ogawa, R. and Bossert, S. (eds) (1997) *Leadership as an Organisational Quality*, Buckingham: Open University Press.

Saarni, C. (2000) 'The social context of emotional development', in M. Lewis and J. Haviland-Jones (eds) *Handbook of Emotions*, New York: Guilford Press.

Southworth, G. (2004) *Primary School Leadership in Context: Leading Small, Medium and Large Sized Schools*, London: RoutledgeFalmer.

Stoll, L. and Fink, D. (1996) *Changing Our Schools: Linking School Effectiveness and School Improvement*, Buckingham: Open University Press.

Strong, T. (2003) 'Getting curious about meaning-making in counselling (1)', *British Journal of Guidance and Counselling*, 31, 3: 259–73.

Sugrue, C. (2005) 'Putting "real life" into school leadership: Connecting leadership, identities and life history', in C. Sugrue (ed.) *Passionate Principalship*, London: RoutledgeFalmer.

Whitaker, P. (1997) *Primary Schools and the Future*, Buckingham: Open University Press.

14 Emotional engagement with leadership

Peter Gronn

> I suppose the ones, when you take those roles on, those leadership roles, they are the ones when you know you are going to be really risk taking...
>
> Respondent #56

This chapter is about an imagined possibility and the probability of its realisation. The imagined possibility is leadership, imagined in the sense that one of the potential rehearsed selves that career mobile individuals may construct when pondering their futures is 'school leader'. Realisation concerns the likely eventuality that not only will a prototype of school leader form part of their mental furniture, but that such prototypes will be utilised and fine-tuned when individuals begin grooming themselves for leadership (Gronn and Lacey 2004). Probability refers to the calculus of combined risk factors and emotions that increases or diminishes the likelihood of the possibility becoming real. This calculus is the main focus of the discussion, for the role of risk perception, assessment and management, and the emotional bases of risk-related decision-making are all curiously neglected aspects of the development of organisational leaders generally and school leaders in particular. As part of this neglect, the question of what it means for individuals to engage with leadership is rarely if ever asked. Perhaps this might be understandable and acceptable when the climate of risk associated with leading schools is relatively benign. If, however, a fundamental shift takes place in the overall balance of the distribution of risk associated with leadership, as has been occurring with devolved schooling reform, then these issues begin to assume some urgency. As a result of what I have recently termed the 'war on schools' (Gronn 2008) – the intermittent although persistent collusion between governments and media in exposing instances of leadership (especially of head teachers) they deem to be unacceptable, ostensibly to appease parents and their children – levels of potential exposure to risk and emotional fall-out for leaders have increased. Evidence of decreasing attractiveness of school leader roles and head teacher supply problems in some systems which have devolved autonomy to schools, while they have simultaneously imposed a regime of accountability, suggests that these two developments may be connected.

In light of gaps in current knowledge, the twofold purpose of the chapter is to provide conceptual clarity about the idea of engagement and, on the basis of some empirical data, to offer a rudimentary understanding of the process of engagement. The first objective is significant for two main reasons. First, while there is a rapidly expanding body of literature on a host of emotional aspects of leadership, and on occupational roles and workplace relations more generally, some of which touches on aspects of engagement, remarkably little of this material has been directed at trying to better understand the experiences of individuals when they seek to become leaders. Second, the positioning and relationship of engagement to a series of closely related ideas and concepts (e.g. self-efficacy, commitment) require clarification and are not well understood. The significance of the second objective derives from the connection between engagement and the changing environment of risk for prospective leaders alluded to in the opening paragraph. Due to restrictions of length and because this chapter is an initial attempt to analyse engagement, the discussion is indicative rather than definitive. It will have achieved its purpose to the extent that it clarifies some of the key issues, maps relations between some of the core concepts, provides a preliminary theoretical grounding of engagement based on an analysis of data from school leader informants, suggests productive avenues for future research, and advances understanding of the role of emotional engagement in leadership.

Risky business

Leaders occupy role spaces. Formal role spaces that entail responsibilities are usually arranged hierarchically in spines or chains and carry with them some degree of exposure to risk. While individuals' sense of their exposure to risk depends partly on subjectively grounded perceptions (Breakwell 2007: 14), changes in the overall social and political distribution of risks alter significantly individuals' level of risk exposure (Beck 1992: 22–3). Thus, while exposure to hazard for role incumbents (e.g. to accountability, litigation, trial by media) in a traditional bureaucratic command-and-control paradigm of delivering public services tends to be lessened due to the seeming invisibility of risk or its pooling and absorption by the system as a whole, as part of the paradigm of quasi-autonomous school site devolution, risk is made highly visible and is focused sharply on the upper level of an organisation. This pattern of re-distribution ensures that, by virtue of her or his overall responsibility, the most senior leader figure stands exposed to the bulk of the risks. That is, diffusion of risk assessment and management to devolved units concentrates the experience of hazard on a handful of identifiable individuals who become objects of public blame and possible humiliation. The significance of this development is that a role space is readily transformed into a risk space. A recent newspaper report illustrates what I mean. Denholm (2008) suggests that Scottish teachers' associations are bitter about local authorities which, when confronted by recalcitrant students and their parents' demands that their offspring have 'rights', capitulate by 'instructing schools not to confront the problem, but to appease complaining parents'. When local authorities side with parents, as part of a supine adoption of a de facto line of least resistance, it is alleged that head teachers intimidate and bully teachers into submission.

As part of this pact to conciliate parents, head teachers are under equal, if not more, pressure from their superiors to comply. Yet this is only one of the pressures confronting heads and principals. Elsewhere, Kathy Lacey and I have documented a range of the emotional challenges experienced by aspiring Australian principals as they consider the possibility of role transition (Gronn and Lacey 2004). But unless and until such aspirations are realised, the principal role remains merely an imagined leadership possibility for potential incumbents. A unique opportunity for imagination to translate into reality, however, is afforded by temporary occupancy of the principal or deputy principal roles. In Scotland, where Draper and McMichael (2002: 299) claimed that 10 per cent of headships were acting at the time of their research, temporary headships may extend to nearly two years. Moreover, the experiences of acting role incumbents are variable. In Victoria, for example, Lacey (2003: 174–5) found that assistant principals mostly regarded their experiences of acting principalship to be satisfying, for which an informant (#25) from another project[1] provided confirmatory evidence:

> I have had six months of being thrown in at the deep end [as acting principal]. I have absolutely learned masses of information. I have to do things myself and by doing it I've learned and I feel so well prepared to move on to a permanent position.

Another informant (#31), however, was dissatisfied:

> It [acting assistant principal] was just huge, huge. I just felt burned out. And I think it has taken me probably until about halfway through this year to feel okay with that. And a lot of times get over the fact that I did feel very used. I really did. I just thought it was shocking, a really poor position to be in. And just to find that the whole answer to everything is: 'It will look good on your CV.' Big deal.

Likewise, Draper and McMichael (2003: 78) found that 11 of 64 Scottish acting heads were deterred by their experience of being 'consumed' by the role from seeking permanent headship appointments.

'Acting up', as it is known in Scotland, and other similar role transitions, for however brief a period, entail identity modification. This is because new roles require commitment and identification or 'time to learn the expected behaviours, attitudes, and even feelings that typify the role identity'. The risk inherent in these requirements is because 'the similarities between previous and current circumstances may be more apparent than real such that one's schemas are outmoded and one's expectations are no longer realistic' (Ashforth 2001: 74, 202). Depending on the anticipated costs of experiencing role transition (e.g. social, psychological), individuals may or may not choose to confront these challenges. More positively, on the other hand, opportunities to 'become' the incumbent of a future possible role provide individuals with the chance to realise a preferred self (Kahn 1990: 701; see Markus and Nurius 1986). The discussion that follows analyses the reflections of a set of Australian school leaders on their experiences as acting principals and assistant principals.[2] At the time of their temporary incumbencies, the 59 participants in the 12 focus interviews were mostly assistant principals or leading teachers. They were asked a series of questions about their career expectations, perceptions of the principalship and whether alternative work arrangements (e.g. shared or part-time roles) were likely to influence their willingness to apply for principal vacancies. The focus of this discussion is mainly on their responses to Q8, which asked: 'Have any of you had previous experience as principals, such as temporarily acting in the role? Describe this experience? Did it affect your aspirations? How?'

Trying it on for size

Acting principals may be external or internal appointees. If they are external to a school, they are most likely to be displaced from another location (displaced, perhaps, due to salary re-grading or school closure) or to be appointed from a pool of relievers. If they are internal, their appointments tend to occur by default. That is, as the persons who may be next in line hierarchically, the (temporary or protracted) absence of a superior virtually guarantees, in the vernacular of the day, that they will 'fill their shoes' or 'step up to the plate'. Persons required to act, therefore, may get little warning of this, may have little choice in the matter, and may be uncertain about how long 'temporary' or 'acting' will endure. All these factors shape their in-role experiences and their feelings about them. In respect of personal and professional self-definition, there is one feature that gives acting incumbencies their distinctiveness. Provided temporary status does not morph without warning into something more permanent, acting positions facilitate reversible self-rehearsal. That is, these are opportunities for people who are role transients to encounter a potentially new sense of self and experiment with an alternative persona, secure in the knowledge that the safety zone of their actual role awaits their impending return. For acting incumbents this impermanence tempers their recently mandated expenditure of emotional labour and sense of exposure to risk.

A self-rehearsal matrix was devised to classify the participants' testimonies. As is evident in Figure 14.1, this comprised two criteria: quality of acting experience and impact on intentions to apply for principal vacancies. Each criterion was sub-divided, according to whether experiences and intentions were deemed affirmative or negative. Four possible outcomes are captured by the matrix: an intention to become a principal because of an

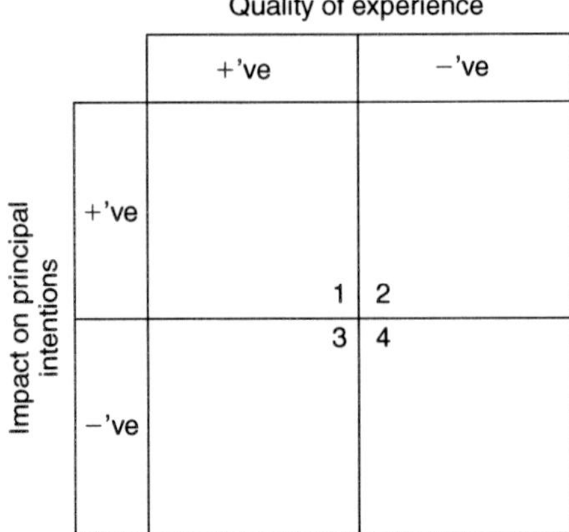

Figure 14.1 Acting principal self-rehearsal outcomes.

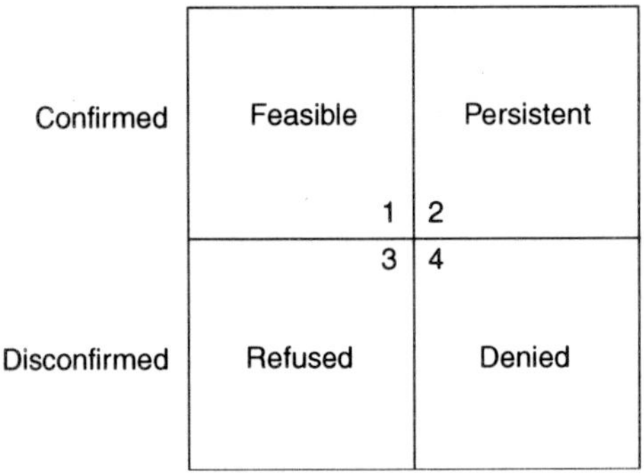

Confirmed	Feasible 1	Persistent 2
Disconfirmed	Refused 3	Denied 4

Figure 14.2 Anticipated selves.

overall positive experience (cell 1) or despite a negative one (cell 2); an intention not to become a principal despite a positive experience (cell 3) or as a result of a negative experience (cell 4). These four possibilities generate a set of anticipated selves which, unless and until such time as these are realised, retain provisional status (see Figure 14.2). Informants' representations of their experiences (cited as #1, #19, etc.) illustrate the four types – strictly speaking, there were no instances of type 2 in the sample,[3] although #43's equivocal comments were close:

1 *Feasible:* I applied for and got an acting position down at [place] as acting principal while the principal was away in second term. And that just gave me a real taste of, of some true leadership. [Later] I think

having that little experience last year has put me there. And I can see myself doing it. (#3)

2 *Persistent:* I am vacillating about my career aspirations. [Later] I can easily visualise myself as a principal and have acted at [school name] a number of times over an extended period of time as well, I didn't like that picture ... So when you are acting there you do tend to take that heat home with you a bit: 'Have I crossed all my t's, dotted all my i's, got this in on time?' ... I got [a] virus, I was very sick for a good 18 months, my father died ... So when you are dealing with the rest of life and then trying to put that on top of it, it wasn't something, I could do it, and I could picture myself doing it, but I didn't want to do it. (#43)

3 *Refused:* I basically probably used it [12 months acting as principal] to find out whether it was something I wanted to do. And I really enjoyed it and that's why I applied for the position because it gave me a whole new perspective on things. [Later] To be quite honest ... without being disrespectful to anyone, at this stage in my career it is not something that I find appealing to be, to be a principal, only because I don't feel that I know enough yet ... (#2)

4 *Denied:* I knew at the start of that three months [as acting principal] that I didn't really want to do it, and I knew at the end of the three months that I definitely didn't want to do it. (#55)

The four cells constitute two sets (i.e. 1–2, 3–4), with the resulting pairings differentiating potential engagers (1–2) from disengagers (3–4).[4] These contrasting calculations about principal leadership are evident in war stories about what it meant to be temporary.

Acceptable risk?

For a person confronting a choice of a career option, the question of whether engagement with it represents an acceptable risk boils down to 'whether or not it is *acceptable to accept the risk*' (Finkel 2008: 134). This is because, regardless of whatever may be thought of generally about the risks associated with a particular occupation, it is the individual in the end who says 'this is what I believe' about riskiness (Breakwell 2007: 259). Thus, even if leadership scores low on a scale of voluntarily undertaken hazardous pursuits (Lyng 1990), it is prospective leaders who have to decide in the end whether a risk assessment is worth undertaking. The following discussion of the data suggests that the less emotionally affirming that participants' temporary incumbency experiences have proved to be, the more likely their leadership reasoning will be prudential in character.

Possible self-confirmation

Among participants for whom acting principal was a positive opportunity, the overwhelming sensation was a boost in confidence. This feeling may be predicated on the need to have arrived at a point of readiness before being willing to take on an acting job: 'I guess it's only this year that I have decided that I would like to be a principal. I feel that, you know, I am suitably qualified, I've gained enough experience to be confident to, you know, lead a school, lead a team of teachers' (#32). A point of significance of being able to occupy the principal's office was that this provided a vehicle for self-exploration (#23):

> I think it's invaluable. It really is. Because at the end of the day, I mean, you are there, you are the person in the job. Not only do you get a better understanding of what the job's about, but you're testing yourself every day. I remember the first day I went in there and I was sitting in the chair thinking: 'I can't wait for the first task' ... because I was really keen to see how I was going to go ... I am a fairly confident person and I had to believe that I was going to be able to do it and I obviously could do it. But if you do, you test yourself. You are in the spot.

For some participants, their sense of confidence about the possibility of principalship originated from within themselves. #3, for example, claimed that the time had been right for her to act and that the acting experience not only gave her the 'self-confidence' but also the 'self-esteem I guess too':

> I am the youngest in this family of you beaut achievers and so: 'Oh shit! I can do it!' ... It was a very positive thing.

In #9's case, confidence meant that 'it was good to act and then have time to reflect'. In the absence of any support from her employer while acting for one term, she resolved that if she was ever to become a principal, then she needed to be 'totally confident of my own ability to cope without expecting the help from outside and, I suppose, totally confident that within the school there's people to support me'.

For other participants, their sense of confident self-confirmation was mirrored back in the reactions of colleagues (#23):

> It was quite amazing ... I thought I can't wait to do this job. And [my principal] was away a term and I loved it. And people said to me: 'God, I've never seen you so happy!' And even though I was happy in my own job and I still am, I really loved it. And ever since I have done that I have thought: 'Isn't that amazing. I almost enjoyed it more than my own job.'

Likewise, #1 said she 'got some nice feedback':

> I would be one to say: 'Oh, you don't have to worry about what other people think', but to be quite honest you do, well I do, and it was nice to get nice feedback. Confidence in me anyway.

Occasionally, role-derived perceptions of oneself as fitting a principal prototype did not register mentally as quickly as others' confirmatory perceptions, as in #17's recounting:

> I had a term acting as the principal and it took me quite a time to realise that, although inside I didn't feel like a principal, some of the people coming in to meet me did see that I was a principal. It was a really: 'Oh, gosh!', funny experience.

On the other hand, while acting may have proved sufficient to generate the added 'confidence to apply' for advertised vacancies (#50), 'positive feedback' from other people in the school community, even though it was 'very supportive', was merely proof that 'Oh yeah, I could do that [job] if I had to do it' but 'didn't mean that I particularly wanted to' (#33).

These remarks suggest that provided people grow in confidence as a result of positive experiences that fulfil or exceed their expectations of themselves then they may be less likely to foresee risks. This omission may occur because a purely rational approach to decision-making is inhibited by a positive emotional over-ride, in which a good outcome does not require attention being given to potentially negative costs (Lakomski 2008: 9). That is, because one's intuition may be that one has risen to the challenge of acting and has what it takes, as it were, then one's internal conversation (or neural representation of the events that make the experience affirming) is scripted so as to indicate that one is well on the way to mastery. This plausible hypothetical reasoning suggests that positive experiences generate a sense of immunity or inoculation from risk and that this then becomes the basis on which individuals engage: the experience feels right and it feels good, and there's a good fit emotionally (Damasio 2000: 239–44;[5] Breakwell 2007: 259). In short, emotional affirmation facilitates identity maintenance and takes priority over the need for precaution.

Possible self-disconfirmation

Contrast the reasoning in those accounts with these next illustrations in which participants were emotionally seared by their experiences – as #57 had been a number of years earlier after having been 'thrust' into being acting principal for six months. This was because

> our principal died early after arriving, so it was sort of being thrown in and left in the, floundering I guess. But we managed to survive the six months and I am still alive to tell the tale. However, that experience told me that I didn't ever want to have, to revisit it.

Those for whom their acting experience turned out to be disconfirming tended in their accounts to dwell on currently experienced benefits which would be put at risk by role transition or to highlight a series of hazardous events to which they had already been exposed.

The prospect of potentially forgone benefits acts as a disincentive that far outweighs any allure that may be attached to principal incumbency. For a number of years, for example, #11 had 'resisted' constant taps on the shoulder and encouragement to move upwards, despite having acted as principal for three school terms and knowing that she could 'manage the day to day things'. She enjoyed her assistant principal role and to have to move to take up an appointment would be disruptive for her 'teenagers who are coming to the end of high school'. Moreover, #10 said that

> if people have to relocate for a principalship that would be a big factor in whether people perceive that the advantages of the role are worth that.... When you like your life, you like your area, you like the climate and all of those sorts of things, if it means having to move a long way it's a hard call.

The implications of a move from a large regional centre to a school in a smaller centre, especially given that her spouse was seriously ill, was a bridge too far for one deputy: 'I am not willing to shift my family for that.' The daily hours were long (7am to 5pm), along with 'some nights', when one needed time with one's family, particularly young children, and 'there is no overtime and people don't recognise the hours you put into the job' (#50).

The list of principal role-associated hazards for those who were conscious of what they might be letting themselves in for was potentially endless. These included: 'the demands on your time' (#34), 'dealing with angry parents' (#48) and relationships – 'it also is probably the worst part of the job as well, when those relationships go wrong' (#42). In this regard, #31 had 'learned to depersonalise the parents thing even when they go ballistic and dump on you big time', but the 'hardest part is the staff stuff, dealing with underperforming staff': 'the staff stuff is the thing that gives you, or gives me, the biggest knot in your guts'. Finally, for (#45) the concerns were the 'sheer pressure and the accountability that is placed onto people and the litigation':

> It is not so bad as deputy principal, but as principal. The principal is accountable for everybody on the work site.... You know ... liable for actions of staff members without even knowing whether they are doing anything wrong. I find that is tremendously astounding.... That's a fairly frightening fact.

Furthermore:

> In the bigger picture there's [sic] other people who are just as accountable and more accountable to cover the principal.... We have a standing

> joke at school, at least we thought it was a joke but it proved to be a bit more serious than a joke. My favourite saying was that my hardest role was keeping the principal, the principal out of prison. And we used to jest about it quite often until of recent times where there was a band of allegations made against people within schools and those allegations didn't stop with the people they were aimed at but extended on to the principal as well, so it's quite a significant factor.
>
> (#45)

The experience of #6, who became an acting principal after a short period as a newly appointed assistant principal, captures more graphically than most how everything that possibly may go wrong sometimes in fact does go wrong:

> The only thing I didn't have happen to me in that acting position, I didn't have a flood. So I had everything else: fire, bomb scare, you name it. I had the whole lot in that eight weeks. So it was a fire and brimstone welcome to principalship.

It was also 'really quite scary' dealing with the paperwork associated with big issues at seven o'clock in the evening. In fairness, some days were 'fantastic', especially periods of relief teaching with the children, but this was not enough to offset the negativity:

> Acting where I, I am, as principal was really difficult. The staff there had gone through real upheaval, so it was a big school that had dropped numbers and so you were left with a hardened core of people that didn't like change, that didn't want to move on. And I had been left two or three little jobs to do, like rewrite the behaviour management policy … And just the antagonism that staff brought to me about that. And I used to go home and really wonder: 'What on earth, why am I here? Why am I doing this job to get all that angst that teachers throw at you?' And it gave me a different perspective on what was professionalism.

To cap it all, on one occasion a departmental official arrived in the school and commandeered the principal's office. This meant that 'I had to excuse myself to actually go into my office and get something, because they were interviewing in my office: "Oh, excuse me. Do you mind if I come in for a minute?" … It's rude … it's blatantly rude.'

Discussion

Prudence and providence

O'Malley (1996: 199–202) has detected an emerging trend of prudentialism in liberal democracies, which is consistent with devolution of risk. It means that governments have sought to diminish risk socialisation by state agencies in favour of privatised approaches to risk management (see Beck 1992: 3). Whereas the socialisation of risk assessment and its management entails spreading the 'costs of unfortunate events' throughout a population (Lupton 1999: 99–100), prudentialism requires individuals to exercise personal responsibility for risk management and to take it upon themselves to be risk averse by calculating the anticipated hazards associated with various personal choices and activities. In short, individuals bear the burden of identifying risks and ensuring that they do not put themselves at risk. The previous data suggest that when people are required to exercise prudence in relation to leadership they will do so. From a systemic point of view, this prudence may come at a cost. First, in relation to those for whom the principalship is a feasible possibility, employers have few grounds for concern and therefore little cost: such people have sufficient incentives to want to do the job of principal that their engagement with leadership, to all intents and purposes, may be characterised as 'rusted on'. But for those whose mindset is one of denial, principal leadership is unlikely to win their hearts and minds, and no incentive is ever likely to be big enough for them to alter their plans. Next, while those with a persistent mentality may draw on their own internally-driven incentives to deal with adversity, there can be little excuse for taking their disposition to persist for granted. Employing authorities and agencies would be well advised to try to identify such people and to provide them with support, for at some point persistence may atrophy into denial and their commitment slip away. Finally, one category among the four potential selves that is of genuine concern is the refuser group: these 'refuseniks' are the able, although unwilling, participants for whom almost no incentive to become principals is sufficiently appealing, as Williams' (2003: 163–4) research showed. For them the temperature in the kitchen feels far too hot and they have no wish to enter it. With their disavowal of leadership they represent a genuine loss of talent to the system.

Rules of engagement

One of the questions raised by the examples discussed in this chapter is: what counts as safe conduct in respect of leadership? Another is: to what extent, given that trust and risk appear to relate reciprocally – so that trust in managers affects perceptions of risk and acceptability of risk helps determine trust in managers (Breakwell 2007: 220) – is it the responsibility of an employer to create an occupationally safe conduct culture for leaders? These questions assume relevance because of the ways that awareness contexts operate for leaders (Glaser and Strauss 1964). While it may be possible in the case of manufactured mass leader cults to manipulate the amount and availability of information that diffuses about public leader identities (Gronn 2006: 202), in the case of prospective organisational leaders, the focus of their awareness is on personal experience in the formation of identity and its 'fit' or otherwise with an imagined role possibility. Unless verbalised, as per the kinds of focus group responses documented above or within the intimacy of one or more confidant relationships, an individual's working through of identity-related emotional tensions and conflicts that form part of leadership transition exists purely as a kind of inner, private leadership. On the other hand, the zone or horizon of awareness as regards information potentially available to prospective leaders is infinitely wide and, in the event that this information encourages risk aversion, is much less amenable to control by others (e.g. employers). Leadership hazards, and the perception and representation of those hazards, then, are all intricately inter-related. But precisely why it is that some prospective leaders perceive, represent, and engage with particular hazards, while others among their peers eschew them, remains a mystery, with Breakwell's (2007: 263) most recent best guess being that, for each individual, four aspects of identity structure are susceptible to the positive or negative impact of hazards: self-esteem, efficacy, sense of distinctiveness, and sense of continuity. Clearly, all these hypothesised links suggest there is considerable scope for further research.

Conclusion

This chapter has examined individuals' beliefs about an imagined occupational possibility, derived from opportunities to rehearse that possibility in tangible and meaningful ways. The discussion has accounted for differences in beliefs about that possibility of leadership in relation to existing identity status, and different levels of vulnerability experienced in relation to acting role status. Incipient or embryonic selves were distinguished, derived from participants' accounts of their passage into and through rehearsed role status, and their exit from it. These permitted the classification of status confirming and disconfirming outcomes concerned with what it meant to spread one's wings. The findings are important because they highlight the interplay of emotion and risk in leadership decision-making. Not only that, but they also suggest that the systematic provision of opportunities for the exercise of senior level leadership through structured temporary role rehearsal may be a prudent means of identifying and fostering leadership talent. The flipside of these advantages, of course, is that temporary leadership role rehearsal also affords a means of avoiding wastage and attrition, particularly by ensuring that people make decisions about whether to be leaders that are experienced-based in some measure, rather than being appointed and having to keep their fingers crossed that all will be well.

Notes

1 'Identifying and Tracking Principal Aspirants' (ITPA) 2004, for which funding was received from the Monash University Small Grant scheme.

2 These data were obtained during Phase 1 of the project: 'Principal Aspirations and Recruitment amidst Leadership Disengagement' (2004–5). The research was supported financially by the Australian Research Council (ARC): Discovery

Project (DP0453405). I am grateful to the ARC for its funding and to my co-researcher, Dr Kathy Lacey, for conducting the focus group interviews.

3 Which was not surprising, perhaps, for to be a 'persister' would have meant attesting publicly to unsatisfactory experiences and being undeterred by them. As this may have meant being adjudged as failures by their peers, such people were presumably reluctant to participate in the focus groups.

4 As #43's extracts suggest, the four cells do not exhaust all the possibilities. A few informants were genuinely undecided about the principalship as a possible career destination.

5 I thank my colleague Professor Gabriele Lakomski for this reference.

References

Ashforth, B.E. (2001) *Role Transitions in Organizational Life: An Identity-Based Perspective*, Mahwah: Lawrence Erlbaum.

Beck, U. (1992) *Risk Society: Towards a New Modernity*, trans. M. Ritter, London: Sage.

Breakwell, G. (2007) *The Psychology of Risk*, Cambridge: Cambridge University Press.

Damasio, A. (2000) *Descartes' Error: Emotion, Reason and the Human Brain*, New York: Harper Collins/Quill.

Denholm, A. (2008) 'Schools pander to "rights" of children, union claims', *Glasgow Herald*, 17 May: 1, 7, 16.

Draper, J. and McMichael, P. (2002) 'Managing acting headship: A safe pair of hands?' *School Leadership and Management*, 22, 3: 289–303.

—— (2003) 'Keeping the show on the road: The role of the acting headteacher', *Educational Management and Administration*, 31, 1: 67–81.

Finkel, A. (2008) 'Perceiving others' perceptions of risk: Still a task for Sisyphus', *Annals of the New York Academy of Science*, 1125: 121–37.

Glaser, B.G. and Strauss, A.L. (1964) 'Awareness contexts in social interaction', *American Sociological Review*, 29, 5: 669–79.

Gronn, P. (2006) 'Aesthetics, heroism and the cult of "the leader"', in E.A. Samier and R.J. Bates (eds) *Aesthetic Dimensions of Educational Administration and Leadership*, London: Routledge.

—— (2008) 'The state of Denmark', *Journal of Educational Administration and History*, 40, 2: 173–85.

Gronn, P. and Lacey, K. (2004) 'Positioning oneself for leadership: Feelings of vulnerability among aspirant principals', *School Leadership and Management*, 24, 4: 405–24.

Kahn, W.A. (1990) 'Psychological conditions of personal engagement and disengagement at work', *Academy of Management Journal*, 33, 4: 692–724.

Lacey, K. (2003) 'Factors that impact on principal class leadership aspirations', unpublished thesis, University of Melbourne.

Lakomski, G. (2008) 'Cognition versus emotion?: Revising the rationalist model of decision-making', unpublished working paper.

Lupton, D. (1999) *Risk*, London: Routledge.

Lyng, S. (1990) 'Edgework: A social psychological analysis of voluntary risk taking', *American Journal of Sociology*, 95, 4: 851–86.

Markus, H. and Nurius, P. (1986) 'Possible selves', *American Psychologist*, 41, 9: 954–69.

O'Malley, P. (1996) 'Risk and responsibility', in A. Barry, T. Osborne, and N. Rose (eds) *Foucault and Political Reason: Liberalism, Neo-Liberalism and Rationalities of Government*, Chicago: University of Chicago Press.

Williams, T.R. (2003) 'Ontario's principal scarcity: Yesterday's abdicated policy responsibility – today's unrecognized challenge', *Australian Journal of Education*, 47, 2: 159–72.

15 The problem of narcissists in positions of power

The grandiose, the callous, and the irresponsible in educational administration and leadership

Eugenie A. Samier and Terryl Atkins

> Narcissism invades the organization one executive at a time. If one narcissist is allowed to rise to power, he inevitably hires reinforcements. Slowly, critical power positions are filled with those who will support his agenda. Some of them are themselves narcissists; others fill the supporting role of the enabler ... One narcissist can create a cluster of narcissism that, if unchecked, can grow to dominate an entire organization.
>
> Downs 1997: 77

Many of the chapters in this collection examine more positive emotions and arguments for their inclusion in our understanding and practice of administration. However, there are many emotions that are destructive, and in some cases, as discussed in this chapter, produce a malignant personality style that causes individual and collective suffering as well as damage to organisational members. One form of leadership that has gained some popularity is that of the charismatic, so potently charged with appeal on the affective level that it can for a time be successfully exploited by narcissists in satisfying their own needs to the exclusion of others (Conger and Kanungo 1998: 211–12).

The growing prevalence of narcissism in organisational leadership reflects a cultural change identified several decades ago by Lasch (1979) and Riesman (1950) who noted a shift from the inner-directed personality type to a peer-oriented other-directed personality. According to Lasch, a culture that rears its children in schools, peer groups, mass media, and the helping professions rather than families, creates a personality type socialised to suit itself (1979: 238). This culturally reinforced other-directedness leads to an inability to conceive of a separation between self and surroundings, what Freud identified as primary narcissism in infant development, and, as secondary narcissism, a pathological condition in adulthood (1914).

In an ethos in which it is assumed that everyone can be a leader, even studies of damaging micropolitics and the 'dark' side of leadership have made little headway in informing scholarship and practice. However, a burgeoning field analysing academic bullying and mobbing, in which intense emotional damage is done, has arisen recently indicating that not all is well in our educational organisations (e.g. Westhues 2005). Structural–functional approaches and new market-oriented imperatives contribute to the suppression of deep considerations of character and personality, the wellspring of moral agency, interpersonal relations, and constructive, sustaining cultures. It is on this level of individual analysis that many emotionally informed problems exist: lack of authentic meaning, misplaced values, and personality disorders that contribute to human pain and dysfunction in organisations.

This chapter examines the problem of narcissism in educational administration and leadership in the form of destructive patterns where positions of power and influence provide motive and opportunity for the damaging character of this personality disorder to negatively affect the work life of colleagues and sabotage organisational effectiveness. The degree of disruption within an organisation can range from mild annoyance to extreme disabling, and, as management theory has recently demonstrated, is far more common than generally recognised. First, a descriptive definition of the nature and structure of narcissism that lends itself to its expression in an organisational context is constructed. It includes typical traits, behaviours, and subtypes of narcissistic manifestations as they affect social interaction, work, and the politics and culture of organisations. Second, a more detailed discussion of the narcissist as an organisational phenomenon will be developed, including misuse of the physical environment and an objectified use of people. Finally, the chapter will discuss recommended strategies on the part of individual organisational actors in identifying and protecting themselves from harmful effects, particularly those in authority positions who bear responsibility for the behaviour of their subordinates, such as setting of formal boundaries in social interaction to disciplinary sanctions, instead of the common reactions of avoidance and inaction (see Downs 1997; Popper 2002).

The nature and structure of narcissism

Narcissism is a complex personality disorder comprising 'a number of overlapping behavioural tendencies rather than a single unitary construct' (Munro *et al.* 2005: 51). The American Psychiatric Association's *Diagnostic and Statistical Manual for Mental Disorders IV-TR* lists the following traits of which a narcissist must have five or more for a diagnosis: a grandiose sense of self-importance; preoccupation with fantasies of unlimited power, brilliance or beauty; believes that s/he is 'special' and unique; requires excessive admiration; has a sense of entitlement; is interpersonally exploitative; lacks empathy; is envious of others (and believes others are envious of him/her); and demonstrates arrogant behaviours and attitudes (2000: 294). It is distinguishable clinically from a number of other personality disorders that on a superficial level may seem similar in an organisational context: paranoid, schizoid, antisocial (or psychopathic), borderline, histrionic, obsessive–compulsive, avoidant, and dependent (2000: 288–95). According to Babiak and Hare, aggressive or malignant narcissism is often difficult to distinguish from psychopathy, lacking only the psychopath's cold-blooded efficiency (2006: 41), and Perry and Perry (2004) have demonstrated that many others with the aforementioned personality disorders share some narcissistic traits. Narcissists constitute 1 per cent of the general population out of a total of 10 to 13.5 per cent of adults with at least one personality disorder (Lynch and Horton 2004: 149). However, due to their limited insight narcissists rarely seek treatment of their own accord indicating a higher actual percentage than is recorded. Their representation in administrative positions in organisations may be disproportionately high, according to a number of management theorists (e.g. Lubit and Gordon 2003), even in universities (see Hill and Yousey 1998; Misch 2002).

The underlying cause of narcissism, according to Kohut (1971; 1977), is the lack of a cohesive self able to mirror to oneself a validation of success causing this personality type to seek external validation, or mirroring, in an attempt to produce an ideal self-image. Since validation cannot be internalised, the narcissist perpetually seeks the praise of others whose opinions are considered valid to counter constant self-doubt, feelings of incompetence, and self-denigration. In turn, others are held responsible for feelings of failure and envy. In this manner, narcissistic traits develop in order to protect the self against underlying shame, loneliness, fear, frustration, and anger (for an overview see Morrison 1989). As part of the childhood developmental experience of coping with a world that does not always provide immediately what a child wants, the 'perfection and bliss' of earlier days is retained through two key constructions: a 'grandiose self' and an 'idealized parent image'. If these cannot develop normally, the resulting adult can be rendered deprived, angry, and empty, transforming his or her needs into an obsession with 'power, beauty, status, prestige, and superiority' (Kets de Vries 2006: 83–5), to which others are expected to serve. In adulthood, they continue to hold a discrepant high self-esteem, exhibited socially to cover for inwardly held low self-esteem, and marking a highly unstable form of confidence vulnerable to insecurities and self-doubt which inevitably makes them volatile in an organisation (Zeigler-Hill 2006).

Destructive narcissism is distinguishable from those with healthy egos in a number of ways. First, the narcissist believes that he or she is consistently and without question superior, exhibiting chronic self-confidence and a sense of entitlement that ignores the needs of or cooperation with others. Harbouring fantasies of power, success, and fame, what Horney called 'neurotic pride' (1950: 86–109, 187–213), this compensatory self-aggrandisement is at the basis of all other behaviours for the destructive narcissist whether in using or denigrating others to elevate the self or by capitalising on opportunities availed through those in charge or the organisation itself. Because destructive narcissists believe they are 'special' and unique, normal organisational rules and behavioural constrictions do not apply. Facts, situations, and people are manipulated in order to curry favour with others considered superior, or to cover up responsibility for the likely failures due to an over-inflated sense of capability coupled with a general lack of creativity, conceptual rigidity, and laziness to detail (Brown 2002; Downs 1997). The narcissist's arrogance is bolstered through the excessive admiration and imagined envy of others. In truth, though, the narcissist is envious of those believed to have garnered the success and fame so greatly desired, disparaging those with actual accomplishments in order to reacquire the needed feeling of superiority. Possible exceptions to this may be accolades for those whose success can be capitalised upon or used as a show of magnanimity performed for a valued audience.

Organisational expression

Initially, narcissists seem to be attractive incumbents for authority roles. They seem to have an abundant self-confidence and vision, however, with increased familiarity, others in the organisation begin to experience disappointment and even assume a strong negative view as the narcissist's insensitivity and self-promotion are discovered (Taylor *et al.* 2003: 166). Unterberg explains how difficult it often is to recognise narcissism in powerful individuals (by virtue of accomplishment or position) since they are able for a time to make real contributions with charm and intelligence; however, their highly personal agenda precludes a genuine concern for others or the organisation's goals (Unterberg 2003: 475). And they may also be skilled in impression management, exhibiting an appearance, grooming, and attirement suited to the high positions they believe they warrant.

Volkan has argued that the 'fit' between a group and narcissistic leader occurs when the group has regressed (possibly due to organisational stresses) and the new leader or leader-candidate promises 'an illusion of safety'. In other words, the narcissistic personality, consisting of 'superior power, intelligence and omnipotence', seems to be an '"antidote" for shared anxiety' in a psychologically dove-tailed dynamic (2007: 6–7). For Kernberg, such a regressed group idealises narcissists, acting out a 'parasitic dependency' (2003: 685). Susceptibility to a narcissistic authority, in itself, can be evidence of a trauma incident, or a long period of stress, in a large group. In an educational organisation it could be caused by downsizing, micropolitics, and/or toxic culture. Volkan explains that there are three symptoms of group regression that lend themselves well to the narcissist: 1) chosen glories – mythologised events and/or persons that increase self-esteem [such as a belief in an extraordinarily high research record]; 2) chosen trauma – a shared representation of tragedies that have befallen the group, such as drastic losses and feelings of helplessness and victimisation [e.g. severe budget cuts]; and 3) purification rituals – discarding perceived contamination elements or individuals, which the narcissist can redirect to remove perceived threats to grandiosity [observable in exercises to replace mission statements, mottos, and symbolic decorative features] (2007: 12–16).

Because destructive narcissists are interpersonally exploitative, their behaviour towards others is essentially manipulative ranging from superficially charming, if they want something, to arrogant and haughty if the other has no apparent value, and finally derisive, contemptuous, and destructive if the individual is in their road or perceived as a threat. Since people are perceived as objects to be exploited, relationships cannot be reciprocal. They will blame others (scapegoat) for their own misjudgements and errors or a faulty system of rules and practices. They will deny giving any wrongful information that someone else may have acted on with negative results. They will be unfair, inaccurate, and will cheat to avoid blame and to save face to superiors (Brown 2002: 33–4) and if this leads to damage of another's reputation, career, or psychic state, they feel no remorse. Rather than imaginative or innovative, their own work is often formulaic, rigid, and sterile so they co-opt others' ideas, whether restating one's idea voiced five minutes previously in a meeting as their own or claim exclusive authorship on more in-depth collaborative work.

Studies by McGregor *et al.* have found convincing evidence that narcissists' organisation style is characterised by defensive tactics to compensate for their own inadequacies or to protect themselves from imagined threats. Their reactions are self-serving, intended to mask vulnerabilities, ranging from exaggerating consensus, expressing defensive pride, to a dismissive–avoidance attachment style, the last leading them to 'arrogantly avoid and dismiss relationships as unnecessary and to see oneself as exceptionally self-sufficient and competent' (2005: 980).

Narcissists have also been examined for their contribution to counterproductive work behaviour, particularly in displaying aggression whenever a threat to ego is perceived. Stucke and Sporer's (2002) studies have shown that they are prone to anger and aggression (often verbal) when their grandiose self-image is threatened by negative feedback or failures, directing aggressive and other antisocial acts, such as derogation, against the perceived source of the ego-threat and to reassert their self-image. Wallace and Baumeister (2002) have also found that narcissists become angry, hostile, aggressive, and derogatory when receiving feedback on failures because it calls their superiority into question. Penney and Spector (2002) surveyed a broad range of literature and research results, finding that aggressive responses are a typical feature of a narcissistic organisational pattern: to punish and discourage others from challenging authority, to signify dominance in response to negative evaluations, and to gain status in a zero-sum approach to self-esteem.

This is a relational disorder in that people are experienced by the narcissist as an extension of his or her needs, indeed of his or her self. Underlying and driving narcissism is a deep lack of self-worth that needs to be bolstered continually by the narcissist's relation to others. According to Herbert Rosenfeld (1987), who first coined the term 'destructive narcissism', the destructive aspects of the omnipotent self are idealised and the aim is to obliterate the separation between the other and the self. The narcissist hides internal feelings of envy, shame, or incompetence by devaluing or eliminating the perceived sources of those feelings – the importance of others. The narcissist's illegitimate sense of entitlement, inappropriate need for admiration and attention, lack of empathy, and projection of negative traits onto others affect the politics and culture of schools and universities, including social interaction and work styles that produce this objectified use of people (Ronningstam 2005). Because they believe that everything should be about them, and have no empathy, they lack choices in their behavioural repertoire and have difficulty learning alternate behaviours. Narcissists will repeatedly dominate conversations or take any form of action to become the centre of attention with no self-reflexive corrections despite criticism. Lacking a sense of humour and irony they can be quick to take offence over what would be considered normal comments on the absurdities of events or life's ironies (Brown 2002: 105).

In addition to requiring love and admiration from subordinates and being unable to accept criticism, on an organisational level they 'tend to transform administrative structures into an inner circle of sycophantic favourites complemented by an outer group of disgruntled, disappointed, resentful, and suspect "enemies"' (Kernberg 1998: 145). While narcissists may initially be regarded as charismatic or consensus leaders, their inability to view others in depth leads to a deterioration of management, a devaluation of valuable colleagues who are not admirers, driving them out of the organisation and others into passive acquiescence (Kernberg 1998: 145–6).

Self-defeating behaviour is common, if not inevitable, for them. Narcissists eventually fail in authority or leadership roles. This is due, in part, to being dispositionally impulsive (Vazire and Funder 2006: 154), an extension of their utter egocentrism and the pressure of shame and worthlessness making them highly reactive to organisational conditions and circumstances. In other words, narcissists are not able to plan well or maintain the deadlines and attention necessary to the administrivia that passes over their desks, even when to the detriment of staff. Their 'egoistic self-deceptive enhancement' (Vazire and Funder 2006: 159) produces self-perceptions that are exaggeratedly positive or even self-delusional so they are unable to see work to be done.

> Among this group [of narcissists] we find those individuals who engage in unacceptable practices in the work situation and thus continually provoke criticism. This narcissistic form of work inhibition characterizes people who are unable to finish their organizational tasks, seem incapable or unwilling to follow up on their promises, make obvious errors, and tend to forget things. An appearance of passivity surrounds their actions.
>
> (Kets de Vries 1980: 17)

They often seek individual rather than collective tasks and avoid routine work in order to achieve self-enhancement, superiority over others, and public display leading to personal glorification and the admiration of others (Wallace and Baumeister 2002).

In an ultra competitive environment of winners and losers, '[t]o flourish, the narcissist must have losers at hand. If they don't exist, he creates them' (Downs 1997: 91). Programmes become centralised around the power domain of the narcissistic leader where those who reinforce this control are rewarded and information must be closely guarded with a whitewashed version meted out to subordinates. The organisational leader(s) coerce employees by demanding increasingly high performance levels, undue competitiveness and partial or skewed information by which to work (Downs 1997: 113–15). Program change is regarded as a threat to this power base. Because of the narcissist's rigid approach to problems and narrow perspective destructive narcissistic leaders will have only a limited range of stereotyped solutions to problems and are unlikely to seek feedback or guidance until it is too late (Babiak and Hare 2006: 40: 131). They then become angry, hostile, aggressive, and derogatory with received feedback on failures because it calls their superiority into question (Wallace and Baumeister 2002).

Farwell and Wohlwend-Lloyd conducted three studies on undergraduate university students, demonstrating that those with strong narcissistic characteristics consistently overestimated their performance in order to enhance their self-image, leading them to attribute positive actions to themselves, and negative outcomes to 'bad luck or uncontrollable circumstances' (1998: 66), compromising their ability to assume responsibility. However, as Wallace and Baumeister point out, 'Narcissists may seek high profile jobs because their self-confidence and desire for glory may overwhelm their fear of failure' (2002: 831). Lubit and Gordon attribute a good portion of micropolitics to personality problems, including narcissists, arguing that administrators and leaders have to be able to discern hidden agendas and boundary issues as part of their effectiveness. Part of the administrative problem is that narcissists can use many of their traits to help them rise within the hierarchy, making them even more difficult to discipline or remove: self-confidence, enthusiasm, and unrelenting drive (2003: 175), although serving self-interest even to the detriment of colleagues, can earn them considerable organisational assets.

Due to their manipulation of others, resources, and organisational goals for self-interest, narcissists may appear to be simply Machiavellian however, Paulhus and Williams demonstrate that the manipulative personality only shares 'a socially malevolent character with behaviour tendencies toward self-promotion, emotional coldness, duplicity, and aggressiveness', with the Machiavellian personality being 'more grounded, or reality-based, in their sense of self' (2002: 557, 561). The Machiavellian will not sacrifice interpersonal relationships simply for ego-enhancement, and would be far more able to follow through strategically and tactically without the strong reactive nature of the narcissist. Narcissism may correlate strongly with leadership style, for example, with authoritarian individuals more frequently being pathologically narcissistic, where gaining power over others compensates for underlying feelings of powerlessness (Jørstad 1996: 18–19). Gender may make a difference, both in styles of narcissists and the success with which narcissists can more easily scapegoat female colleagues than male, particularly in fields that are still dominated by men where a strong old boys' network still exists. Jørstad argues that narcissism may be far more acceptable in men, whose 'masculine' traits are closer to narcissism than stereotypic views of women (1996: 22).

Narcissists have a rather slippery hold on the truth and a highly personal ethic. Their sense of entitlement extends to an arbitrary use of rules, including those regarding the rights and well-being of others (Lubit and Gordon 2003: 179). This means that they are likely to violate policies, principles of administrative law, and natural justice. The truth in relation to these is what serves their ends, particularly when a threat to ego-image is perceived. Their own perception of their truth telling and policy adherence is a function of self-deception, unless vigorously challenged by authorities they cannot manipulate or undermine. The unwarranted attacks on others, in verbal or written form even to the extent of manufacturing dismissal, could be seen instead by narcissists as warranted staff discipline.

Conclusion: recommended strategies

It seems to be very difficult for most to believe that a colleague or superior may have more than a lack of knowledge, a difficult personality, etc., and may, in fact, have a serious personality disorder. In part, this is accounted for in Hannah Arendt's (1977) banality of evil thesis – that people generally resist accepting that those causing suffering to others cannot resemble themselves, in this case, people who can be reasoned with, encouraged, or taught. In effect, all of the strategies one would use with 'normal' colleagues and superiors are considered by most writers in the field as ineffectual, and should be replaced with strategies and tactics for maintaining distance, disengagement, and individual survival. Educational organisations may be more vulnerable in this respect, since the ethos of support and learning can over-ride other considerations.

Unterberg (2003) recommends approaching the narcissist in a non-threatening manner in order to avoid further reaction. However, other authors have a much dimmer expectation of success with a narcissist. Lubit and Gordon recommend a number of strategies, depending upon one's relationship organisationally. To superiors, 'do not try and change their behavior; avoid doing things that bother them; don't criticize them; flatter them; be deferential; document your work; [and] find a new position'. To a narcissistic peer: 'avoid borrowing from them or gossiping with them; don't share good ideas until you have told your boss in writing; set clear boundaries; [and] avoid arguments'. For narcissistic subordinates: 'set clear limits on their behavior; [and] hire an executive coach skilled in working with narcissistic managers, or tell them they need to for their career to progress' (2003: 179).

Hotchkiss concurs, however, with a more optimistic view of strategies that allow one to adequately protect oneself. The first strategy is to protect oneself by becoming more aware of one's own emotional reactions and detach emotionally in order to deflect the potential shame, discomfort, and anger produced by engaging with a narcissist (2003: 66–7). Second, embrace reality by rejecting the narcissist's 'manufactured images, illusions, distortions of fact, catastrophising or other kinds of exaggerations, denial, or outright lying' (2003: 69) and abandon attempts to change their behaviour (2003: 73). Third, set boundaries to prevent the narcissist from using and exploiting others to their own ends (2003: 76). Finally, cultivate compensatory reciprocal relationships with others (2003: 81–2).

Brown reviews a range of possible strategies, all of which are inadequate or can contribute to problems with narcissists. The first, withdrawal, can remove frustration that may lead to more constructive relationships with others; however, one is then out of the communication loops that could cause one to lose out on important information regarding promotions and other important activities. The second, attacking, often does cause the narcissist to leave one alone, but the disadvantages are significant – authorities may perceive one as aggressive and hostile providing the narcissist with organisational ammunition. Third, confronting, has no advantages, and this will be perceived as an attack. Fourth, smoothing (or yielding) can effectively avoid conflict; however, it may require one to discard or devalue one's own goals. Finally, compromising has no advantages, causing the narcissist to become incensed and seek to marginalise one from others (1996: 267).

Kets de Vries and Miller recommend reducing their influence, transferring them out of others' harm's way, and keep inexperienced and insecure subordinates out of their reach (1997). More cynically, Downs suggests that the rules for operating in a narcissistic organisation are relatively simple: 'Always look good and do anything to make your boss look good; take as much for yourself as you can; constantly watch your back, and, in the end, remember that results are all that really matter' (1997: 77–8). Once successfully in senior administrative positions, however, narcissists can assume that they have all the answers and stop listening to others, insulating themselves with circles of 'yea-sayers', many of whom may be emergent narcissists themselves, who tell them only what they want to hear. Once such a narcissistic organisational climate is created, only the removal of narcissists can improve the organisation (Kets de Vries 2006: 50–1).

The imposition of New Public Management neo-liberal ideology since the early 1980s, which involves importing private sector management practices and commercialisation, has made public sector type administration including public education more vulnerable to excesses in producing a fertile ground for narcissists, and in mis-diagnosing and mistreating the problem. One of its fashions to which educational administration is not immune is the widespread use of executive coaches. However, as Berglas (2002) has recently warned, few of them have the background to detect deep-seated psychological problems, and in many cases exacerbate the problems of such individuals in their organisations. He views the problem as threefold: 1) many coaches, drawing from sports, try to provide 'simple answers and quick results'; 2) they tend to rely upon behavioural solutions that aren't appropriate; and 3) unschooled in psychotherapy, they often 'exploit the powerful hold they develop over their clients' (2002: 88). The more educational organisations become corporatised and commercialised, the more likely narcissists will successfully arrive at senior positions in which they can do great harm. Unfortunately, narcissists can initially appear to be very productive, with the destructive nature of their character flaws becoming apparent only over time. They can appear to operate well with those outside organisations, but be abusive with their own staff (Berglas 2002: 88). By the time organisational authorities realise there is a problem, narcissists have become entrenched and may have produced irreparable damage.

> Narcissistic managers, in particular, tend to rise to management positions in organizations in disproportionately large numbers. Being particularly self-absorbed, they are known to use (and abuse) their subordinates and play up to their superiors to assure their own personal career success.
>
> (Babiak and Hare 2006: 131)

References

American Psychiatric Association (2000) *Diagnostic and Statistical Manual of Mental Disorders: DSM-IV-TR*, Washington, DC: American Psychiatric Association.

Arendt, H. (1977) *Eichmann in Jerusalem: A Report on the Banality of Evil*, Harmondsworth: Penguin.

Babiak, P. and Hare, R. (2006) *Snakes in Suits: When Psychopaths Go to Work*, New York: HarperCollins.

Berglas, S. (2002) 'The very real dangers of executive coaching', *Harvard Business Review*, 80, 6: 86–92.

Brown, N. (1996) 'The destructive narcissistic pattern', *Social Behavior and Personality*, 24, 3: 263–72.

Conger, J. and Kanungo, R. (1998) *Charismatic Leadership in Organizations*, Thousand Oaks: Sage.

Downs, A. (1997) *Beyond the Looking Glass: Overcoming the Seductive Culture of Corporate Narcissism*, New York: American Management Association.

Farwell, L. and Wohlwend-Lloyd, R. (1998) 'Narcissistic processes: Optimistic expectations, favourable self-evaluations, and self-enhancing attributions', *Journal of Personality*, 66, 1: 65–83.

Freud, S. (1991 [1914]) *On Narcissism: An Introduction*, New Haven: Yale University Press.

Hill, R. and Yousey, G. (1998) 'Adaptive and maladaptive narcissism among university faculty, clergy, politicians, and librarians', *Current Psychology*, 17, 2–3: 163–9.

Horney, K. (1950) *Neurosis and Human Growth: The Struggle Toward Self-Realization*, New York: Norton.

Hotchkiss, S. (2003) *Why Is It Always About You? The Seven Deadly Sins of Narcissism*, New York: Free Press.

Jørstad, J. (1996) 'Narcissism and leadership: Some differences in male and female leaders', *Leadership and Organization Development*, 17, 6: 17–23.

Kernberg, O. (1998) *Ideology, Conflict, and Leadership in Groups and Organizations*, New Haven: Yale University Press.

—— (2003) 'Sanctioned social violence: A psychoanalytic view – Part I', *International Journal of Psychoanalysis*, 84: 683–98.

Kets de Vries, M. (1980) *Organizational Paradoxes: Clinical Approaches to Management*, London: Tavistock.

—— (2006) *The Leadership Mystique: Leading Behavior in the Human Enterprise*, 2nd edn, Harlow: Prentice Hall.

Kets de Vries, M. and Miller, D. (1997) 'Narcissism and leadership: An object relations perspective', in R. Vecchio (ed.) *Leadership: Understanding the Dynamics of Power and Influence in the Organization*, Notre Dame: University of Notre Dame Press.

Kohut, H. (1971) *The Analysis of Self: A Systematic Approach to the Psychoanalytic Treatment of Narcissistic Personality Disorders*, New York: International Universities Press.

—— (1977) *The Restoration of the Self*, New York: International Universities Press.

Lasch, C. (1979) *The Culture of Narcissism: American Life in An Age of Diminishing Expectations*, New York: W.W. Norton.

Lubit, R. and Gordon, R. (2003) 'Office politics: The good, the bad, and the ugly', in J. Kahn and A. Langlieb (eds) *Mental Health and Productivity in the Workplace: A Handbook for Organizations and Clinicians*, San Francisco: Jossey-Bass.

Lynch, T. and Horton, L. (2004) 'Personality disorders', in J. Thomas and M. Hersen (eds) *Psychopathology in the Workplace: Recognition and Adaptation*, New York: Brunner-Routledge.

McGregor, I., Marigold, D.C., Nail, P.R., and Kang, So-jin (2005) 'Defensive pride and consensus: Strength in imaginary numbers', *Journal of Personality and Social Psychology*, 89, 6: 978–96.

Misch, D. (2002) 'The "as if" faculty/student advocate', *Educational Management Administration and Leadership*, 30, 4, 461–7.

Morrison, A. (1989) *Shame: The Underside of Narcissism*, New York: The Analytic Press.

Munro, D., Miles, B., and Powis, D. (2005) 'Personality factors in professional ethical behaviour: Studies of empathy and narcissism', *Australian Journal of Psychology*, 57, 1: 49–60.

Paulhus, D. and Williams, K. (2002) 'The dark triad of personality: Narcissism, Machiavellianism, and psychopathy', *Journal of Research in Personality*, 36: 556–63.

Penny, L. and Spector, P. (2002) 'Narcissism and counterproductive behavior: Do bigger egos mean bigger problems?' *International Journal of Selection and Assessment*, 10, 1/2: 126–34.

Perry, J.D.C. and Perry, J.C. (2004) 'Conflicts, defenses and the stability of narcissistic personality features', *Psychiatry*, 67, 4: 310–30.

Popper, M. (2002) 'Narcissism and attachment patterns of personalized and socialized charismatic leaders', *Journal of Social and Personal Relationships*, 19, 6: 797–809.

Riesman, D. (1950) *The Lonely Crowd: A Study of the Changing American Character*, New Haven: Yale University Press.

Ronningstam, E.F. (2005) *Identifying and Understanding the Narcissistic Personality*, Oxford: Oxford University Press.

Rosenfeld, H. (1987) *Impasse and Interpretation: Therapeutic and Anti-Therapeutic Factors in the Psycho-Analytic Treatment of Psychotic, Borderline and Neurotic Patients*, London: Tavistock.

Stucke, T.S. and Sporer, S.L. (2002) 'When a grandiose self-image is threatened: Narcissism and self-concept clarity as predictors of negative emotions and aggression following ego-threat', *Journal of Personality*, 70, 4: 509–32.

Taylor, S., Lerner, J.S., Sherman, D.K., Sage, R.M., and McDowell, N.K. (2003) 'Portrait of the self-enhancer: Well adjusted and well liked or maladjusted and friendless?' *Journal of Personality and Social Psychology*, 84, 1: 165–76.

Unterberg, M. (2003) 'Personality: Personalities, personal style, and trouble getting along', in J. Kahn and A. Langlieb (eds) *Mental Health and Productivity in the Workplace: A Handbook for Organizations and Clinicians*, San Francisco: Jossey-Bass.

Vazire, S. and Funder, D. (2006) 'Impulsivity and the self-defeating behavior of narcissists', *Personality and Social Psychology Review*, 10, 2: 154–65.

Volkan, V. (2007) 'Some psychoanalytic views on narcissistic leaders and their roles in large-group processes'. Online at www.austenriggs.org/Senior_Erikson_Scholar (accessed 14 February 2008).

Wallace, H. and Baumeister, R. (2002) 'The performance of narcissists rises and falls with perceived opportunity for glory', *Journal of Personality and Social Psychology*, 82, 5: 819–34.

Westhues, K. (2005) *The Envy of Excellence: Administrative Mobbing of High-Achieving Professors*. Lewiston: Edwin Mellen Press.

Zeigler-Hill, V. (2006) 'Discrepancies between implicit and explicit self-esteem: Implications for narcissism and self-esteem instability', *Journal of Personality*, 74, 1: 119–43.

Index